Criminal Justice
An Overview

Criminal Justice
An Overview

Alexander B. Smith
Harriet Pollack

John Jay College of Criminal Justice

Holt, Rinehart and Winston
*New York Chicago San Francisco Dallas
Montreal Toronto London Sydney*

The authors would like to express their appreciation to the following authors and publishers for permission to reprint their work:

Excerpts from: *The Blue Parade*, by Thomas A. Reppetto. Copyright © 1978 by The Free Press, a Division of Macmillan Publishing Co., Inc.

Excerpt from: *Agency of Fear*, by Edward J. Epstein. Reprinted by permission of G. P. Putnam's Sons. Copyright © 1977 by Edward J. Epstein.

Excerpts from: *Introduction to Parole*, by Alexander B. Smith and Louis Berlin. Copyright © 1979, West Publishing Company. All rights reserved.

Excerpts from: *Civil Liberties and Civil Rights in the United States*, by Harriet Pollack and Alexander B. Smith. Reprinted by permission of West Publishing Company.

Excerpt from: *Journal of Criminal Law and Criminology*, by Alexander Smith and Harriet Pollack. Reprinted by special permission of the *Journal of Criminal Law and Criminology*, copyright © 1977 by Northwestern University School of Law, vol. 68, no. 2.

Excerpt from: *Some Sins Are Not Crimes*, by Alexander B. Smith and Harriet Pollack, copyright © 1975 by Alexander B. Smith and Harriet Pollack. Used by permission of the publisher, Franklin Watts, Inc.

Selection entitled "What Do James St. Clair and Abe Fortas Have in Common?" by Alexander B. Smith and Harriet Pollack. Originally published in *Juris Doctor Magazine for the New Lawyer*, July 1975.

Library of Congress Cataloging in Publication Data

Smith, Alexander B.
   Criminal justice: an overview.

Includes bibliographies.
1. Teaching.   2. Criminal Justice.
I. Pollack, Harriet, joint author. II. Title.

LB 105-.G196   1979   371.3   78-27645
ISBN: 0-03-046586-9

To Jennie and Joe

Preface

In 1972, the first edition of this book appeared under the title *Crime and Justice in a Mass Society.* We have since changed the title to *Criminal Justice: An Overview* because the latter title seems more descriptive of the contents of the book. The subject matter of the book, and our approach to it, has not changed at all. Indeed, the first paragraph of the original preface said:

> This book is about criminal justice in the large cities of the United States. Our concern is with large cities because it is in urban America that our criminal justice system is perilously close to breakdown. Our smaller communities and rural areas may still be able to cope with the problems caused by law-breaking, but our big cities are in trouble. Most of the available data, moreover, comes from the large cities. In the 1970 election campaigns only the economic recession and the Viet Nam War took precedence over "law and order" as an issue of concern to the public. We are all against crime in the streets and for justice in the courts. But how we are to achieve these noteworthy goals is, of course, the unanswered question. There are at least as many suggested solutions as there are politicians running for office, and approaches run the gamut from the give-em-hell repressiveness of Vice President Agnew to the Lincolnian pleas for justice and mercy of former Attorney General Ramsey Clark.

If we were to replace "Viet Nam War" by "energy crisis" and change the names of the politicians, the statement is as applicable to 1980 as it was to 1970.

We still have crime in the streets; we still want law and order; we still want courts that dispense justice; and we still do not know how to achieve these goals. As in the earlier edition, our purpose is not so much to suggest solutions as to ask informed questions, and to point out, on the basis of historical evidence, what will *not* work. We have updated and expanded the material of the earlier edition, especially in relation to the post adjudicatory process: sentencing, probation, parole, and the rights of incarcerated prisoners. We have also added a section on capital punishment, an issue which has received extensive consideration at the United States Supreme Court level since 1972, and upon which a somewhat uneasy legal closure has been reached.

Once again we wish to thank our colleagues who have helped in the preparation of this book. Arthur Niederhoffer, our friend and colleague of long standing, gave us invaluable advice and criticism in relation to the chapter on the police. Thomas Reppetto, Vice President of John Jay College, was similarly generous in sharing some of his insights into the historical development of the police. Michael Farrell, of the Vera Institute of Criminal Justice, suggested new perspectives on the operations of the courts. Sylvia Rothberg did her usual superb job in typing the manuscript and Betty Goldstein performed innumerable secretarial stints cheerfully and efficiently. The John Jay library staff headed by Eileen Rowland was extraordinarily helpful and Gerald Lynch, President of John Jay College, has followed in the footsteps of his predecessor Donald H. Riddle in creating, at John Jay, a pleasant and supportive milieu for scholarly activities. Last but not least, we thank our students who are the sounding board for our ideas, and who frequently bring us back with a thud to the real world from our flights of academic fancy. We share whatever is good in this book with those mentioned above; the errors belong only to us.

Alexander B. Smith
Harriet Pollack

Contents

Criminal Justice
An Overview

chapter **1**

justice, law, and the courts

"Let right be done!"
From the English *Petition of Right*

"The prophecies of what the courts will do in fact and nothing more is what I mean by law."
Oliver Wendell Holmes, Jr., *The Path of the Law* (1897)

"The final cause of the law is the welfare of society."
Benjamin N. Cardozo, *The Nature of the Judicial Process*

One can look at justice in two ways, either theoretically or pragmatically. A theoretical inquiry into the nature of justice must answer questions such as "Is justice absolute or relative? Are there fixed principles of justice that transcend time, place, and circumstance?" A pragmatic inquiry, on the other hand, asks "Is this accused innocent or guilty? Does the punishment given this defendant fit the crime he has committed?" A successful criminal justice system must attempt to deal with justice on both levels: the conduct which a particular society labels as criminal must violate an ethical system, and the accused who is judged guilty must be the actual perpetrator of the alleged offense.

The society whose criminal justice system achieves both these goals will have arrived at the millenium. Certainly no such society exists.

In the United States today, we are painfully aware that our criminal justice system is in trouble, that we are handling crime and criminals badly. The torrent of criticism these inadequacies have aroused suggests, however, that the ancient urge to "do justice" still persists.

When the victorious allies tried the leaders of the Hitler regime at Nuremberg, the defendants were indicted on four counts: 1) The Common Plan or Conspiracy; 2) Crimes Against Peace; 3) War Crimes; and 4) Crimes Against Humanity. The fourth count included murder, extermination, enslavement, deportations, and other inhumane acts committed against civilian populations, before and during the war.[1] The Nazis' defense was that they were simply obeying the commands of their superiors, who in turn were enforcing the accredited, duly enacted statutes of the sovereign state of which they were all citizens. The prosecution's response was that however "legal" the statutes in question may have been, they were illegitimate and not to be obeyed because they had violated the fundamental tenets of decency and justice. The government of Germany, in other words, had had no "right" to enact such monstrous laws, and the defendants had had no "right" to obey them.

The Nuremberg principle was applied more recently in the case of Lieutenant Calley who was convicted in March 1971 of having massacred civilian women and children at My Lai during the Viet Nam War. Like the Nazi defendants, Lieutenant Calley's defense was that he was "following orders" —to clear out territory which the American Army needed to secure. The military court which convicted Calley responded that Calley's duty was to follow *legitimate* orders; the shooting of defenseless women and children who had been herded into a ditch could not possibly have been legitimate.*

Similarly, many of President Nixon's aides who were convicted of offenses in the Watergate scandal claimed to have been led astray by the fact that their superiors were countenancing clearly illegal behavior and obviously expected them to do the same. Jeb Stuart Magruder, for example, described his horror at hearing Gordon Liddy's plan for breaking and entering, kidnapping, blackmail, and even political assassination discussed in the presence of John Mitchell, the Attorney General of the United States. When Mitchell merely responded that the plans were impractical and too expensive, Magruder concluded that lawbreaking was an accepted way of doing business in the executive branch.[2] Magruder, like most of the Watergate defendants, eventually pleaded guilty, acknowledging that despite Mitchell's reaction he should have known that crimes were crimes, however logical and expedient they seemed at the time.

A still more recent example of "authorized" government illegality is the

---

*Many critics have commented that Calley was unfairly singled out as a scapegoat for the sins of the entire military hierarchy, and that at least his immediate commanding officers should have been tried and convicted as well. Leaving aside the complex question of where responsibility in such a case begins and ends, the point, nevertheless, is that the military court held that it is the duty of individuals committing such acts to assess, not only their legality in the technical sense, but their *moral* legitimacy.

conduct of the FBI which is revealed to have grossly and frequently violated the rights of individuals under their surveillance. Not only were unauthorized wiretaps placed on the telephones of unsuspecting people, but homes and offices were burglarized, *agents provocateur* were infiltrated into political groups, and illegal searches and seizures of all kinds were made. Again, the defense of those accused has been that, in the name of national security, they were ordered to do the things they did by their superiors—up to, and in some cases including, the president of the United States himself. (The FBI cases have not yet been resolved largely because of the problem of tracing responsibility upward and fixing blame at the appropriate executive level. There has been in both the public at large and the Carter administration's Department of Justice a reluctance to punish agents at the operating level while allowing their superiors to go free. Nevertheless, in the wake of Watergate, there is considerable pressure to end "legal" illegalities.)

Underlying the prosecution at Nuremberg, and the more recent prosecutions in the United States, is the thought, presumably, that somewhere immanent in the universe are rules for human conduct that are absolute and untransgressable, no matter how persuasive the circumstances or what the formal institutional justification to the contrary. These "rules"—whether called justice, natural law, higher law, or whatever—have eluded definition since the beginning of human society. Two thousand years before Christ, Hammurabi's code attempted to define socially impermissible conduct and prescribe punishment for it. Centuries later, the Ten Commandments which formed the nucleus of the Mosaic Code were given to mankind—allegedly by God himself. Later still, Plato defined the "just" state as one in which each individual was assigned a status and a code of conduct commensurate with his abilities. Thomas Aquinas taught that justice was embodied in natural law, that is, in that part of the mind of God which human beings could comprehend. Hobbes, Locke, and Kant all wrestled with the same problem: What are the ultimate standards for good and evil? Perhaps we can do no better than to agree with the British philosopher T. D. Weldon who said that while he couldn't define evil, when he saw a storm trooper beating up an old Jew, he knew that was wicked.*

There are in reality very few, if any, behavioral prohibitions which are universal. Though the deliberate killing of a human being, for example, is

---

*T. D. Weldon, *The Vocabulary of Politics* (London: Penguin Books, 1953), p. 43. The complete quote is: "But then you might have seen an S. A. man (or a lot of them) beating up a Jew and you might have said *'Das ist verbrecherisch'* (That is criminal). Your teacher would have said *'Durchaus nicht verbrecherisch. Eine ehrenwerte Tat'* (Not at all criminal, an honorable deed). And what could you say then? You might accept the correction in the same way as that in which in the United States you accept the correction 'We don't call them braces, we call them suspenders, and what you call suspenders, we call garters.' But if you did your friends would not have said 'You have learnt German very well.' They would have said, 'You are a liar and a hypocrite. You know it is wicked to behave like that, yet you are saying that it is praiseworthy. You are pretending in order to avoid trouble.' "

forbidden in most all societies, Eskimos put their old and infirm people on ice floes to float away to their deaths when the community could no longer support them. The Greeks and others practiced infanticide, and Europeans in the name of protecting religion (that is, the moral code) and civilization perpetrated the horrors of the Crusades and the Spanish Inquisition. Incest, encouraged among Incan and Egyptian royalty, is taboo in the modern world, but many marital arrangements permitted by us were forbidden to certain North American Indian tribes. Western civilization permits only monogamy, but in parts of Africa polygyny is encouraged, and in Tibet polyandry is an acceptable way of life. The variety of property arrangements accepted as correct varies from the state capitalism of the Fascists, through the modified capitalism of the United States, to the democratic socialism of the Scandinavian countries and the state socialism of the Soviet Union and mainland China. In the United States we are permissive with regard to the consumption of alcohol, but highly restrictive of the use of opium derivatives and marijuana. Moslem society, on the other hand, prohibits the use of alcohol, but generally accepts the use of the drugs that we find so threatening. In America there is a noteworthy amount of freedom of expression, even for ideas which are politically heretical or sexually lewd; the Soviet Union insists upon political orthodoxy and considers pornography Western decadence. Spain, over the years, has continued to resist twentieth-century impulses toward sexual permissiveness, and strictly prohibits "obscene" literature.

That concepts of justice, and their external manifestations which we call law, vary in different cultures is unquestionable. It is fallacious, however, to conclude from this that there are no universal principles of right and wrong underlying the legal systems of most societies. It may be very difficult to define these universal principles of justice in terms of universal patterns of behavior. Nevertheless, there are few societies which do not sanctify and legitimize their actions through reference to a code of moral conduct which, in its basics, varies surprisingly little from ancient society to modern, and from country to country throughout the world today. In former times as well as now, even despotically ruled countries which may in fact have violated these basic principles of justice have been highly defensive about such actions, and have attempted either to hide or to so describe such actions as to legitimize them by making them compatible with these professed, if ignored, principles.

PRAGMATIC PROBLEMS

Justice in the mind of the layman is seldom conceived in terms of natural or higher law. His view is a pragmatic one: Is the outcome of a particular case "right"? On a mundane level practitioners of the criminal justice system must be concerned not only that their decisions be in accord with formal law but that they meet the expectations of the relevant community. For example, a judge who is insensitive to these expectations may find himself sharply criticized for what may seem to him a logical, strictly legal decision. Judge Nathan R. Sobel, one of the most respected judges of the New York State Supreme Court, was horrified at the storm of protest which arose when he ordered the severance from each other of the trials of two defendants who had been indicted for the murder of a young rabbinical student in Brooklyn in 1952. The crime occurred in a low-income, high-crime area populated mainly by Chassidic Jews, blacks, and Puerto Ricans where considerable hostility existed among the groups. The student in question, who was unknown to the two defendants, was walking through a park about 1 A.M of a June night when he was sighted by two youths, Baldwin and Ferrick, who were skulking in some bushes some one hundred yards away holding an old .22 caliber rifle. Both had been drinking, and when Baldwin dared Ferrick to shoot the rabbi, the latter pulled the trigger. The rabbi fell mortally wounded, and was clinically dead before he hit the sidewalk. As a result of fine police work, the two youths were soon apprehended, and after indictment for murder, both were arraigned.[3]

A question immediately arose in the judge's mind as to the legal responsibility of Baldwin. A prepleading investigation was ordered to establish the facts of the killing which convinced him that, although Baldwin was morally guilty because he had urged Ferrick to pull the trigger, he was not legally responsible. Sobel then severed the action against Baldwin and subsequently dismissed the severed indictment. The Jewish community in Williamsburg reacted very strongly to the judge's handling of the case. Sobel was inundated with letters and telegrams. Community protest meetings were held at which speakers accused the judge of having succumbed to "pressures." Whatever the legal niceties of the decision, it obviously did not square with the community's sense of justice.

By way of contrast to the rabbi's case, an unusual disposition in a murder case in Brooklyn met with a surprising degree of community acceptance. One Bernard Lewis, a thirty-six-year-old maintenance man, became involved in an argument with his drunken wife while he was cutting up meat for stew. Using the same kitchen knife with which he had been preparing dinner, Lewis stabbed and killed his wife. He was subsequently arrested and indicted for the killing. Lewis was characterized in his probation report as a somewhat rigid individual who never drank to excess, had a regular work record, and no previous criminal record. The deceased, a thirty-year-old mother of three, was a "fine girl" when sober but frequently became intoxicated, and on occasion, according to a social work agency's records, had left her small children at home unattended, remaining away from home for as long as three or four days. The defendant had frequently been notified at work of his wife's defection, and had often had to leave his job to go home to care for the children. The defendant pleaded guilty to Manslaughter 1, and was referred to the Probation Department for a presentence investigation. During the investigation, in an interview with the probation officer, the mother of the deceased declared that while she loved her deceased daughter, the latter was a "nuisance" when drunk, and although she (the mother) could not forgive the defendant, the children had no mother and needed a father. After due consideration, the judge placed the defendant on probation so that he could return home to care for his three children.[4] There was no comment by the community on the judge's sentence. The man returned to his children, adjusted very well on probation, and was discharged from supervision some years later.

An acceptable system of criminal justice obviously must take into account community expectations as well as formal law when disposing of cases. Not only judges, but policemen, prosecutors, probation officers, prison officials, and parole officers, if they are to avert criticism or even obstructionism on the part of the public, must make decisions which avoid offending community mores or expectations.* No matter how rigidly prescribed are the formal procedures of indicting, trying, and sentencing defendants, there remain substantial areas of discretion which prudent judicial and administrative officials normally use in accordance with the consensus of public opinion. In a very real sense then, justice may lie not so much in the mind of God as in the collective mind of the community.

If it is true that, on a day-to-day basis, justice is pragmatically determined, is there any validity in the "higher law" notion of justice? Is there any relationship between what a community considers the right disposition of a case and the immutable principles of Judeo-Christian morality? On the lowest court levels on many occasions there is no such relationship.

The 1931 conviction on rape charges of the illiterate, friendless Scottsboro boys, unrepresented in any real sense by counsel, by a jury on which it was impossible for any black to serve, was heartily approved by the people of Lowndes County, Alabama, and was upheld by the Alabama appellate courts. Similarly, lower court decisions upholding segregation of school children along color lines conformed to local public opinion in most areas of the country where such cases arose. Certainly, racism, whether manifested in the form of an unfair trial, or the exclusion of children from schools on the basis of color, violates higher law principles. Yet these decisions were right by contemporary community standards.

Communities, however, do not exist in a vacuum, but are parts of larger communities less affected by local idiosyncracies. The United States Supreme Court decisions twice setting aside the convictions of the Scottsboro defendants reflected the revulsion of the country as a whole for the unfairness of the trials.[5] The traditional Southern fear of an uncontrollable wave of rapes

---

*This is especially obvious with regard to parole boards. Consider the cases of Alger Hiss, James Hoffa, and Morton Sobell, none of whom posed threats to the security or safety of the community, but all of whom were denied parole.

of white women by black men in the wake of an acquittal was not persuasive at the national level, as it had been at the local level. The lily-white classroom, in the end, came to be seen as more objectionable than the dangers of black-white socializing among grade school children when *de jure* segregation of the public schools was ended by the United States Supreme Court in *Brown v. Board of Education of Topeka.*[6]

To summarize, when the pragmatic justice rendered locally tends, for reasons peculiar to the locality, to wander too far from the principles of natural justice, the loser in the battle may appeal to the larger outside community in an attempt to redress the balance of forces against him.[7] On the simplest level the defendant may ask for a change of venue; on a more complex level, he may try to move from the state to the federal court system, or up the appellate court line to the United States Supreme Court. His ultimate goal is to present his case at the level where decision makers are most likely to be talking about the basic immutable principles underlying American society (which principles, presumably, will benefit his cause). To the extent that American society is based on such immutable principles, it will be Supreme Court justices, rather than local civil and criminal court judges, who will most likely be concerned with such principles.

Students of constitutional law might object that during much of American history, the decisions of the local courts were considered to be closer to the principles of natural justice than were those of the appellate courts, because the lower courts were more concerned with human rights than with property rights. The reverse was true of the higher courts. The United States Supreme Court, for example, from 1880 to 1937, invalidated virtually all state and local attempts to mitigate the lot of the working classes. It is of course true that during this period the higher courts were more concerned with property rights than with human rights. One could argue, however, that this was an era when the sanctity of property was widely held to be the most important of all personal rights since it was only through independence of means that the individual was able to protect himself from a slavish dependence on higher authority or other people. It is only since 1937 that this philosophy has been replaced by a belief that the economy must be socially controlled for the benefit of all. Indeed, the basic reason for the bitterness of the conservative judges and their resistance to the validation of the New Deal program was that they sensed they were witnessing a major shift in the popular perception of natural justice, from *laissez faire* to welfare state. The United States Supreme Court is frequently considered to function as a legitimizer of the resolution of group conflicts precisely because the Court tends, through its legalistic discussion of due process, to base its decisions on its (and hopefully society's) notion of natural justice.

In the American system, pragmatic justice and natural justice, if they do not coincide at the lowest level, may become reconciled at the highest court levels. This is not to say, of course, that such reconciliation is always, or even frequently, accomplished. It is a utopian goal, not a reality, that man-made and natural law coincide.

ENGLISH ROOTS OF AMERICAN LAW

When the English colonists first came to North America they brought with them, in addition to their material possessions, a cultural heritage not the least part of which was English law, especially the Common Law. The development of the Common Law started under the Norman and Angevin kings during the eleventh and twelfth centuries. It replaced earlier tribal and feudal law in which justice had been in the hands of popular assemblies known as folk-moots. As feudalism developed, folk-moots evolved eventually into shire-moots, local courts whose membership included the elite of feudal society: large landowners, bishops, lords, and shire-reeves. The first step in the nationalization of these courts was taken when William the Conqueror attempted to consolidate his power by sending his own representatives to the local shire-moots. William also separated lay from ecclesiastical courts, so that two distinct legal systems emerged: state law and canon law. State law came to be called Common Law, was judge-made (as opposed to king-made, or parliament-made), and was common to all England in the same way that canon law (church law) was common to all Christendom. The law was also "common" because it had been derived by the royal justices from the customary practices of the realm.

Ultimately, three great courts of common law developed: the Court of Common Pleas, which heard minor cases where the king's presence was not required; the Court of Exchequer, for tax and fiscal cases; and the Court of King's Bench, for important cases where the presence of the king was mandatory. By the time of Henry II the administration of justice in England had been centralized, and it was the king's peace, rather than the local lord's peace, that was preserved.

> The king was now a territorial king, and his peace extended throughout the land. The king was now the source of law. He had jurisdiction in every case. The State, and not the family or the lord, was now the proper prosecutor in every case.[8]

It was during the same period that crime ceased to be a tort, that is, a dispute between private individuals which could be resolved by the direct action of the aggrieved party, and became instead an offense against the state to be resolved only by state procedures involving the courts and other state officials.

The Common Law is thought to have developed over approximately four centuries from about 1100 to 1500 A.D. During this period, judges, in deciding cases brought before them, relied heavily on decisions made by other judges in handling similar earlier cases. This heavy reliance on precedent is known as the doctrine of *stare decisis*. The Common Law developed a pragmatic orientation: decisions were based on the facts of a case rather than on a generalized statement of principle. It also rested solidly on centuries of local practice apparently sanctified into acceptability by time. The Common Law, however, suffered from two basic flaws: it tended toward rigidity, since new sets of facts were difficult to handle under the old precepts; and it could not handle satisfactorily cases where damage inflicted by a wrongdoer could not be compensated by money. These two defects of the Common Law led to the growth of Equity, a parallel system of judge-made law which originated in the appeals of litigants to the royal chancellor (the keeper of the king's conscience) for justice. It was in the courts of Equity that such devices as the injunction, to prevent the commission of a wrong rather than compensate for it later on, originated. The trust, wherein one may manage the property of another for the benefit of a third, also is a product of the system of Equity. Thus by the end of the fifteenth century a fairly comprehensive system of law had developed in England based on large part on the decisions of generations of judges in the Crown's courts of Law and Equity.

The English settlers of the seventeenth century brought with them the courts of Law and Equity with which they were familiar. The Common Law, by that time fully developed, formed the underlying bedrock on which the system of colonial law was based. It was, however, supplemented and modified by the royal charters issued to the governing body of each colony and, later on, by the edicts of the royal governors and the statutes enacted by the colonial legislatures. However, most law in the colonies, just as in England, continued to be made by the courts rather than by either the executive (king or royal governor) or the legislature (colonial or Parliament).

THE AMERICAN REVOLUTION, NATURAL RIGHTS, AND JUDICIAL REVIEW

Every modern society has many lawbreakers, most of whom (if they are not too numerous) are relatively easily handled by the police because even while breaking the law they do not challenge its legitimacy. A burglar, while he may wish fervently that he had not been caught, will not plead that the law which defines burglary as a crime is unreasonable or morally wrong. More troublesome to society are those who break the law because they feel the law is morally improper. Consider, for example, the thousands who violated the South's segregation laws in the civil rights demonstrations led by Martin Luther King. Of such disbelievers in the law's legitimacy political heretics and ultimately revolutionaries are made. The stability of American government over almost two hundred years is, however, testimony to the existence of a fair degree of consensus as to the legitimacy of our form of government.

Probably the best single statement of the political beliefs underlying this sense of legitimacy is still the Declaration of Independence. Jefferson's statements then, as now, are highly acceptable to most Americans, and indeed seem to be only common sense.

> We hold these truths to be self-evident, that all men are created equal, that they are endowed by their Creator with certain unalienable Rights, that among these are Life, Liberty and the pursuit of Happiness.—That to secure these rights, Governments are instituted among Men, deriving their just powers from the consent of the governed,—That whenever any Form of Government becomes destructive of these ends, it is the Right of the People to alter or abolish it.

John Adams, stung by the acclaim his rival Jefferson received for writing the Declaration, remarked resentfully that he did not understand why Jefferson was so widely praised, since he simply repeated in the Declaration the things that everyone was saying anyway. Historically, this appears to have been true, but why? How did it happen that the principles of the Declaration, being, of course, almost a paraphrase of Locke's *Second Treatise on Civil Government,* were so widely known and accepted? Locke's treatise was an attempt to justify the Glorious Revolution in England wherein Parliament removed James II from the throne and installed his daughter Mary and her consort William as king and queen of England. Locke attempted to explain why this drastic departure from the normal accession pattern should be accepted, and he justified the parliamentary action on the basis of his theory of social contract. In the state of nature, men, according to Locke, were created by God —free, equal, independent, and with inherent inalienable rights to life, liberty, and property. As a concomitant of these rights each individual had the right of self-protection against those who would infringe on his personal liberties. While most men, in the Lockean view, were basically good, content to live and let live, some would be likely to prey on their fellows, who in turn would have to be constantly on guard against such wrongdoing. To avoid this brutish existence, men joined together to form governments to which they surrendered their rights of self-protection; in return, they received governmental protection of their lives, liberty, and property. As in any proper contract there are benefits and considerations on both sides: men give up their rights to protect themselves and receive protection in return. Governments give protection and receive loyalty and obedience in return. Government, in its control over men, cannot exceed the stated aims of the contract, however. Once it controls men more than is necessary for the protection of the mutual welfare it becomes illegitimate and no longer deserving of loyalty or obedience.

Locke, of course, had no notion of when or how the state of nature existed. Nor did he specify the mechanism by which the social contract was entered into. Like other Enlightenment thinkers, Locke derived this theory inductively, that is, by reasoning how it ought to have been. Although his theory reflected the desire of the rising mercantile middle class in England to have done with the absolutist, divine-right Stuart kings, it was enthusiastically, if perhaps unconsciously, adopted by the American colonists with whose experience and aspirations it fitted remarkably well. After all, could there have been anything closer to the state of nature than the New England shore that greeted the first Pilgrim settlers? To the men who carved a society out of a wilderness through their unaided individual efforts, the fruits of this society seemed surely to belong to themselves and not to a sovereign over whom they exercised no control. To a society that practiced, at least initially, equality of opportunity, it was only self-evident to preach that all men were created equal.

Thus the Declaration of Independence became the blueprint for American notions of governmental legitimacy: government must be representative, that is, based on the consent of the governed, but the majorities thus represented must be restricted in the exercise of their power so that basic individual freedoms are not impaired. These sentiments were not only noble and utopian, they were, unfortunately, mutually contradictory, since to preserve minority rights of necessity impaired the immediate desires of the majority; and to enforce the will of the majority required, at least for the moment, that the minority forego its protections. American history has been from this vantage point a balancing act, an attempt to fix the point at which majorities prevail and minorities yield.

The political embodiment of the Declaration of Independence was the government created by the Articles of Confederation. Power lay in the hands of the popularly elected state legislatures, a radical state of affairs in the highly class-conscious world of the eighteenth century. When the weak federal government proved unable to maintain the climate of order and stability necessary for the growth of commerce and industry, the representatives of the middle and upper classes met at Philadelphia to create a new central government. The Constitution which was the fruit of that convention was essentially a counterrevolutionary document one of whose main purposes was to prevent the formation in a short period of time of popular majorities on any single issue. The purpose of fragmenting power among the executive, legislative, and judicial branches of the federal government, and between the states and national government, was to insure that no wave of popular sentiment could infringe the rights of property as some debtor-controlled state legislatures had already done. The Bill of Rights was not part of the original Constitution, and was added by those more interested in personal than property rights as the price of ratification. Thus the Constitution with its Bill of Rights emerges as a plan for a central government with ambiguous and, as it turned out, extensive powers, but with distinct limitations on majority domination of the rights of either persons or property.

The founding fathers meeting in Philadelphia in 1787 created a form of government which was, at the time, structurally unique. The importance they attached to the legislative branch is reflected by the fact that fully one-half of the text of our Constitution is taken by Article I which deals with the structure and powers of Congress. Article II, on the presidency, was perhaps the most difficult for them to draft since no one seemed to have a clear idea what role an executive who was neither a hereditary monarch nor a popularly elected governor ought to play, or indeed, how he was to be chosen. However, it was in Article III, establishing a Supreme Court, that the founding fathers created a really new institution: a court that could sit in judgment on the actions of both legislature and executive. This power—judicial review—is nowhere spelled out in the text of the Constitution, which simply gives the Court the power to hear all cases in law and equity arising under the laws, treaties, and Constitution of the United States; but it was assumed for the Court by Chief Justice John Marshall in the famous case of *Marbury v. Madison*:

> If an act of the legislature, repugnant to the Constitution is void, does it, notwith-standing its validity, bind the courts and oblige them to give it effect? This . . . would seem, at first view, an absurdity too gross to be insisted on. . . . It is emphatically the province and duty of the judicial department to say what the law is. . . . So if a law be in opposition to the Constitution; if both the law and the Constitution apply to a particular case, so that the court must either decide the case conformably to the law, disregarding the Constitution, or conformably to the Constitution, disregarding the law; the court must determine which of these conflicting rules governs the case. This is the very essence of judicial duty.[9]

Scholars have long argued the question of whether the founding fathers intended for the Supreme Court to have the power to sit in judgment on its coequal legislative and executive branches. Neither the Constitution, nor the Federalist Papers, nor any official documents of the times indicate unequivo-cally that it was intended for the Supreme Court to have this power. On the other hand, that part of the *Marbury v. Madison* decision which enunciated judicial review excited very little opposition even among Jeffersonians. Con-temporary evidence seems to indicate that the notion of judicial review was well understood and expected of the Supreme Court. By 1803, state high courts had on previous occasions sat in judgment on the actions of their state legislatures, and, during colonial times, disputes over whether actions of a colonial legislature violated the colony's charter had been referred to the Privy Council in England for resolution. On balance, the preponderance of historical evidence tends to favor Marshall's interpretation of the powers of the Court, and the argument today has become almost totally irrelevant in view of the firm establishment of judicial review as an accepted practice.

However, there is still an ongoing debate today as to how activist the Court ought to be. Those who favor judicial self-restraint, perhaps influenced by lingering doubts as to the legitimacy of judicial review, argue that the Court is essentially an antidemocratic institution inasmuch as it is elitist (drawn from the upper socioeconomic groups), unrepresentative (not elected), and not responsible to the public (justices appointed for life). For all these reasons, they conclude the Court ought to confine its activities to the bare minimum required for it to act as umpire of the federal system. The Court should avoid, wherever possible, involvement in disputes that can be handled by the popularly elected branches of government.

The judicial activists, on the other hand, claim that an uninhibited, fully active court is necessary to maintain a balance within the system between the right of the majority to govern and the right of minorities to preserve their inalienable rights from infringement by the governing majority. Democracy, the activists reason, is not simply majority rule. Individual rights are an important part of the question, and in a government where both the legislature and the executive are essentially instruments of the majority, it is essential that one branch respond to the needs of those who cannot succeed in influencing either president or Congress. Were the Court to be unduly modest the democratic balance would be upset.

Like the argument over the historical validity of the Court's assumption of the power of judicial review, the argument over whether the justices should be restrained or activist cannot be resolved. It is clear, however, that whichever course of action the Supreme Court chooses in a particular controversy, it of necessity influences the outcome of that controversy. Whether it chooses to intervene or modestly declines to participate, the outcome of the dispute will be affected. For the Court there is no neutral middle ground. Once it is agreed that the Court could, if it would, intervene, failure to do so is as much a decision as direct intervention. Most partisans in the judicial activism—judicial restraint controversy choose sides according to their preference for certain substantive results in a current dispute. While it is perfectly proper to advocate that the Court not intervene in a given situation because one hopes to preserve the ruling of the lower court, there is no moral superiority in the nonintervention position. It is, in a negative way, as activist as a more aggressive stance on the part of opponents of the status quo. The ongoing argument over whether the Supreme Court ought to be more or less active generally resolves itself into a question of whose ox is being gored.

STATE AND FEDERAL JUDICIAL SYSTEMS

The United States has fifty-one court systems: fifty state and one federal. Typically, most court systems operate on three levels: courts of original jurisdiction (trial courts); intermediate appellate courts; and final appellate courts. Unfortunately for students and laymen, there is no uniform terminology for the designation of these courts. In most states, and in the federal system, the highest appellate court is called the Supreme Court, and the intermediate appellate court is called the Court of Appeals. In New York

State, however, the lowest state-wide court of general jurisdiction is the Supreme Court, and the final appellate court is called the Court of Appeals. Despite the lack of uniformity in terminology, however, there are widespread uniformities of practice in both state and federal systems.

Most state courts of general jurisdiction are called superior or county courts. It is in these courts that important civil and criminal actions are initially heard, that is, suits involving large sums of money, and felonies. They also hear, on appeal, minor cases which originated in local magistrates' courts or with justices of the peace. The intermediate courts of appeal hear cases appealed from the county, superior, or other courts of original jurisdiction. Above this level appeal may be had to the highest court of the state, although such appeal may be of right (not at the discretion of the court) only if certain procedural or other requirements are met. State judges are generally elected rather than appointed, usually for seven to fourteen years.

The federal court system parallels that of the states. The lowest federal court of general jurisdiction is the district court, of which there were ninety-four in 1978, handling all criminal cases arising under federal law and civil suits in excess of $10,000. Cases from the district courts are appealed to the federal Courts of Appeal, of which there were eleven in 1968, ten for the states and one for the District of Columbia. An exception to this appellate jurisdiction is that the decisions of certain specially constituted federal district courts, known as three-judge courts, are appealed directly to the Supreme Court, bypassing the Courts of Appeal. These three-judge district courts are convened on an *ad hoc* basis to consider important cases usually involving constitutional principles, and are comprised of two district judges and one judge from the Court of Appeals. All federal judges are appointed for life except those in the so-called legislative (as opposed to constitutional) courts, such as, the United States Court of Military Appeals, and some Territorial courts.

The highest court in the federal hierarchy is the United States Supreme Court, whose docket encompasses a small number of cases, arising under a constitutionally prescribed original jurisdiction, which must be heard, and a very much larger number of cases on appeal which may be heard. The great bulk of the Court's agenda comes to it on appeal from the lower state and federal courts. Technically, there are two major methods* by which cases may be appealed to the United States Supreme Court: by appeal or by writ of *certiorari*. Cases come on appeal generally when they involve: federal courts which have declared state laws unconstitutional; state courts which have declared federal laws unconstitutional; or two federal Courts of Appeal which have made conflicting decisions on the points of law. All other cases come on

---

*A minor method of appealing to the United States Supreme Court is by certification where a lower court asks for instructions on a question of law in any civil or criminal case. This method is rarely employed.

writ of *certiorari,* that is, a petition from the appellant to the Supreme Court for an order from the high court that the lower court, which had previous jurisdiction over the case, send up the records of the case for review. Although technically the Supreme Court is required to hear all cases which come up on writ of appeal, in practice it dismisses those cases it does not wish to consider with the brief notation, "Dismissed for want of a substantial federal question." Petitions for *certiorari* are granted at the option of the Supreme Court. The net effect, thus, is to make the appellate caseload of the Court almost entirely that of the Court's own choosing. The Court tends to select for review those cases which present questions of national importance. All cases in the federal courts must arise under the laws, treaties, or Constitution of the United States; must allege the infringement of a federal right; or must present problems of diversity of citizenships between litigants, that is, must involve actions between citizens of different states, or between citizens and foreigners.

The state and federal systems overlap. It is possible for a given civil or criminal case to be handled by either system or by both. The overlap affects the actions of both public officials and litigants. On the whole, the relationship between state and federal law enforcement officials is one of somewhat distant politeness. Most cases are handled exclusively by one jurisdiction or the other. In those cases which are handled simultaneously at both levels, problems arise on occasion either because of over-competitiveness or, even worse, over-cooperativeness.

The Weinberger kidnapping case was one which created hostility between the local police and the FBI. The Weinberger infant was kidnapped from his carriage in front of his parents' Long Island home in July 1956. Seven days later (in accordance with the traditional presumption that the victim might, after one week, have been transported across state lines in violation of federal law) the FBI entered the case.[10] From an analysis of handwriting samples taken from the ransom note, it was determined that one Angelo LaMarca was the likely kidnapper. Federal agents accompanied by Nassau County detectives thereupon arrested LaMarca. The baby was found dead and subsequent investigation disclosed that the child had never left New York State. Since no federal law had been violated, the suspect was turned over to county officials who succeeded in convicting LaMarca of the crime. He was electrocuted two years later. Despite the successful outcome of the case in terms of apprehending and punishing the criminal, strained relations developed between Nassau County officials and the FBI because the local authorities felt that the federal agents had unfairly taken all the credit for the results.

An interesting footnote to the LaMarca case was the 1974 kidnapping of Jack L. Teich, a wealthy Nassau County businessman, who was taken from the driveway of his Nassau County home by four masked men. Teich was kept in the closet of a dwelling for one week and was released upon the payment of $750,000 ransom in one hundred dollar bills. The Nassau County police and the FBI worked cooperatively on the investigation, and two years later, in September 1976, one Richard Williams was arrested in California, at which time $38,000 of the original ransom money was recovered. In May 1978, Williams was returned to Nassau County, indicted, and found guilty of fraud and conspiracy to kidnap.[11] In contrast to the friction present in the LaMarca case, in the Teich kidnapping the interaction between the two police forces was smooth. The FBI agents and Nassau County detectives whose relationship in the LaMarca case had been unpleasant, had, by the time of the Teich case, become supervisors in their respective agencies and developed sufficient assurance to be able to work well together. (In addition, by 1974, J. Edgar Hoover was dead. Hoover had a reputation among local police agencies for claiming excessive credit in cases in which the mass media were interested.)

Sometimes over-cooperativeness, rather than over-competitiveness, becomes a problem, and relations between the state and federal agents become too close for legality. Until quite recently, it was a fairly common practice for state police to illegally seize evidence of a federal crime and turn it over to the federal authorities, who were then permitted to use it against the accused. While the rules of procedure in federal court did not permit the introduction of evidence illegally obtained by federal agents, under the terms of the notorious "silver platter" doctrine, such evidence could be used if obtained by nonfederal agents. State officials working on a state case that was also of interest to federal agents were thus permitted to commit illegal acts in the name of "law enforcement." In 1960, however, the United States Supreme Court put an end to this practice by excluding from federal court all illegally seized evidence.*

Private litigants, too, are affected by the bifurcated state-federal structure. It is, for example, a common practice among attorneys handling civil suits which procedurally could be heard in either state or federal court, to shop for the court that will provide the most favorable forum for the client's interests. In the criminal field, defense attorneys, by use of the appropriate writ, will sometimes shift a case from the state court system, where appeals have been decided unfavorably to the client, to the federal system in the hope that a federal judge will be more sympathetic to the client's cause. When Dr. Samuel Sheppard contended vainly in the Ohio courts that he had been unable to receive a fair trial because of prejudicial pretrial publicity engendered by a Cleveland newspaper, his attorneys were able to appeal to the federal courts

---

*Elkins v. United States, 364 U.S. 206 (1960). It should be noted that the Fourth Amendment prohibition against illegal search and seizure applies only to government officials, both state and federal. In 1921, in Burdeau v. McDowell, 256 U.S. 465, the U.S. Supreme Court (Holmes and Brandeis dissenting) ruled that stolen, incriminating evidence might be used in federal courts if the evidence had been seized by private parties and government officials had played no part in the theft. No further Supreme Court review of this question has occurred since 1921. State and lower federal courts have reaffirmed the Burdeau doctrine over the years.

on the ground that Sheppard's due process rights had been infringed. Sheppard's appeal went up the federal judicial ladder, and ultimately succeeded when the Supreme Court ordered that he be released from custody unless the state of Ohio retried him within a reasonable time.[12] On retrial in 1966, he was acquitted, twelve years after the murder.

In recent years the use of the federal courts to overrule actions of the state courts has become frequent enough that some observers, including Chief Justice Burger of the United States Supreme Court, have become concerned lest the federal courts become a general overseer of the state judicial systems. A reflection of this concern was the United States Supreme Court decision in *Stone v. Powell*[13] where the Court ruled, 7–2, that where a state has provided an opportunity of fully and fairly litigating a Fourth Amendment claim of illegal search and seizure, a state prisoner may not be granted *habeas corpus* access to the federal courts for the purpose of litigating that claim. In other words, had Sam Sheppard's grievance related to an illegal search on the part of the state authorities rather than to the improper conduct of his trial, he would not have been able to appeal his case through the federal courts. Burger and his supporters argue that the state courts are sufficiently honest and reliable to provide justice for criminal defendants without intervention by the federal courts. Critics of the *Stone v. Powell* decision point to the many examples of miscarriage of justice due to local prejudice, and argue that it is unfair to foreclose the availability of a federal forum for vindicating federally guaranteed rights. In any case, court shopping is still a phenomenon of the American legal system, although some legal restrictions may limit such practices in the future.

The dual state-federal judicial structure of the United States can also, on occasion, act like twin millstones grinding a hapless defendant between them. As of the present writing, a man tried and convicted in federal court for an offense such as robbery of a federally insured bank (a violation of both state and federal law) can be retried and reconvicted in the state court for the same offense.[14]

Only since 1964 has the Supreme Court held that testimony compelled under a grant of immunity by one jurisdiction may not be used by the other to try and convict a defendant.[15] Sometimes, however, the possibility of dual federal-state prosecution for the same offense leads not to injustice, but to justice, as for example, in the shocking murder of three civil rights workers in Philadelphia, Mississippi in 1964. The local sheriff, who was accused of the murder, was acquitted by a jury made up of local residents clearly prejudiced against the victims who were regarded as intruders and troublemakers in the community. It was apparent that no conviction at the state level would be obtained given the state of public opinion in Mississippi at the time. The United States Department of Justice, however, meticulously prepared a case which, when tried in federal court, resulted in the sheriff's conviction for violation of the victims' civil rights.[16] Although the formal charges against the defendant sheriff were different in the state and federal cases, they related to the same criminal act. If it had not been possible to prosecute the sheriff in the federal courts, he could not have been convicted of the murder which the available evidence indicates he almost certainly committed.

In a similar type of situation in 1977, three Houston policemen were brought to trial in state court because they were alleged to have beaten to death a Chicano prisoner in their custody. They were found not guilty of murder charges, but were convicted of negligent homicide, a misdemeanor. The outraged Mexican-American community protested vigorously. As a result, the three policemen were brought to trial in federal court on charges of having violated the federal civil rights of the victim. They were convicted, but the judge, to the great disappointment of local Mexican-American leaders, sentenced the three to only one year in prison though the charge carried with it the possibility of a life sentence. The judge was roundly denounced by the community, though the courage of the prosecutor and the jury were praised.[17]

Judicial review of state and federal practices has not only affected the substance of our criminal justice systems, but has tended to make them more uniform. Increasingly, the substantive and procedural guarantees of the Bill of Rights (originally conceived as applicable to the federal government only) have, through the due process clause of the Fourteenth Amendment, been made applicable to the states also. This evolving national standard concerns not only the courts, of course, but police, prosecutors, and corrections officials as well. Even local and state legislatures are bound by the evolving national standard of what a fair law is, and what kinds of activities can be labeled crimes. Whether for good or for ill, the days when Connecticut could make the use of a contraceptive a crime, or Massachusetts declare *Fanny Hill* obscene, or any state convict a felon unrepresented by counsel in court, are gone. Whether this tendency will become oppressive because of the overcentralization of judicial law-making in Washington remains to be seen. Local option and local flexibility has been curtailed at least in those instances where a determined litigant (especially one supported by appropriate interest groups) is able and willing to carry his case to the highest level. This nationalizing thrust tends to lessen the disparities among the fifty-one systems of criminal justice in this country; and, in the process of removing controversies from local forums to the federal arena, parochial standards for the dispensing of justice have tended to give way to more broadly based conceptual notions of justice.

Selected Readings

Abraham, Henry J. *The Judicial Process*, 3rd ed. New York: Oxford,1975.
Arendt, Hannah. *Eichmann in Jerusalem.* New York: Viking, 1963.
Arendt, Hannah. *On Revolution.* New York, Viking, 1963.

Berman, Daniel. *It Is So Ordered.* New York: Norton, 1966.

Chambliss, William J. *Crime and the Legal Process.* New York: McGraw-Hill, 1969.

Clark, Ramsey. *Crime in America.* New York: Simon & Schuster, 1970.

Cole, George F. *Criminal Justice: Law and Politics.* Belmont, Calif.: Duxbury Press, 1972.

Commager, Henry S. *The Empire of Reason.* Garden City, N. Y.: Doubleday, 1978.

Devlin, Patrick. *The Enforcement of Morals.* New York: Oxford, 1965.

Hall, Jerome. *Theft, Law and Society.* 2nd ed. Indianapolis: Bobbs-Merrill, 1952.

Harris, Richard. *Justice: The Crisis of Law, Order and Freedom in America.* New York: Dutton, 1970.

Krislov, Samuel. *The Supreme Court in the Political Process.* New York: Macmillan, 1965.

Levy, Leonard W. *Against the Law: The Nixon Court and Criminal Justice.* New York: Harper & Row, 1974.

Lieberman, Jethro K. *How the Government Breaks the Law.* Baltimore, Md.: Penguin, 1973.

Morris, Norval, and Hawkins, Gordon. *The Honest Politician's Guide to Crime Control.* Chicago: University of Chicago Press, 1970.

President's Commission on Law Enforcement and Administration of Justice. *The Challenge of Crime in a Free Society.* Washington, D.C.: U.S. Government Printing Office, 1967.

Pound, Roscoe. *The Development of Constitutional Guarantees of Liberty.* New Haven: Yale University Press, 1957.

Pritchett, C. Herman. *The American Constitution.* 3rd ed. New York: McGraw-Hill, 1977.

Quinney, Richard, ed. *Crime and Justice in Society.* Boston: Little, Brown, 1969.

Rawls, John. *A Theory of Justice.* Cambridge, Mass.: Harvard University Press, 1972.

Samaha, Joel. *Law and Order in Historical Perspective.* New York: Academic Press, 1974.

Schattschneider, E. E. *The Semi-Sovereign People.* New York: Holt, Rinehart and Winston, 1960.

Smith, Alexander B., and Pollack, Harriet. *Some Sins Are Not Crimes: A Plea for Reform of the Criminal Law.* New York: New Viewpoints/Franklin Watts, 1975.

Wilson, James Q. *Thinking About Crime.* New York: Basic Books, 1975.

Notes

1. *New York Times,* October 19, 1945, pp. 1, 11–14.

2. Jeb Stuart Magruder, *An American Life: One Man's Road to Watergate* (New York: Atheneum, 1974).

3. *New York Times,* June 28, 1952, p. 10; July 19, 1952, p. 1.

4. *New York Times,* December 25, 1958 , p. 2.

5. *Powell v. Alabama,* 287 U.S. 45 (1932); *Norris v. Alabama,* 294 U.S. 587 (1935)

6. 347 U.S. 483 (1954).

7. For an interesting exposition of the relationship of the widening of conflict to decision making, see E. E. Schattschneider, *The Semi-Sovereign People* (New York: Holt, Rinehart and Winston, 1960), Chapter 1.

8. Clarence Ray Jeffrey, "The Development of Crime in Early English Society," as quoted in William J. Chambliss, *Crime and the Legal Process* (New York: McGraw-Hill, 1969), p. 27.

9. *Marbury v. Madison,* 1 Cranch 137 (1803), at 177–178.

10. *New York Times,* July 5, 1956, p. 27; July 12, 1956, p. 12.

11. Ibid., May 24, 1978, p. 7.

12. *Sheppard v. Maxwell,* 384 U.S. 333 (1966).

13. 428 U.S. 465 (1976).

14. *Bartkus v. Illinois,* 359 U.S. 121 (1959); *Abbate v. United States,* 359 U.S. 187 (1959). See also discussion, Chapter 9.

15. *Murphy v. Waterfront Commission,* 378 U.S. 52 (1964).

16. *New York Times,* November 21, 1967, p. 1.

17. Ibid., March 29, 1978, p. 12.

apiece to addicts; in the *Behrman* case, the physician had issued a prescription for a large quantity of narcotics to be used at the addict's discretion. In both cases, although the actions of the doctors were questionable in terms of legitimate medical practice, the prosecution proceeded on the assumption that such prescriptions were made in good faith for the treatment of addiction. The net result was to obscure the distinction between the honest physician, trying to relieve the addict's withdrawal distress, and the unethical practitioner who indiscriminately sold narcotics prescriptions for personal profit.

The issue was joined in 1925 in the *Linder* case[8] where a reputable Seattle practitioner provided four small narcotics tablets to ease the withdrawal symptoms of an addict who subsequently turned out to be a federal agent posing as a patient. Dr. Linder was convicted under the Harrison Act, and after extensive litigation (said to have cost Linder $30,000) achieved Supreme Court review of his case. The court unanimously reversed the doctor's conviction, on the ground that addicts were diseased persons, and proper subjects for *bona fide* medical treatment. Although this decision would appear to have opened the way for treatment by reputable physicians of addicts and the diseases incident to their addiction, the effect of the earlier decisions, together with the vigorous enforcement policies of the Federal Bureau of Narcotics, has apparently had an effect sufficiently intimidating to cause physicians to be unwilling to prescribe narcotics for addicts under any circumstances. As the rights of the doctor under federal law remain ambiguous, no doctor has been willing to risk his livelihood and his professional reputation in a case testing the validity of the Federal Bureau of Narcotics' rigorous interpretation of the Harrison Act.

The net result of current federal and state regulations is that addicts have no legal access to drugs. Far from curing the addiction problem, the rate of addiction is thought to have increased in recent years, despite the fact that

> The average sentence of the Federal offender against these statutes has increased by more than 300 percent within the last decade, and with the denial of probation and parole many narcotics violators are now being punished more severely than the average murderer.[9]

Worse than the growing number of addicts is the tremendous social problem of their criminal activities, a concomitant of their inability to obtain drugs legally. Thus the punitive restrictive attitudes encompassed in federal and state law enforcement have accomplished little, if anything, more than the earlier (pre-1914) permissive attitudes toward drugs. Many authorities go so far as to consider present punitive programs counterproductive in that they aggravate rather than relieve the problem. Most interesting of all, perhaps, is that the change from permissiveness to punitiveness in the drug field was unaccompanied by any scientific demonstration of a correlation between drug use and antisocial conduct. To this day there is no unanimity of professional

opinion on how drug use affects the individual, either physically, psychologically, or socially. There is little evidence that drug use (at least in relation to
marijuana and heroin), in and of itself, leads to criminal conduct.[10]

In contrast to the dearth of scientific evidence linking drug use *per se*
directly to crime (excluding, of course, crime committed by addicts in order
to obtain drugs), there is voluminous evidence linking the consumption of
alcohol to all kinds of antisocial conduct. The President's Commission on Law
Enforcement and the Administration of Justice states that "two million arrests
in 1965—one of every three arrests in America—were for the offense of public
drunkenness."[11] While some of these arrests were, no doubt, merely for the
offense of being intoxicated in public, others involved assaults, boisterous
conduct, and committing public nuisances. In addition to arrests for drunkenness, alcohol is involved in an undetermined number of detentions for murder, rape, vagrancy, loitering, disorderly conduct, and nonsupport of families.
Accident statistics also indicate that a high proportion of drivers involved in
both fatal and nonfatal motor vehicle accidents, had been drinking shortly
before. More recently, statistics show the same to be true for crashes involving noncommercial aircraft.

Twentieth-century public attitudes toward consumption of alcoholic bev-
erages, in contrast to attitudes toward drug use, have, however, changed from
punitive to permissive. The early part of the century saw the full flowering
of the nineteenth-century temperance movement whose underlying philosophy was that the use of alcohol was morally evil. The ultimate victory of the
WCTU and its allies was, of course, the Eighteenth Amendment and the
ill-fated era of Prohibition. With the collapse in 1933 of the "noble experiment," public attitudes toward social drinking softened markedly among
almost all social groups. Such drinking today is a widely accepted part of our
social mores, and the readily apparent abuses of such drinking, which take
the form of antisocial and even criminal conduct, tend to be treated therapeu-
tically rather than punitively. Excessive drinking and alcoholism are looked
upon most commonly today as diseases or personality disorders rather than
as the results of moral weakness, or as illegal conduct.

The contrast between public attitudes toward the use of marijuana or
heroin and the consumption of alcohol is marked. One can only speculate as
to why the public is tolerant toward drinking, which is known to produce
antisocial conduct, but is almost rabidly intolerant of heroin and until recently, marijuana use, which is far less obviously connected to aggressive
antisocial behavior. While a large proportion of those imprisoned in our
metropolitan jails are there because of drug-related offenses, almost all of this
crime stems from the need to procure either the drugs or the money for the
drugs. Very little criminal conduct occurs as a direct result of the taking of
marijuana or heroin as distinguished from the criminality associated with
drunkenness.

The contradictory and irrational quality of these attitudes may, however, be seeping into the public consciousness to the extent that, in many jurisdictions, drug laws have been modified. At the federal level, and in some states, criminal penalties for possession of small amounts of marijuana have been removed, although selling is still a crime. Most urban areas have methadone programs in which an addictive drug, methadone, is given to heroin addicts registered with the program, enabling them to carry on normal activities. Slowly, the notion that drug use may only be *malum prohibitum* rather than *malum in se* is becoming acceptable to larger segments of the public.

Another type of deviant conduct viewed more sympathetically and less punitively in recent times by the general public is homosexuality. The law in Western society has until recently considered sodomy a crime against nature, and homosexual behavior a serious perversion. Moreover, judges and legislators have labored under the impression that such proscribed forms of sexual behavior are comparatively rare. Present-day research has cast doubt upon these premises. The Kinsey Report,[12] which contains an analysis of the incidence and frequency of orgasm through six sexual outlets (masturbation, nocturnal emissions, heterosexual petting, heterosexual intercourse, homosexual outlets, and animal outlets), indicates that at some period in their lifetimes more than one third of American males have experienced homosexual activities resulting in orgasm. In spite of the implications of this report, attitudes in the United States toward homosexual behavior have remained on the whole disapproving and highly punitive until comparatively recently.

In England on the other hand, a more reasonable approach in the handling of such sexual offenses evolved somewhat earlier. In 1957, the Wolfenden Report was published, indicating a general measure of agreement on two propositions: first, that there exists in certain persons a homosexual propensity that varies quantitatively according to the individual, and second, that this propensity can affect behavior in a variety of ways, some of which are not overtly sexual.

> Although homosexual behavior in some cases may result from disease, the evidence placed before us has not established to our satisfaction the proposition that homosexuality is a disease. This does not mean, however, that it is not susceptible to treatment. . . . [Psychiatrists] deal regularly with problems of personality which are not regarded as diseases. It seems to us that the academic question whether homosexuality is a disease is of much less importance than the practical question of the extent to which, and the ways in which, treatment can help those in whom the condition exists.
>
> In this connection, it is important to consider what the objectives of this help should be. It seems to us that these may be one or more of the following. First, a change in the direction of the sexual preference; secondly, a better adaptation to life in general; and thirdly, greater continence or self-control.[13]

In 1967, ten years after the publication of the Wolfenden Report, and after protracted and heated parliamentary debate, the laws relating to homosexual

offenses in England were finally repealed so as to legalize homosexual relations in private between consenting adults.[14]

Similar attempts at restructuring the law have occurred (though less successfully) in the United States within the past ten years. Illinois and several
other states have already decriminalized adult consensual sodomy, and in
New York, the 1967 revision of the Penal Code was the occasion for a
concerted effort to remove from the code those provisions making unorthodox private sexual conduct a crime. Although these efforts were unsuccessful,
they were on the whole greeted sympathetically, and as a matter of New York
police practice, it is almost unheard of for homosexual relations in private
between consenting adults to form the basis for a prosecution. Typical of
present-day attitudes is a comment in an *Albany Law Review* article on legislation regulating deviant sexual behavior.

> It is believed that the proscription of deviate sexual behavior between consenting
> adults is not within the proper scope of legislative endeavor. The fact that such
> acts are considered by many to be immoral does not prove sufficient reason for
> state regulation. In addition, the various harms resulting from their criminal
> sanctions far out-weigh their questionable deterrent effects.[15]

A concomitant of the "disease view" of homosexuality is psychological
treatment of homosexuals. An interesting experiment of this nature was the
group therapy program carried out from 1953 to 1957 at the Brooklyn Association for the Rehabilitation of Offenders' Civic Center Clinic in Brooklyn,
New York. The BARO Clinic was, at the time, the only full-time licensed,
privately endowed, mental hygiene clinic devoted exclusively to the psychiatric treatment of adult offenders. In 1954, a group therapy program for
offenders was established, designed to treat individuals referred by various
criminal courts, agencies, and other sources. While at first the therapy groups
included homosexuals as well as other kinds of offenders, later, at the request
of homosexual patients, separate groups were organized for homosexuals.
After several years of work with male homosexual offenders, the therapists
conducting the sessions came to the conclusion that while it was probably not
possible to change the sexual proclivities of most patients, it was possible to
make the homosexual a more comfortable and law-abiding member of society. If his sexual problems could not be solved, at least the homosexual could
be helped to accept his condition, and to lead a reasonably satisfying, law-
abiding life in other areas of his day-to-day existence.[16]

Many homosexuals today, however, reject the "disease theory" of homosexuality and consider themselves to be no more deviant than people who put
salt on their grapefruit rather than sugar. They argue that the question of
sexual preference is a private matter which should have no bearing on public
policy, and that homosexuals who are, in fact, discriminated against in matters of employment, housing, and tax policy should have treatment fully

equal to that of heterosexuals. Implicit in this attitude is the assumption that homosexuality is as desirable a sexual orientation as heterosexuality. While public opinion appears to be increasingly supportive of efforts to remove the legal disabilities attendant upon homosexuality, it is not yet ready to concede that homosexuality is not a pathological condition. The American Psychiatric Association, for example, has stated that homosexuality *per se* should no longer be considered as a "psychiatric disorder" but should be defined instead as a "sexual orientation disturbance."[17] Liberal laymen, unconcerned about terminology, frequently support gay rights campaigns, but are nevertheless disturbed by the prospect of homosexuals in the army where large groups of men live in close physical proximity, or as teachers who may influence susceptible youngsters. In the public mind, homosexuality is not only a disease, but a contagious disease, and however much the public may sympathize with victims, they are not yet willing to accept the self-image that gay activitists have of themselves.

CRIMINAL LAW: THEORIES OF ORIGIN

The criminal law, thus, seems to relate to two kinds of proscribed conduct: those acts which are *mala in se* and those acts which are *mala prohibita*. The offenses we call *mala in se* are related to our notions of natural law; the *mala prohibita* reflect social consensus but in narrower terms, more closely related to time, place, and circumstance. How are these two types of social consensus translated into legislative, judicial, and administrative action?

Several theories have been advanced to explain how our criminal law evolved. A purely historical approach suggests that criminal law developed from the private law characteristic of the far simpler social systems (*Gemeinschaft*)* prevailing before the Middle Ages. Law in those systems was private law, that is, it prescribed redress for torts (private wrongs committed by one individual against another). Attacks, assaults, and stealing were originally thought to be offenses which concerned only the perpetrator and his victim, and redress was usually arranged in terms of compensation to the victim, his family, or his clan. Subsequently, as social organization became more complex in the later feudal era (*Gesellschaft*),** offenses of this nature became offenses against the state: wrongdoers became disturbers, not of the victim's

---

*A concept developed by Ferdinand Tönnies, defined as a society in which "people feel they belong together because they are of the same kind." For a full discussion, see Leonard Broom and Philip Selznick, *Sociology*, 5th ed. (New York: Harper & Row, 1973, p. 149).

**In sociology, the typology constructed by Ferdinand Tönnies—*Gemeinschaft* and *Gesellschaft* —illustrates this point. *Gemeinschaft* was used by Tönnies to typify group relationships which developed unconsciously or subconsciously and which were familistic in nature, whereas *Gesellschaft* was used by him to indicate "group relationships entered into deliberately to achieve recognized ends." Alvin L. Bertrand, *Basic Sociology* (New York: Appleton, 1967), p. 50.

peace, but of the king's peace. Crime, and the punishment therefore, became matters of public rather than private concern. According to the classical historical theory criminal law thus developed directly from the laws relating to private torts, and changed, as our social system changed, into a system of public law. However, not all wrongs in primitive society were torts; some, such as sacrilege and treason, were always crimes against the group. Furthermore, even to say of torts that they developed into crimes is not to explain the pattern of development.

Another theory of the origin of criminal law is that it represents the considered, orderly thinking of society as to what regulations are necessary to maintain order. Just as John Locke hypothesized that governments came into being to insure order, tranquility, and the inalienable private rights of individuals, so one may theorize that the substance of our criminal law resulted from the intellectual assessment of social problems, and considered judgment as to the best remedies possible. Few practitioners familiar with criminal law and its idiosyncracies, contradictions, and irrationalities could accept this theory except perhaps in very general terms.

A more promising theory is that criminal law is a crystallization of the mores of a society, that is, that normative behavior upon which society places a high evaluation. Sabbath blue laws and those laws relating to gambling, prostitution, obscenity and pornography, alcohol and drug use are all reflections of public opinion regarding such modes of conduct at the time the legislation was placed on the books. American legislatures are notorious for their failure to repeal outmoded morals legislation, and therefore, as social attitudes towards these practices change, it is left to the judiciary, and even to the police and prosecutors, to modify the stated law in accordance with the changing consensus of society. Such modification is achieved through "interpretation" by the courts and through either selective enforcement or nonenforcement by police and prosecutors.

This changing social consensus is frequently given form, direction, and impetus by interest groups which promote a particular point of view regarding desirable social goals. Such groups operate essentially as educational institutions, that is, through mass media and other instruments of social communication. They educate the public as to the "rightness" of their views and urge public support for them. Thus, as the public comes to accept the innocuousness of private homosexual behavior between consenting adults, less and less pressure is placed on police and prosecutors to take action against such conduct, and judges are freer to impose minimal or suspended sentences. Ultimately, if and when public opinion becomes sufficiently mobilized, the legislature may be moved to take action to modify or repeal the formal statute. In some areas of legislation, such as abortion and birth control, pressure groups have been markedly successful in bringing "test cases" to court to afford the judiciary an opportunity to reinterpret old statutes in the light of more modern standards.

The operations of interest groups are extremely complex and subtle, and extend for example, to efforts to influence the curricula of law schools and the training of lawyers.* New emphases on labor law, poverty law, and criminal law in the law schools have been the product in the first instance, at least, of the persuasive efforts of interest groups concerned with social problems such as the improvement of the position of the working man, the rights of the poor, and the equalization of the treatment of defendants in our criminal justice system. Critics of our legal system, and especially of our criminal law, sometimes charge that the more politically powerful middle- and upper-class groups are able to define law in terms that regulate the conduct of the lower classes but leave them free to act in ways often just as reprehensible. From this point of view, the nature of criminal law and the enforcement processes are dependent upon the outcomes of struggles between various social classes (rich-poor, landlord-tenant, urban-rural, debtor-creditor, propertied-propertyless) for power. Those groups which win the political struggle get to decide what are and who commits crimes. Who is a criminal, and what is a crime are, in this view of the matter, a function of the social stratification system. While this is at least partially true, the interests of the disadvantaged have been championed by interest groups which have attempted to redress the balance. For example, by the successful fight for countervailing rights, the rights of property have been modified to permit the recognition of the rights to collective bargaining, safe and healthful working conditions, minimum wages, controlled rents, and equal opportunity employment.

Thus upon examination, crime, far from being the exact mode of forbidden conduct it superficially seems to be, is really a highly philosophical concept, reflecting nothing less than a *Weltanschauung* (world outlook) as to the kind of society we ought to live in. The definition of crime in the first instance is found on the statute books, but it is highly modified, sometimes to the point of extinction, by both administrative (police and prosecutorial) action and by judicial interpretation. Moreover, the modes of conduct proscribed by the formal law have found their way there from a variety of sources: either as vestigial historical remains, or as a result of a rational effort at problem solving, or as a crystallization of widely held notions of natural law or, on a less lofty plane, of notions of proper social conduct. Criminal law, like all law, is in a state of flux, reflecting the movements of a dynamic society. Much of this movement is channeled and focused through the mechanism of *ad hoc* or ongoing interest groups which educate or inform the general public in the process of serving their own causes.

*For an excellent discussion of the relationship of class interests to the structure of the legal profession and the curricula and admissions policies of law schools, see Jerold S. Auerbach, *Unequal Justice,* New York: Oxford University Press, 1976.

Selected Readings

Becker, Howard S. *Outsiders: Studies in the Sociology of Deviance.* New York: Free Press, 1963

Brecher, Edward M., et al. *Licit and Illicit Drugs.* Boston: Little, Brown, 1972.

Chambliss, William J. *Crime and the Legal Process.* New York: McGraw-Hill, 1969.

Committee on Homosexual Offenses and Prostitution. *Wolfenden Report,* Command Paper 247. London: Her Majesty's Stationery Office, September 1957.

Dealing with Drug Abuse: A Report to the Ford Foundation. New York: Praeger, 1972.

Erikson, Kai T. *Wayward Puritans.* New York: Wiley, 1966.

Ferri, Enrico. *Criminal Sociology.* New York: Appleton, 1896.

Grinspoon, Lester. *Marijuana Reconsidered.* New York: Bantam, 1971.

Lindesmith, Alfred R. *The Addict and the Law.* New York: Vintage Books, 1967.

Mannheim, Hermann. *Pioneers in Criminology.* 2nd ed. Montclair, N. J.: Patterson Smith, 1972.

McNamara, Donal E. J., and Sagarin, Edward. *Sex, Crime, and the Law.* New York: Free Press, 1977.

Non-Medical Use of Drugs: Interim Report of the Canadian Government Commission of Inquiry. Baltimore, Md.: Penguin, 1971.

President's Commission on Law Enforcement and Administration of Justice. *Task Force Reports: Police; Courts; Corrections; Juvenile Delinquency and Youth Crime; Organized Crime; Science and Technology; Assessment of Crime; Narcotics and Drugs; Drunkenness.* Washington, D.C.: U.S. Government Printing Office, 1967.

Quinney, Richard, ed. *Crime and Justice in Society.* Boston: Little, Brown, 1969.

Schur, Edwin M. *Crimes Without Victims.* Englewood Cliffs, N.J.: Prentice-Hall, 1965.

Sutherland, Edwin H., and Cressey, Donald R. *Criminology.* 10th ed. Philadephia: Lippincott, 1978.

Notes

1. *People v. Friedman,* 302 N.Y. 75 (1950), as quoted in Leo Pfeffer, *Church, State and Freedom,* rev. ed. (Boston: Beacon Press, 1967), pp. 283–284.
2. E. H. Sutherland and D. R. Cressey, *Criminology,* 10th ed. (Philadelphia: Lippincott, 1978), p. 4.
3. *Griswold v. Connecticut,* 381 U.S. 479 (1965).
4. 410 U.S. 113 (1973).
5. For an extended discussion of the concept of the "outsider," see Howard S. Becker, *Outsiders* (New York: Free Press, 1963).
6. Harrison Act, 1914. For a more complete discussion of the development of federal policy toward drug use, see Alfred R. Lindesmith, "Federal Law and Drug Addiction," in William J. Chambliss, *Crime and the Legal Process* (New York: McGraw-Hill, 1969), pp. 63–73; and Edwin M. Schur, *Crimes Without Victims* (Englewood Cliffs, N.J.: Prentice-Hall, 1965), pp. 120–168.
7. *Webb v. United States,* 249 U.S. 96 (1919); *United States v. Behrman,* 258 U.S. 280 (1922).
8. *Linder v. United States,* 268 U.S. 5 (1925).
9. Lindesmith, p. 63.
10. For an excellent discussion of this topic, see Edward M. Brecher, et al., *Licit and Illicit Drugs,* Boston: Little, Brown, 1972.
11. President's Commission on Law Enforcement and Administration of Justice, *Task Force Report: Drunkenness* (Washington, D.C.: U.S. Government Printing Office, 1967), p. 1.

12. Alfred C. Kinsey, Wendell B. Pomeroy, and Clyde E. Martin, *Sexual Behavior in the Human Male* (Philadelphia: Saunders, 1948).

13. Committee on Homosexual Offenses and Prostitution, *Wolfenden Report,* Command Paper 247 (London: Her Majesty's Stationery Office, September 1957), p. 66.

14. *New York Times,* July 5, 1967, p. 1.

15. R. M. Fritts and F. V. Smith, "Deviate Sexual Behavior: The Desirability of Legislative Proscription," 30 *Albany Law Review* 304 (1966).

16. For fuller discussion, see Alexander B. Smith and Alexander Bassin, "Group Therapy with Homosexuals," *Journal of Social Therapy* 5, no. 3 (1959):225–232.

17. Charles Hite, "APA Rules Homosexuality not Necessarily a Psychiatric Disorder," *Psychiatric News,* January 2, 1974, p. 1.

chapter 3

criminals: status groups and differential handling

"Equal Justice Under Law"
  Inscription over U.S. Supreme Court Building,
  Washington, D.C.

"Our constitution is color-blind, and neither knows
nor tolerates classes among citizens."
  Justice John Marshall Harlan dissenting, *Plessy v.
  Ferguson* (1896)

"The law, in all its majestic equality, forbids the rich as
well as the poor to sleep under bridges on rainy nights,
to beg on the streets and to steal bread."
  Anatole France, *Le Lys Rouge*

Superficially, the neatly bound volumes of statutes in the law libraries may seem to be rocks of stability and objectivity in a bewildering, rapidly changing world. The heavy books with their precise, stilted language, describing seemingly every contingency, every mode of proscribed conduct imaginable, seem the very essence of certainty and immutability. This appearance is deceptive. In the long run, societal perceptions of natural law and the changing standards of approved conduct will affect the substance of the law. In more immediate terms, the content of the law will change with the enactment of new laws, repeal of old laws, and shifting judicial interpretations in cases adjudicated under the penal code.

It is not only the formal substance of the law that varies, however. Were it fixed (and it is of course fixed during relatively short periods of time) an additional variable would exist in the way the law is applied to those over whom it has jurisdiction. Is the law really the same law for rich and poor, black and white, child and adult, blue-collar and white-collar, homosexual and heterosexual, rational and insane, normal and retarded? The impact of the law is obviously not the same, and few people would argue that it should be. The five-year-old who unthinkingly locks a playmate in an abandoned refrigerator ought not to be treated in the same manner as the hold-up man whose gagged victim suffocates. The mental incompetent cannot be questioned in the same manner as the normal suspect; the results of the interrogation as well as the evaluation of the intent of his conduct must make allowance for his mental capacity.

Most people would nevertheless indignantly reject the notion that social position, education, affluence, or political connections warrant specially favorable treatment at the hands of the law. In reality, however, the law works differently not only for the child, the mentally incompetent, and the insane, but also, to some extent, for those whose status is other than white and middle- or upper-class. On the whole the poor, alcoholics, hippies, addicts, homosexuals, nonwhites, and political radicals are frequently treated more severely for the same kinds of conduct than white, middle-class, conventional defendants would be.

DIFFERENTIAL HANDLING: RICH AND POOR

Case 1.   Tobacco heiress Doris Duke, while intoxicated, drove her car along a private road on her Rhode Island estate, hitting and crushing to death against a wall a male employee, one Tirella, reputedly her lover. The police refrained from interrogating her for three days until she recovered her composure. At that time she was questioned at home. No indictment was handed down.[1]

Case 2.   In an affluent, upstate New York, suburban community residents reported being annoyed by a peeping Tom. The police knew the culprit to be one of the town's leading citizens. The complaint was handled by calling the suspect's wife and asking her to take care of the matter.[2]

Case 3.   Mrs. Anne Woodward, a Long Island socialite, was allegedly awakened from sleep at about three A.M. on October 30, 1955. She claimed that she was frightened, grabbed the family shotgun, and on seeing a shadow nearby, let go with both barrels, hitting and fatally wounding her husband. She was handled very gently by the police. On November 22, 1955, she voluntarily left the hospital for the questioning at Nassau County Police Headquarters. On November 26, 1955, the Grand Jury cleared her, after she and thirty-one witnesses testified.[3]

Case 4. On April 6, 1966, the Reverend Harold L. Elliott of North Babylon Center, Long Island, was arrested on a charge of luring a seven-year-old girl into a station wagon and committing sodomy in the presence of a nine-year-old girl. The police reported that, in the one year Elliott had been in charge of his church on Long Island, he was involved in at least forty to fifty similar cases in Nassau and Suffolk counties. The Reverend Elliott had previously been arrested in Elizabeth, West Virginia, on March 26, 1964, charged by a fifteen- and a sixteen-year-old-girl with indecent exposure. He posted a small bond which he forfeited, and then moved to Levole, Maryland, with a new church position. There, less than a year later, on February 16, 1965, he was again arrested for indecent exposure, this time on complaint of a number of twelve- and thirteen-year-old girls. These charges were dropped with the understanding that Elliott would undergo psychiatric treatment.

Elliott was indicted in Nassau county on seven counts of sodomy. The court ordered a succession of psychiatric examinations, after which Elliott was found sane. Finally, he was permitted to plead guilty to one count of Sodomy, First Degree by Nassau County Judge Martin Kolbrener. Although the district attorney asked that a life sentence be imposed, Judge Kolbrener gave Elliott a five- to ten-year suspended sentence, on condition that the latter commit himself to a state hospital until certified as cured. Elliott was thereupon admitted to Central Islip State Hospital. The newspaper commented that the sentence imposed was very lenient.[4]

All of the above cases have one thing in common: the treatment of the offenders was extraordinary in that it differed markedly from treatment given to ordinary suspects. It is inconceivable, for example, that a lower-class or lower-middle-class woman involved in a vehicular homicide case would have been accorded the courtesy of three days respite from questioning in order that she might regain her composure. Most peeping Toms are arrested, questioned, publicly arraigned, plead guilty to a minor charge, and are given a short sentence or probation. Householders who fatally wound alleged intruders are, normally, rigorously and promptly questioned by the police. Sex offenders who are not upper-middle-class clergymen of established religious denominations are seldom treated gently and sympathetically. In short, to state the matter baldly, every criminal justice practitioner from the policeman to the parole officer knows that the law in practice is not the same for rich and poor.*

*While it is generally true that the law handles the rich more gently than the poor, there is a latent hostility in the United States, which occasionally surfaces towards those who are considered to be economically and socially privileged. Two cases come to mind. Sam Sheppard, the wealthy osteopath who was charged with the murder of his wife and whose conviction was ultimately set aside because of prejudicial pretrial publicity (Chapter 8), was vilified and convicted by the *Cleveland Plain Dealer* which harped continuously on his wealth and the possibility of his family's purchasing his acquittal through bribery and covert influence on public officials. Sheppard's account of the events on the night of his wife's murder was sufficiently credible that one can hardly account for the reaction of the police and the public except on the basis of sheer prejudice against Sheppard because of his high status in the community. A second case is that

One of the results of this differential handling is probably an overrepresentation of the poor in official statistics relating to crime. Figures indicating arrests, convictions, and commitments show that poor people (lower-class people) commit crimes in numbers vastly disproportionate to their numbers in the population at large. Criminologists have long viewed these figures with some skepticism. Research, based on data gathered from anonymous questionnaires given to middle-class people, has indicated a surprising incidence of criminal conduct, including the commission of felonies, among groups the official statistics would lead us to believe are virtually crime-free. A study made by Herbert A. Bloch, a prominent sociologist, indicated that 91 percent of a group of college juniors and seniors admitted to having knowingly committed both misdemeanors and felonies. Women students were as delinquent as men. All those interviewed came from at least middle-class homes. An extension of the study, directed at professional men and women including physicians and lawyers, reported similar results.[5] An even more well known study by Austin L. Porterfield found that middle-class college students, very few of whom had ever been charged or arrested, had committed virtually the full range of crimes with which juveniles in the Texas courts had been charged. These offenses averaged out at no less than eleven per student.[6]

Not only do middle-class people apparently commit the same kinds of crime as lower-class people, but in addition, they are prone to a considerable degree of what Edwin H. Sutherland, the late dean of American criminologists, has labelled "white-collar crime." These crimes, so called because they are perpetrated in the normal course of business by those in managerial or professional positions, include, in the business world, such practices as "misrepresentation in financial statements of corporations, manipulation in the stock exchange, commercial bribery, bribery of public officials . . ., misrepresentation in advertising and salesmanship, embezzlement, short weights . . ., and misapplication of funds in receiverships and bankruptcies."[7] Each profession has its own variety of illegal practices; for example, physicians have been known to sell narcotic drugs and prescriptions illegally, treat criminal fugitives and underworld characters, file fraudulent reports, prejure themselves in court, and split fees. A similar list could no doubt be drawn up for attorneys and other professionals. The money value of these crimes no doubt exceeds the total money value of traditional crimes, and their social effects

---

of Patricia Hearst who, following her kidnapping and imprisonment by the Symbionese Liberation Army (SLA), a group of political terrorists, committed an armed robbery for which she was subsequently convicted. While the conviction was justified, the sentence appeared to have been excessive given the fact that she was only twenty at the time of the kidnapping and had been subjected to frightful mistreatment and psychological pressure from her captors. The movement to obtain executive clemency and remission of part of her seven year prison sentence met, at least initially, with tremendous public hostility, with many critics describing her as a spoiled, rich girl whose parents could buy anything, even a pardon for their daughter. President Carter ultimately commuted her prison sentence shortly before she became eligible for parole.

may well be very harmful. Yet perpetrators of white-collar crimes are seldom so much as charged, and are even more rarely committed to correctional institutions.

In assessing the unfairness of differential handling of middle-class as opposed to lower-class accused persons, one must guard against comparing apples and oranges. In general, offenses by middle-class people tend to be property crimes rather than crimes against the person, while lower-class crime tends to incorporate elements of personal violence. It is true, of course, that many lower-class people commit property crimes, such as burglary and larceny, but these property crimes frequently have elements of violence or potential violence, as for example, when a householder surprises a burglar who thought the premises to be empty. White-collar crimes, on the other hand, at least as conceived by Sutherland, were, by definition, nonviolent: embezzlement, trademark infringements, stock exchange manipulation, and the like. There are, however, white-collar offenses which do have potential for crimes against the person as well as property: the landlord who bribes the fire inspector to overlook the inadequate fire escapes, the physician who sells prescriptions for dangerous drugs, the contractor whose shoddy concrete results in an unsafe structure, and so on.

Thus, in comparing the handling of lower-class with middle-class defendants, it is necessary to ascertain the degree of violence or potential violence in the acts committed. Violent crime is far more dangerous to society and harmful to its victims than crimes which result simply in the loss of property, and the handling of those who commit violent crimes should be qualitatively different from the handling of those who commit nonviolent crimes. If middle-class defendants who commit white-collar crimes which may cause bodily harm are treated differently from lower-class defendants who have committed violent crimes, then the criminal justice system is clearly exhibiting a class bias. If, however, middle-class, nonviolent property crime is treated more leniently than lower-class crimes against the person, such differential handling is not necessarily unjustified.

Police as a group have their own variety of white-collar crime. The charges made by Lincoln Steffens in *The Shame of the Cities* (1904), of police connivance with and protection of racketeers, gamblers, prostitutes, and other criminals, have been repeated frequently since, and were not novel when made. Periodically, exposure is made of some particularly corrupt department which cooperates with underworld elements. These crimes fit Sutherland's definition of white-collar crime in that they arise out of the normal course of legitimate police business. They are regarded by the public at large and by most police practitioners as illegal, immoral, disfunctional activities. There is, however, another set of police activities which are in violation of the formal statutes, but which nevertheless are considered both moral and functional by almost all working policemen. These are the kinds of actions policemen take in acquiring and using informers. Many informed observers have described such police malpractice as harrassment through illegal arrests and detentions, nonfeasance of duty in refraining from arresting criminals, bribery and illegal wiretapping. Some of these activities are related to the process of using petty criminals to inform on their bigger and more dangerous colleagues. Few policemen would deny the validity of this description of the informer system; fewer still would deny the necessity for the use of informers in police work. The evasions of the law necessitated by the informer system do, nevertheless, create a large body of lawbreakers within the police department.

The public at large is, for the most part, only dimly aware of the advantages that the well-to-do lawbreaker enjoys in contrast to his lower-class fellow criminal. In recent years, due in part to the publicity given to such cases as *Gideon v. Wainright* and *Miranda v. Arizona*,[8] there has been an increasing appreciation of the importance of adequate legal counsel in every criminal case. Access to such counsel is obviously easier for the rich man than for the poor. However, differential handling is a much more subtle and complex phenomenon than the relatively simple matter of providing counsel. The entire criminal justice system reacts differently to the rich man: he is less likley to be arrested; if arrested he can make bail; he will be treated considerately, if not deferentially, by the police; every avenue of legal appeal will be available to him; and should he be convicted, his punishment will be less severe, at least in terms of imprisonment.

Does society really wish it otherwise? While the average, strongly egalitarian-minded American would, in principle, vehemently reject the notion of one law for the rich and another for the poor, how many people really want to see rich and poor treated alike? In Philadelphia, Federal District Court Judge Ganby sentenced seven executives of leading electrical equipment manufacturers (including General Electric and Westinghouse vice-presidents) to jail for thirty days. He fined thirty-six men and twenty-one companies $931,500 for criminal violation of the anti-trust laws. The government had brought charges against forty-five individuals and twenty-nine companies for fixing prices and rigging bids for government contracts. Twenty received suspended jail terms.[9] Should these executives of the country's leading electrical manufacturers have received prison terms commensurate with the money value of the crimes they committed? In Case 2, cited above, involving an affluent peeping Tom, or in Case 4, concerning a middle-class sodomist, would any social purpose beyond simple vengeance have been served by committing the suspects to prison? If an offender is so situated that he can be rehabilitated and prevented from doing further social harm without being publicly disgraced and punished, is there a reason why he should be handled in a harsh and punitive manner?

Most people, except for those who think of justice in retributive terms, would probably agree that it is socially desirable to use only that degree of force and official action needed to accomplish the primary social goals of deterrence and reform. If this is so, then differential handling for the rich has considerable practical validity. What must not be overlooked, however, is that the poor are in many cases punished, disgraced, and publicly pilloried, not only because of the offenses they committed, but because their social position is such that other, less harsh alternatives are not available to the system of criminal justice. Lower-class, storefront clergymen simply don't have the strong families and resources that guarantee they will be kept out of trouble in the future. Poor people who commit violent crimes usually don't have relatives, business associates, and friends who will see to it that they are restrained in the future. The police and the jails must play the part that the psychiatrist and the good lawyer play in the lives of the rich. Thus the criminologist's skepticism as to the validity of official crime statistics is, in large part, justified.*

DIFFERENTIAL HANDLING: BLACK AND WHITE

Black Americans bear a special relationship to our criminal justice system. They are more likely to become suspects or defendants in criminal cases than are white Americans, and once having become suspects, they suffer the double handicap of being both poor and black. All the disabilities suffered by a poor person in defending himself against a criminal charge are suffered by the poor black, and in addition, his color will add still another dimension of disadvantage to his case.

The incidence of crimes among blacks is disproportionately high,[10] especially with regard to crimes of violence. The President's Crime Commission Report indicates that the arrest rate of blacks for FBI Index Offenses** in 1965 was four times as great as that for whites; the black arrest rate for murder was almost ten times as high; and for burglary it was almost three and one-half times as high. We may not conclude from this, however, that a tendency toward crime is a genetic quality inherent in blacks. One variable accounting for the disparity between white and black crime rates is a difference in level of income. There is a strong correlation between poverty (and especially slum living) and crime, and blacks are disproportionately poor. Studies of ethnic groups in America have shown that crime rates decrease as the group moves from the core city to the suburbs. The difference in arrest rates between blacks and whites living under similar conditions is far less disparate.

Secondly, the statistics which indicate these differential crime rates are incomplete, and therefore unreliable. The figures of the President's Crime Commission Report cited above are based on arrests. Other figures showing the disproportionate amount of black criminal activity are based on convic-

*See appendix for a brief discussion of crime statistics.
**The FBI Index lists seven offenses: Willful Homicide, Forcible Rape, Robbery, Aggravated Assault, Burglary, Larceny, and Motor Vehicle Theft.

tions. Neither of these figures bears any precise relationship to offenses committed. All that can be said with certainty is that far more crimes are committed than are known to the police, and infinitely more than result in arrests or convictions. The differential in crime rates between blacks and whites can thus mean one of two things: either that blacks commit disproportionately more crime, or that they are arrested and convicted disproportionately more frequently than whites. Probably both are true, but the discriminatory factor in the criminal justice system which leads to disproportionate arrests and convictions has received far less attention from the public than the hypothesis that blacks are more prone to crime than whites.

Poor people, as indicated in the previous section, do not and cannot receive the same handling in the criminal justice system as well-to-do people. They are more likely to be suspected and arrested than the middle class. When arrested, they are less likely to be admitted to bail or discharged on their own recognizance. If tried, they are less likely to have the assistance of good quality counsel; if convicted, they are less likely to appeal; if sentenced, they are more likely to receive prison sentences rather than fines or probation; and, when sentenced to prison, their sentences tend to be longer than those given well-to-do defendants. All these disabilities apply to most black suspects enmeshed in the toils of the law, because most blacks are poor. There is however, an added dimension to the problem for the black: his color alone, aside from his class, will make him more likely to be suspected, arrested, convicted, and committed, especially if his victim is white. On the other hand, the police may under-enforce the law where black preys upon black, thus reducing the protection of the law for black victims.[11]

The motion picture *In the Heat of the Night* depicts the classic problem of the black *vis-à-vis* the police. When a mysterious murder takes place in a small southern town, the police, in searching for a suspect, automatically consider first a strange black who was passing through the town. It is quite clear that their decision to question him was based almost entirely on his color, combined with the fact that he was an outsider. Blacks have become increasingly bitter in their complaints that police will arrest or at least stop to question them under circumstances under which whites would not be approached. In Louisville, Kentucky, one Thompson,[12] a black handyman waiting in a café for a bus, passed the time by "shuffling" to the music of the juke box. Despite the fact that neither the proprietor nor the other customers complained, city police officers on a routine check arrested Thompson for loitering, and when he protested verbally, added the charge of disorderly conduct. Thompson was convicted and fined in Louisville Police Court. Ultimately, the Supreme Court reversed the conviction on the ground that an arrest and conviction based on no evidence is a violation of due process rights under the Fourteenth Amendment.

Not many cases are as extreme as the *Thompson* case fortunately, but many blacks feel that their color singles them out for especially harsh treatment by the police. One of the most troublesome problems in this area arises when the police decision to arrest or to question on the street is motivated largely by color. In *People v. Rivera*[13] two Puerto Rican youths were stopped, questioned, and searched by the police because their conduct seemed suspicious. The conduct in question consisted of looking intently for an extended period of time into the window of a bar and grill located in New York City's East Village. The police suspicions in this case were justified, in that Rivera was found to be carrying a revolver. The relevant question, however, is whether the very same conduct on the part of two students from nearby New York University would have produced the same reaction on the part of the police. There is some probability that it would not. From the police point of view, it is both logical and proper that poorly dressed Puerto Ricans should be regarded with more suspicion than well-dressed college boys. The statistical likelihood that a boy of Rivera's type would stick up a bar and grill is greater than that a college student would do so. From the point of view of the black or Puerto Rican this attitude is simply a reflection of the bitter truth that he is suspect because of his color or ethnic background.

Merely being out of the ghetto is enough, on occasion, to single out the black man for attention. In 1969, in a case involving robbery and murder, two suspects were apprehended by the police, and subsequently convicted of homicide. In a second trial of one of the defendants on charges of felonious possession of a weapon arising out of the same incident, the conviction of the defendant was set aside by the appellate court because of inflammatory, allegedly racially biased remarks by the prosecutor. The basis for these remarks (which were in rebuttal to accusations of racial bias by the defense attorney) was that suspicion had fallen on the two suspects initially because they were black men in a white neighborhood.[14] Again, from the vantage of the police, black men running through a white neighborhood are unusual and suspect; to the law-abiding black, however, such law enforcement simply means that he is judged by standards more rigorous than those applied to his white counterparts.

Another area in which blacks feel they are at a disadvantage *vis-à-vis* the police is with respect to the question of identification. To the white man, all blacks tend to look alike. Certainly, there is a far greater chance of error when a black suspect is identified by either a white victim or a white policeman, so much so that an authority on the problems of eye-witness identification suggests that far greater weight be given to identification of blacks by other blacks than to identification of blacks by whites.[15] In practice, however, it is doubtful that judges and juries are aware of the somewhat dubious validity of interracial identification.

The grievances of blacks against the criminal justice system are not, however, confined to complaints about over-zealous or unduly harsh enforcement of the law. Curiously enough, precisely the opposite complaint may be made: that the police do not enforce the law vigorously enough when crimes are committed against blacks by other blacks. It is notorious, for example, that assaults, especially those arising out of domestic quarrels, frequently do not end in arrest and prosecution when the parties involved are black unless the victim insists on filing a complaint and following through. LaFave states:

> This kind of unequal enforcement of the law frequently occurs when Negroes are involved, particularly in large metropolitan areas such as Detroit. Such offenses as bigamy and open and notorious cohabitation are overlooked by law enforcement officials, and arrests often are not made for carrying knives or for robbery of other Negroes. However, the practice is most strikingly illustrated by the repeated failure of the police to arrest Negroes for a felonious assault upon a spouse or acquaintance unless the victim actually insists upon prosecution.[16]

Similarly James Q. Wilson, in his study of police behavior in eight different American communities, says that:

> In Newburgh every Negro interviewed . . .agreed that the overriding characteristic of the Newburgh police was their tendency to under-enforce the law in Negro areas. One lawyer told an interviewer:
> "We can't get police protection in this [Negro] community. They [the police] ignore the crowds. There's a bar right next to where my parents live. . . . Every night there'll be a big crowd . . .that will gather in the streets in front of this place. Sometimes we'll have to call the police four and five times before they even come. When they do come, they often get out of their cars and just start joking with people standing there. The police are supposed to break up those crowds and move them along, but they don't do it."
> Another Negro . . .complained . . .:
> "Not long ago five men broke into my house. Five men! They came upstairs. . . . If I didn't have a .22 rifle with me, I don't know what would have happened. I called the police three times, and it took them a half hour to get there. . . . When you complain to the police about their not giving you any kind of protection, you get answers like the one X gave me. He said, 'I'll deny I ever said this if you repeat it, but you know how this police department is run. Our motto is, let the niggers kill each other off.'"[17]

The police rationale for such under-enforcement is generally that the mores of the black community are different, that blacks don't regard those offenses as crimes, and that they want to be let alone by the police. They cite as evidence that black complainants are frequently uncooperative, refusing to file complaints or withdrawing complaints already filed. Some policemen see blacks as preferring to take the law into their own hands and discipline the offender personally. Wilson quotes a Newburgh detective as saying that the police would permit this "discipline" only in "small cases . . . no more than fifteen to twenty stitches." The policeman will almost always deny that the under-enforcement of the law in black communities stems from contempt for the black community and a lack of concern for its well-being. He will justify his department's policy on the ground of suiting official conduct to the needs and desires of the client served. However, law-abiding blacks, victimized by crime, see only that the law does not afford them the same protection it affords law-abiding whites. The policeman's case is somewhat weakened by the fact that an official *laissez faire* attitude towards crime by blacks rarely exists when whites are the victims.

It is not only in the area of detention and arrests that color is a factor in official actions. Sentencing of black defendants also shows a differential pattern. In 1969, a study of the criminal justice system by Marvin E. Wolfgang of the University of Pennsylvania and Bernard Cohen of Queens College was published by the American Jewish Committee. It concluded that: "More blacks are arrested, jailed, convicted and given more severe penalties than whites." A specific example cited was that,

> between 1940 and 1964 in Florida 125 white men were convicted of raping white women and 68 black men were convicted of raping black women. In each category, approximately 4 percent of those convicted were sentenced to death. However, during that same period, 84 black men were convicted of raping white women and 54 percent of them were sentenced to death. Eight white men were convicted of raping black women and none was sentenced to death.[18]

To cite the most extreme example, in the South the death penalty for rape was reserved almost exclusively for blacks; white men convicted of the same offense received varying terms of imprisonment.

Black juvenile defendants are more often committed to institutions, where white children are usually returned to their parents or are handled by unofficial agencies. Discriminatory attitudes on the part of those officials involved in handling such young offenders are only partially to blame for the situation; the lack of access by black children to the private agencies that service whites (especially Jewish youngsters) is also a highly significant factor. Nevertheless, studies show that black children are frequently committed at younger ages than whites, for less serious offenses, and with more promising case histories.[19] Thus, the criminal justice system for the black man, especially the poor black, is harsh and punitive to a degree experienced by relatively few whites. The black's consequent alienation from the system on which the white middle class pin their hopes of peace, order, and stability is easily understandable. As Professor Bloch has eloquently said:

> This is the inevitable price we pay for the social and cultural disenfranchisement of minority peoples, and the story can be duplicated in various parts of the country. The groups may change from time to time, but the effects of the cultural pattern of marginality remain largely the same.[20]

DIFFERENTIAL HANDLING: PARIAHS

In the discussion of deviance in Chapter 2, it was suggested that deviance was tentatively defined by some authorities as behavior that is pathologically different, pathological in the sense that it causes harm or disruption to society. Much of this antisocial behavior we label crime. There are, however certain kinds of activities which are more distasteful than disruptive, and social attitudes towards the handling of such activities are frequently highly ambivalent. Most enlightened people today, for example, claim to look upon alcoholism as a disease. Alcoholics, thus, are not criminals but sick people. However, the sight of a drunk in the gutter arouses disgust rather than compassion in most onlookers, and their immediate reaction to the sight of the derelict inebriate is not so much "Help him" as "Get rid of him." Drug addicts, overt homosexuals, obvious prostitutes, mental defectives, hippies, skid row bums, and alcoholics all share a pariah status. Society wishes not so much to punish these people as to get them out of sight where they will cease to offend the sensibilities of "decent" people. We may agree that homosexual behavior in private between consenting adults is permissible, but we object to seeing a mincing, effeminate, rouged male on the streets. We may ultimately decide that smoking marijuana should not be punished, but we don't like to see groups of glassy-eyed adolescents wandering around in public. We may chuckle privately at extramarital sexual dalliance, but we object to the sight of groups of bizarrely dressed prostitutes soliciting clients in our downtown areas. In short, we object to the public display of conduct that good taste demands be kept private.

The police share the negativism of societal attitudes toward these types of deviants. The police, after all, are individuals drawn from the common ranks, and share the common ranks' prejudices. The public, furthermore, having no other agency to turn to in its effort to be spared the discomfort of seeing these deviates, turns to the police. The police reaction mirrors that of the community, but only more intensely.

Paul Chevigny of the American Civil Liberties Union discusses police reactions to undesirables:

Bohemians, homosexuals, political activists (particularly of the left), derelicts, prostitutes, and narcotic users all evoke police action. A member of one of these outcast groups will not be harmed if he obeys the orders of the police, unless there is a drive on to round up homosexuals, derelicts or prostitutes....On the other hand, the police do tend to take some action, short of arrest, against a member of such pariah groups, even without any verbal challenge or other threat. His mere presence seems to be enough challenge to make the police tell him to move on. Any sort of defiance of the police action in such cases is likely to be answered with violence.[21]

On the whole the aim of police conduct towards these outcasts is to get them out of sight: to get them to move on, beat it, get lost. Occasionally, in response to complaints from merchants, tourists, and others, there will be clean-ups of particular areas frequented by undesirables, in which case drunks, homosexuals, prostitutes, and others will be arrested and sentenced to short terms in jail. The police may also be rougher in their handling of these individuals than they are of other suspects, for very few of these pariahs complain. Most complaints, according to Chevigny at least, come from middle-class citizens who witness and are affronted by police conduct.

This type of police conduct, moreover, is typical of the handling of any minority group that has not yet achieved full acceptance. Blacks, Jews, Italians, Puerto Ricans, and even the Irish in the nineteenth century have experienced the underlying hostility of society towards them as filtered through the medium of police behavior. Conceivably, some of the groups mentioned by Chevigny will eventually lose their outcast status and be accepted as unusual but not necessarily distasteful members of society (as some ethnic groups eventually have). In the interim, however, students of the criminal justice system must be aware that police handling of these individuals is by no means evenhanded or comparable to the handling of commonplace suspects.

DIFFERENTIAL HANDLING: POLITICAL HERETICS

Another group that frequently receives unusually harsh and punitive handling by the criminal justice system is the politically unorthodox, especially radicals of the left. There are two principal reasons why this type of differential treatment occurs: first, many law enforcement officials are unaware of the public policy implications of a commitment to the classical theory of democratic government on which the United States Constitution purports to be based; and second, radicals do not only speak—they act—and their actions sometimes pose real threats to the public order.

To many policemen and judges, the hortatory dogma of groups such as Communists, black militants, and student protestors is a threat, not only to the stability, but to the very existence of the social order that law enforcement officials are sworn to protect. Such violent critics of the system are, moreover, not only dangerous but ungrateful. As many policemen see it, the freedom of speech that radicals enjoy is a gift bestowed upon them by a generous society, and when radicals use it to the detriment of that society, they are surely violating the rules of the game and behaving despicably.

This reasoning, though superficially plausible, is fallacious in terms of classical democratic theory. Freedom of speech is not a gift from society to the individual. On the contrary, freedom of thought, speech, and conscience are inalienable rights which inhere in every individual, and which no society may abridge. Moreover, such rights are socially justified only partially because of the fulfillment individuals may find in them. Their more important justification is that they are the salvation of a free society.

> The peculiar evil of silencing the expression of an opinion is, that it is robbing the human race; posterity as well as the existing generation; those who dissent from the opinion, still more than those who hold it. If the opinion is right, they are deprived of the opportunity of exchanging error for truth: if wrong, they lose, what is almost as great a benefit, the clearer perception and livelier impression of truth, produced by its collision with error. . . . We can never be sure that the opinion we are endeavoring to stifle is a false opinion; and if we were sure, stifling it would be an evil still.[22]

The practical implications of Mill's theory are that every idea must be heard —primarily for the benefit of society. However silly, destructive, hateful, or strange, no idea may be suppressed, because no one in society is capable of rendering an *a priori* judgment as to its worthlessness. History bears witness to the number of radical thinkers reviled in their own time whose thought is now revered and accepted. Moreover, the persecution of such thinkers has invariably resulted in a great loss to the society which suppressed them. The Athens which executed Socrates and the Hitler regime which drove Jewish scientists from Germany enfeebled their own civilizations. Thus, the radical is not an individual to be simply tolerated. He is a necessity to a society in a state of flux.

Most confrontations between police and radicals do not involve abstract questions of freedom of speech. They center on the policeman's duty—as he sees it—to maintain public order and the radical's right—as he sees it—to publicize his message wherever and however he can. Most such clashes involve public assemblies wherein a mixture of speech and action occurs. Action, unlike speech, may be legitimately repressible by a democratic government. The dispute between radicals and the police normally concerns where the line should be drawn. The radical interprets his action as incident to his speech, hence beyond control; the police see the radical's speech as incident to his action, hence subject to restraint. No easy resolution of these disparate viewpoints exists. The best that can be done, perhaps, is to attempt to achieve some perspective on the dispute by reviewing some of the history and theory of our Constitution.

The absolute terms of the First Amendment to the United States Constitution reflect the healthy appreciation the founding fathers had for freedom of speech and conscience. "Congress shall make no law . . .abridging the freedom of speech, or of the press; or the right of the people to peaceably assemble. . . ." Despite this clear prohibition, however, certain kinds of speech—libel, obscenity, and sedition—have been legally suppressed in varying degrees by both the state and federal governments.

Although the first ten amendments to the Constitution, as originally passed, were restrictions on only the federal government, since 1925 the United States Supreme Court has increasingly applied these restrictions to the states, on the theory that the phrase *due process* in the Fourteenth Amendment means that which is unfair action for the federal government is equally unfair for the states. There is an ongoing controversy among members of the Supreme Court as to whether the phrase due process is the precise equivalent of the guarantees encompassed in the Bill of Rights, or whether the phrase can mean something either more or less than these guarantees. There is nevertheless agreement at this point that the First Amendment is applicable to the states. While libel and obscenity laws have caused relatively little political controversy, attempts to regulate sedition, that is, the bringing of the government into "hatred and contempt," have caused far greater problems.

The first federal attempt to regulate such speech was in the infamous and unpopular Alien and Sedition Laws, passed in 1798, and repealed two years later. From 1800 to 1917, the federal government had no peacetime regulation whatever of political speech. In 1917, however, coincidental with both our entry into World War I and the outbreak of the Russian Revolution, the federal government passed two statutes limiting speech that was disloyal and contemptuous of the United States government or that interfered with military operations. Since then the federal government has enacted several other similar laws, perhaps the most famous of which is the Smith Act of 1941. It is understandable that, in light of the absolute prohibition on regulation of speech in the First Amendment, challenges to these laws should have come to the United States Supreme Court in the form of cases involving individuals convicted under this restrictive legislation. The Supreme Court has had great difficulty in establishing a single yardstick for the test of the constitutionality of restrictive speech legislation. It has instead delivered opinions which range along a spectrum marked by two extreme positions. The more liberal of these positions is the famous so-called clear and present danger test; the more conservative position is the "bad tendency" or "gravity of the evil discounted by its improbablity" test. In recent years the more customary position taken by the Supreme Court in cases involving "pure speech" has been the "clear and present danger" position, that is, all speech is permissible that does not create an imminent likelihood of antisocial action—riot or revolution. Although imminence is not readily definable, the Court appears to think of the time span involved in terms of days or hours rather than months or years. This standard refers to "pure speech," that is speech unmixed with action. The best example of such speech might be publication of ideas in a book. Speeches before audiences, picketing, demonstrating on the streets, and distributing handbills are all examples of speech mixed with action, and are regulated in a somewhat different manner.

While the clear and present danger standard is the more usual position of the Court, at least since the late 1930s, there have been notable and significant exceptions. During the McCarthy era, from the end of World War II until well into the first Eisenhower administration, the Court refused to permit the advocacy of revolutionary ideas even though they were expressions of sentiment or desire rather than plans for overt action. Thus, Eugene Dennis and his codefendant Communist party leaders were convicted for having preached the dogma embodied in such classical works of Communist literature as Marx's *Communists Manifesto* and Lenin's *State and Revolution*.[23] The reasoning of the Court seemed to be that a society had a right to protect itself from ideas which might in the future produce dangerous results—that there was no obligation on the part of the authorities to wait until the plans of the revolutionaries had been laid and action was about to take place. This standard is, of course, far more restrictive since it depends for its application on subjective judgment by administrators of the likelihood of events in the indefinite future. Timid or fearful officials, or those under political pressure, may easily see danger in every expression of dissent or dissatisfaction.

It is not surprising that, historically, the more restrictive standard of permissibility for speech has been invoked in times when the nation has, correctly or incorrectly, felt itself to be in danger, such as during and after World War I and during the McCarthy era following World War II. Interestingly, in the United States, the turmoil and criticism surrounding the Viet Nam War and the Civil Rights movement did not lead to a retreat by the Supreme Court from the more liberal clear and present danger standard. If the historical parallel is correct, we may expect to experience such a retreat when and if our problems, internal or external, are perceived as a threat to our national integrity and stability.

The determination of a standard for the permissibility of pure speech is difficult conceptually, and controversial even theoretically. To the criminal justice system, however, difficult pragmatic problems are presented by situations where speech is mixed with action, and public-safety and crowd-control considerations present themselves. Even the most innocuous speech can, under the wrong circumstances, cause a riot; and flaming revolutionary rhetoric delivered over coffee cups to two sympathetic listeners is harmless in terms of danger to public order. Clearly, a speaker who waves an ideological red flag before the enraged bull of a hostile audience will provoke disorder. The problem presented to the criminal justice system under these circumstances is: who is to be restrained—the speaker or the audience?

As in the case of pure speech, the guidelines handed down by the Supreme Court have been ambiguous. In 1948, one Terminiello addressed eight hundred members of the Christian Veterans of America in a Chicago auditorium. In his address he referred to "Queen Eleanor Roosevelt, Queen of America's Communists," and referred to Jews and blacks as "slimy scum," "snakes," and "bedbugs." Outside the hall two thousand opponents of Terminiello's Fascist adherents staged a riot, throwing bricks and bottles, and breaking into the hall. Terminiello was arrested and convicted of disorderly conduct.[24]

During the 1948 presidential campaign, one Feiner, a student at Syracuse University, addressed a crowd of seventy-five to eighty people on a street corner in a black residential section of Syracuse, New York. He urged his audience to attend a meeting supporting the candidacy of Henry Wallace, and referred to President Truman as a "bum" and to the American Legion as a "Nazi Gestapo." He also made some remarks urging blacks and whites to join in and fight for their rights. His statements stirred up a little excitement and some muttering and pushing. A bystander with an infant in his arms approached one of the two policemen in the audience and said that if the police did not get that "s.o.b." off the stand he would do so himself. The policemen thereupon arrested Feiner who was ultimately convicted of disorderly conduct.[25]

Both cases were appealed to the U.S. Supreme Court. The Court held that, in the *Terminiello* case, where an actual riot was in progress, the conviction should be reversed because it was the duty of the police to have restrained the crowd and protected the rights of the speaker. In the *Feiner* case, on the other hand, the court upheld the defendant's conviction on the ground that the police had the right to arrest a speaker who was threatening the peace, even though the imminence of the disorder was by no means clear.

These two cases, although both involve speakers and hostile audiences, are not identical. Terminiello was speaking inside a closed auditorium, rented and paid for by his supporters; Feiner was speaking on the street, where problems of traffic obstruction, noise, and crowd movement presented themselves. Terminiello was speaking to an invited sympathetic audience. Feiner was speaking to an uninvited, somewhat unsympathetic, audience. Nevertheless, the two Supreme Court decisions taken together are somewhat contradictory and present grave problems. If the *Feiner* rationale is followed, there is freedom of speech only for those speakers who do not displease their audiences. This is, in effect, to limit street meetings to those who love mother, the home, and the flag. On the other hand, while the two thousand people who howled for Terminiello's blood might have been controlled by a police force the size of Chicago's, what if that size crowd had gathered in a small town with an inadequate police force, or for that matter, what if the Chicago crowd had numbered twenty thousand or two hundred thousand instead of two thousand?

The probabilities are that no court can draw *a priori* hard-and-fast rules for the guidance of police, prosecutors, and judges in such situations. Each case must be judged in terms of the realities of the situation: the actual ability of the existing law force to handle a realistically perceived threat to the public peace. On the other hand, the feeling on the part of many police officers, that a speaker who is inflammatory is *ipso facto* liable to arrest for disorderly conduct or disturbing the peace, does not square with the need of an open society for gadflies and critics. If the First Amendment is to be something more than a pious platitude, speakers who express the sentiments we most loathe must have protection comparable to that afforded speakers who preach the gospel of love, peace, and patriotism.

It is worth noting that even at the Supreme Court level there appears to be differential handling of political offenders of the right and of the left. There is no conviction of a right-wing speaker that has been upheld by the United States Supreme Court. On the other hand, left-wing speakers such as Schenck, Abrams, Gitlow, and Dennis have been convicted of abstract advocacy of ideas, and on review these convictions have been affirmed by the high court. Similarly, left-wing agitators are normally treated with more hostility than their right-wing counterparts by the police. Why this is true is not entirely clear, but two reasons suggest themselves. Many policemen conceive it their duty to maintain the *status quo.* The radical who threatens the *status quo* by advocacy of armed revolution is therefore more dangerous than the radical who threatens to protect the *status quo* from social change, albeit in an equally violent manner. A new left student group advocating Maoism is more dangerous than a Minuteman group, even though the Minuteman group may advocate the arming of private citizens. That the forcible slowing down of the normal process of social change can be as subversive of stability as the forced acceleration of such change is perhaps not obvious to many police officials. At the Supreme Court level, the dearth of right-wing convictions may stem from the fact that liberals will oppose such convictions on civil libertarian grounds, and conservatives do not perceive right-wing ideology as sufficiently dangerous to warrant restraint.

Problems posed by public meetings aside, a technique which has gained increasing popularity in recent years presents the criminal justice system with new problems. The use of civil disobedience, that is, the deliberate violation of a law to dramatize profound disapproval of the existing state of affairs, has been utilized increasingly by reformers of many political hues. Martin Luther King's leadership of the Montgomery bus boycott, the march to Selma, Alabama, the sit-ins at Selective Service headquarters, the demonstrations in Grant Park in Chicago at the Democratic National Convention in 1968 all involved conduct at least partially illegal in terms of existing local law. All were designed to bring to public attention conditions perceived as unjust and inexcusable by the demonstrators. The chief result of police attempts to break up such demonstrations was frequently the spread of social unrest. To justify their actions, demonstrators claim that there is a law higher than the statutes on the books, higher even than the Constitution. Such law is "natural law," "justice," "the principles of morality." The police, on the other hand, are paid by the public to enforce the very law the demonstrators claim is not binding on them. Inevitably, confrontation and conflict must result from these two opposing positions.

Civil disobedience takes two forms. In one, the demonstrators disobey a law which they hold to be basically unjust or even unconstitutional; for example, civil rights demonstrators' violation of southern segregation statutes. When the demonstrators were arrested for such violations they appealed their cases to higher courts in the hope of obtaining a declaration of unconstitutionality. This technique was very successful in eliminating legalized segregation throughout the United States.

The second type of civil disobedience is the deliberate breaking of a law to which one has no objection in order to demonstrate one's disapproval of some unrelated social policy. During the Viet Nam War, students who seized college buildings were not protesting the criminal trespass laws. They seized buildings in order to make it impossible for the Establishment to ignore their objections to the war, research sponsored by the military, or racist admission policies.

Should such demonstrators be punished? And if so, to what extent? It must be appreciated at the outset that the Judeo-Christian morality on which this country claims to be based clearly holds that there is a law higher than the stated law of the political sovereign, and that therefore, each individual has a moral right to resist injustice where he finds it. Demonstrators have a strong moral basis for their actions. The problem, however, in terms of the criminal justice system, is whether they have a legal basis for their actions, that is, whether they can pursue their chosen course of conduct without the imposition of legal sanctions. As for those who, like Martin Luther King, challenge laws they feel are unconstitutional, if they win favorable verdicts in the appellate courts, they are clearly entitled to be free from legal punishment.

The situation with regard to the second type of demonstrator, the one who breaks a "legitimate" law, is far more complex. The great writers who developed theories of civil disobedience, Thoreau and Ghandi, held that such violators should offer themselves to the civil authorities for punishment in much the same way that Jesus offered to be crucified for the sins of mankind. Hopefully the sympathies of the uncommitted will thereupon be stirred to rectify the underlying social injustice and to prevent further punishment of the demonstrators. In the real world, however, not too many people are capable of Christ-like conduct, and many demonstrators seek to avoid punishment. The uncommitted public, moreover, is seldom effectively stirred from its apathy. The problem thus usually takes forms such as: Should students be punished for disrupting universities, though their cause is admittedly just, if the disruption is clearly illegal and produces great hardship to innocent people? Or, should anti-war protestors be permitted to disrupt the military operations of the government if they truly believe that we are engaged in an unjust war?

Once again, there are no clear guidelines for the police. Certainly, to exempt automatically all sincere protestors from punishment for their law-breaking is an invitation to anarchy. No society can realistically aid in the process of its own dissolution. Chaos would reign if each individual were free to exempt himself at will from the laws governing social conduct. On the other hand, to treat sincere moral protest in the same manner as the unprinci-

pled violation of law for private gain is counterproductive in terms of achieving a just society. Probably some balance between the social costs of forgiving
violations and the social benefit of the reform proposed is in order. The
mothers who obstruct traffic in order to force the installation of a traffic light
at a dangerous school crossing must be forgiven, because the social cost of
their protest is small and the social gain proposed is great. The forcible
kidnapping of school officials in order to change university policy with regard
to military recruiting is probably indefensible because of the enormity of the
social wrong involved in kidnapping and the marginal utility of the act in
rectifying the alleged social wrong.

Thus, in civil disobedience situations the police become the men in the
middle. They are the visible agents of a society which must decide on its
proper course of action. It is those who make social policy who must determine the extent to which the civilly disobedient must be punished. The
greater the extent of society's recognition and approbation of the protestors'
cause, and the more defensible the techniques employed, the more lenient
must be the instructions given the criminal justice system for the handling
of demonstrators. If there is no public identification with the cause in question, harsh treatment may be meted out without risk of causing widespread
social disorder. In any case, policy in regard to the treatment of the civilly
disobedient cannot be made by the police, local prosecutors, or the courts. It
must be made at far more politically responsive and responsible levels such
as the presidency, Congress, and the state legislature. Police cannot function
intelligently in this area unless they accept the fact that they are only agents
of a policy that must be determined elsewhere.

Selected Readings

Abraham, Henry J. *Freedom and the Court.* New York: Oxford, 1967.

Bloch, Herbert A. *Disorganization: Personal and Social.* New York: Knopf, 1952.

Bloch, Herbert A., and Geis, Gilbert. *Man, Crime and Society.* 2nd ed. New York:
Random House, 1970.

Chafee, Zechariah, Jr. *Free Speech in the United States.* Cambridge: Harvard University
Press, 1967.

Chevigny, Paul. *Police Power: Police Abuses in New York City.* New York: Pantheon,
1969.

Clinard, Marshall B., and Quinney, Richard. *Criminal Behavior Systems.* 2nd ed. New
York: Holt, Rinehart and Winston, 1973.

Clor, Harry M. *Obscenity and Public Morality.* Chicago: University of Chicago Press,
1969

Conklin, John E. *The Impact of Crime.* New York: Macmillan, 1975.

Devlin, Patrick. *The Enforcement of Morals.* New York: Oxford, 1975.

Hart, H.L.A. *Law, Liberty and Morality.* Stanford, Calif.: Stanford University Press,
1963.

Haskell, Martin R., and Yablonsky, Lewis. *Criminology.* 2nd ed. Skokie, Ill.: Rand
McNally, 1978.

Hughes, Graham. *The Conscience of the Courts.* Garden City, N.Y.: Anchor Press, 1975.

Krisberg, Barry. *Crime and Privilege: Toward a New Criminology.* Englewood Cliffs, N.J.: Prentice-Hall, 1975.

LaFave, Wayne R. *Arrest.* Boston: Little, Brown, 1965.

Lindesmith, Alfred R. *The Addict and the Law.* Vintage Books, 1967.

Mill, John Stuart. *On Liberty.* New York: Appleton, 1947.

Nettler, Gwynn, *Explaining Crime.* 2nd ed. New York: McGraw-Hill, 1978.

Packer, Herbert L. *The Limits of Criminal Sanctions.* Stanford, Calif.: Stanford University Press, 1968.

President's Commission on Law Enforcement and Administration of Justice. *Challenge of Crime in a Free Society.* Washington, D.C.: U.S. Government Printing Office, 1967.

Radzinowicz, Leon, and Wolfgang, Marvin E., ed. *Crime and Justice, Volume I: The Criminal in Society.* 2nd ed. New York: Basic Books, 1977.

Reid, Sue Titus. *Crime and Criminology.* 2nd ed. New York: Holt, Rinehart and Winston, 1978.

Reppetto, Thomas A. *The Blue Parade.* New York: Free Press, 1978.

Silver, Isidore, ed. *The Crime Control Establishment.* Englewood Cliffs, N.J.: Prentice-Hall, 1974.

Smith, Alexander B., and Pollack, Harriet. *Some Sins Are Not Crimes.* New York: New Viewpoints/Franklin Watts, 1975.

Steffens, Lincoln. *Shame of the Cities.* New York: Sagamore Press, 1957.

Sutherland, Edwin H., and Cressey, Donald R. *Criminology.* 10th ed. Philadelphia: Lippincott, 1978.

Toch, Hans. *Violent Men.* Chicago: Aldine, 1969.

Wilson, James Q. *Explaining Crime.* New York: McGraw-Hill, 1975.

Wilson, James Q. *Varieties of Police Behavior.* Cambridge: Harvard University Press, 1968

Wolfgang, Marvin E., and Cohen, Bernard. *Crime and Race.* New York: Institute of Human Relations, 1970.

Notes

1. *New York Times,* October 8, 1966, p. 27.

2. James Q. Wilson, *Varieties of Police Behavior* (Cambridge, Mass.: Harvard University Press, 1968), p.220.

3. *New York Times,* October 31, 1955, p. 19; November 26, 1955, p. 1.

4. *Newsday,* April 6, 1966, p. 1; December 22, 1966, p. 7.

5. Herbert A. Bloch, *Disorganization: Personal and Social* (New York: Knopf, 1952), pp. 259-260.

6. Austin L. Porterfield, *Youth In Trouble* (Fort Worth: Leo Potishman Foundation, 1946), p. 38ff.

7. Edwin H. Sutherland, "White-Collar Criminality," *American Sociological Review* 5, no. 1 (February 1940): 1-12.

8. *Gideon v. Wainwright,* 372 U.S. 335 (1963); *Miranda v. Arizona,* 384 U.S. 436 (1966).

9. *New York Times,* February 7, 1961, p. 1; February 26, 1961, p.3

10. For fuller treatment of this subject, see President's Commission on Law Enforcement and Administration of Justice, *Challenge of Crime in a Free Society* (Washington, D.C.: U.S. Government Printing Office, 1967), .p. 44ff; Thomas F. Pettigrew, *A Profile of the Negro American*

(Princeton: Van Nostrand, 1964), Chap. 6; Walter C. Reckless, *The Crime Problem,* 4th ed. (New York: Appleton, 1967), pp. 103-107; Edwin H. Sutherland and Donald R. Cressey, *Criminology,* 10th ed. (Philadelphia: Lippincott, 1978), pp. 137-155.

11. See Wayne R. LaFave, *Arrest: The Decision to Take a Suspect into Custody* (Boston: Little, Brown, 1965), pp. 110-114.

12. *Thompson v. Louisville,* 362 U.S. 199 (1960).

13. 14 N.Y. 2nd 441 (1964).

14. *New York Times* November 30, 1969, p. 53.

15. Patrick M. Wall, *Eye-Witness Identification in Criminal Cases* (Springfield, Ill.: Charles C Thomas, 1965), pp. 122-125.

16. LaFave, p. 111.

17. Wilson, pp. 161-162.

18. Marvin E. Wolfgang and Bernard Cohen, *Crime and Race* (New York: Institute of Human Relations Press, The American Jewish Committee, 1970), pp. 80-81.

19. Herbert A. Bloch and Frank T. Flynn, *Delinquency* (New York: Random House, 1956), pp. 45–46.

20. Ibid., p. 47.

21. Paul Chevigny, *Police Power: Police Abuses in New York City* (New York: Pantheon, 1969), p. 114.

22. John Stuart Mill, *On Liberty* (New York: Appleton, 1947), pp. 16-17.

23. *Dennis v. United States,* 341 U.S. 494 (1951).

24. *Terminiello v. Chicago,* 337 U.S. 1 (1949).

25. *Feiner v. New York,* 340 U.S. 315 (1951).

criminal responsibility: juveniles

"Under our Constitution the condition of being a boy does not justify a kangaroo court."
  Abe Fortas, *In re Gault*

"Juvenile proceedings are not criminal trials. They are not civil trials. They are simply not adversary proceedings."
  Potter Stewart dissenting, *In re Gault*

Horace Mann, the famed educator, was once invited to make a dedicatory address at an institution for the reclamation of juvenile offenders. At one point in the address he stated, with much enthusiasm, that all the money spent for that institution would be worthwhile, if only one boy was reclaimed. When the address was over, a rather cynical listener came to Mann and said: "Didn't your enthusiasm run away with you today, Sir? Do you really mean that it is worthwhile spending all the money for this institution if the end were to be the reclamation of one boy only? Didn't you exaggerate, Sir?" Horace Mann quietly but firmly replied: "Not if it were my boy."
  Richmond News Leader, in *Federal Probation* 18, no. 2 (June 1954): 10

The classical school of criminology (which developed during the eighteenth century as one manifestation of the egalitarianism underlying the French Revolution) held that individuals were free actors who deliberately chose their paths of conduct, guided only by the relative amounts of pleasure and pain each chosen act produced. Therefore, to deter men from criminal acts it was necessary only for society to prescribe punishment of sufficient severity to make the pain of punishment outweigh the pleasures of crime.

Punishment should be identical for identical crimes, and, since all individuals are basically equal, punishment for each should be the same, regardless of age, sex, physical condition, or class. Although this superficially plausible theory was intended to reform the criminal law by removing its class bias, it had grave weaknesses. It failed to cope with the problem of crimes committed by those who almost by definition were not equal to others: juveniles, idiots, and the insane.

THE JUVENILE JUSTICE SYSTEM

Historically, all societies have recognized that preadolescent youngsters are different from adults, and cannot be held accountable in the same way adults are. Rites of passage, such as puberty rites in primitive societies and confirmation ceremonies in modern Western religions, are indications that the child must be somehow transformed before he is deemed worthy of acceptance as a full member of society with full responsibility for his actions. In English Common Law, a child under the age of seven was considered incapable of *mens rea* (guilty intent), and since without intent there could be no crime, small children were thus immune from criminal prosecution for their acts. Below the age of fourteen (but over seven), the presumption of criminal responsibility was rebuttable; over that age, every person assumed full responsibility for criminal acts.

The recognition of the differential status of children came to the United States as part of the English Common Law.[1] Efforts to improve the handling of juvenile offenders were made as early as 1825 in New York and in 1826 in Boston with the establishment of houses of refuge for children. At first, reformers were more concerned with the postconviction handling of children than with the processes that led to their detention and conviction in the first place. Gradually, however, attention began to shift from postconviction handling to preconviction handling, and for example, in Massachusetts in 1869, statutes required that a state agent or his deputy be present in court, "whenever application for commitment is made for any child, to any reformatory maintained by the Commonwealth." An 1879 Suffolk County (Massachusetts) statute required that cases against children under sixteen should be heard in courts, "separate from the general and ordinary criminal business." In New York in 1892, "cases involving violations of the Penal Code that would ordinarily fall within the jurisdiction of a police court or the court of Special Sessions might be heard . . . separate and apart from the trial of other criminal cases." The first specialized court established specifically for the handling of juvenile cases (as distinguished from ordinary criminal courts with separate juvenile parts) was established in 1899 in Cook County, Illinois, to deal with neglected dependent as well as delinquent children. The approach of the court was the salvaging of children in trouble. As Judge Julian W. Mack, a pioneer in the juvenile court movement, said:

> The problem for determination by the judge is not, Has this boy or girl committed a specific wrong, but What is he, how has he become what he is, and what had best be done in his interest and in the interest of the State to save him from a downward career.[2]

The fruits of this humanitarian movement have been the establishment in the United States of a separate juvenile justice system. In every state of the union children are handled separately from, and by standards different from those applied to adult criminals. The development of this system has, however, been highly idiosyncratic, and there are few uniformities in jurisdiction and procedures. In most states juveniles are handled in separate courts, but in some areas they are still handled in special parts of the adult courts. Some juvenile courts are state-wide, some county-wide, some purely local. The names of these courts vary: juvenile court, children's court, family court. While the lower age limit for the court's jurisdiction over children is usually seven years of age, the upper age limits vary. Eighteen is the customary upper age limit, but New York and several other states have established sixteen or seventeen as the appropriate cut-off point for the court's jurisdiction. A few states have extended the upper age limit to nineteen, and even to twenty-one in special cases.

Some states, on the other hand, have lowered the upper limits for the handling of juveniles in order to make it possible for particularly violent offenders to be tried in the adult courts and sentenced as adult criminals. In some jurisdictions, such offenders are taken initially to the juvenile court which then decides either to hold the accused or transfer the case to the adult felony court. In other jurisdictions, the process is reversed and the juvenile charged with a specified serious felony will be initially arraigned in the adult criminal court. Subsequently, as the case progresses through the adult court system, at any point up to the time of trial, the judge (usually with the consent of the prosecutor) may, "in the interests of justice," make the decision to remand the case to the juvenile court. In New York state even thirteen-year-olds who have committed murder may be tried in an adult felony court. Fourteen- and fifteen-year-olds may be tried for crimes such as assault in the first degree, manslaughter in the first degree, and rape in the first degree.

From the point of view of continued development of the juvenile justice system, the movement to lower age limits in special circumstances is regressive. It is the result, unfortunately, of the increasing frequency of violent crime, including murder, by very young offenders. The notion underlying the juvenile justice system is the premise that children who commit antisocial acts are young, impetuous, and unthinking rather than vicious, and the acts that they commit are mischievous and annoying rather than venal. It also assumes that the offender is capable of rehabilitation. The thirteen-year-old who casually murders a passer-by for a trivial, or indeed, no reason does not fit into the conceptual framework on which the juvenile justice system was built. In many jurisdictions, the public has reacted in such cases against the ideals of minimal sentences and nonpunitive handling, and has demanded greater protection from this type of violent offender.

On the other hand, some states have extended the special handling of young offenders beyond the cutoff age for the juvenile courts, and set up special procedures for the handling of young adults who are first offenders. New York, for example, provides for special judicial processing of youthful offenders between the ages of sixteen and nineteen so that they may avoid the stigma of an adult conviction. This is not part of the juvenile court system, but is a modification of the adult criminal court procedure.

Juvenile court jurisdiction in most areas extends not only to children accused of committing unlawful acts, but to children who behave in socially, rather than legally, unacceptable ways; for example, truants, runaways, and incorrigibles, as well as to neglected and dependent children (those whose welfare has not adequately been provided for by appropriate adults). In recent years there has been a tendency to label as delinquent only those acts which, if committed by adults, would be called crimes. Other behavioral offenses are given other labels, but the jurisdiction of the juvenile court remains broad and includes all problems relating to children, both criminal and noncriminal: those stemming from the child's behavior, and those stemming from the behavior of the adults responsible for him.

Unfortunately, despite the complexity of juvenile court problems, the judges who serve in juvenile court are, on the whole, less qualified than the judges who sit in adult felony courts. Though some progressive states have placed highly qualified persons on the bench, there are wide variations in the stated qualifications for the position. A 1973 survey conducted for the National Council of Juvenile Court Judges indicated that one-third the incumbent judges lacked undergraduate college degrees and 10 percent had never attended law school. Almost none were full time: eighty-six percent devoted half of their time or less to juvenile matters, and two-thirds spend one fourth of their time or less. The average salary for full-time judges was slightly more than $24,000. Over 50 percent of the judges complained of inadequate facilities for detention or shelter care of juveniles pending disposition, and half complained of insufficient home placement facilities. More than one quarter found the probation and social service staffs to be inadequate. These statistics, though distressing, mark a distinct improvement over a survey conducted ten years earlier which showed the level of services and staff provided by the juvenile courts to be substantially lower. Juvenile court judges still lag behind their colleagues in the adult courts, but the disparity is lessening.[3]

As a result of the fine work of Judge Mack and other reformers, juvenile courts exist in one form or another all over the United States. The peak period of development of the juvenile justice system was in the 1920s. Since then, the talented and compassionate individuals that shaped and gave impetus to the movement have died and with them some of the high hopes and idealism that inspired the movement. As a result, public interest has waned markedly and the juvenile courts generally suffer from a lack of adequately qualified personnel and services to their child clients. Even worse has been the emerging reality that while the philosophy underlying the juvenile court continues to be rehabilitative, in practice, these courts have become, and are frequently, punitive. In practical terms, children don't need protection from government officials who are helping them, but they certainly do need protection from judges and probation officers who are hurting them. The juvenile court conceptually is like a kind but firm parent prescribing treatment for the child that, while possibly somewhat unpleasant, is rationally designed to help the child as quickly as possible. In practice, the court is usually far more like the adult court which, while it holds pious hopes for the ultimate rehabilitation of the offender, quite openly sentences for punitive and deterrent reasons rather than therapeutic ones.

The nonpunitive handling of children perhaps comes closest to realization in advanced states such as New York. New York City, in common with many other cities and counties, has had difficulty in establishing and maintaining a satisfactory system of detention facilities for juveniles awaiting hearings or placement. There has been frequent criticism of these centers because of outbreaks of violence, mistreatment of inmates by inmates, and a lack of security which enables juveniles to escape. Handling such disturbed and aggressive children is very difficult and very few jurisdictions satisfactorily solve the problem. Nevertheless, intake in the New York juvenile courts is handled by trained probation officers who have both the ability and the legal power to arrange for informal handling of the child. Those cases which cannot be handled in this manner are passed on to a full-time qualified juvenile court judge who has at his command the auxiliary services of psychologists, psychiatrists, and social workers. He has a wide range of options available to him in the disposition of a case: the child can be released on probation to his parents, to a social work agency, or to an institutional or outpatient setting. As a last resort he may be committed to a training school, some of which, at any rate, have a high ratio of professional staff to patients and are highly reputed for their sensitive and humane treatment of their child inmates. At the opposite end of the spectrum are juvenile court systems, such as the one which existed in Arizona in 1967, which gave rise to *In re Gault,* [4] the first case in which the United States Supreme Court held up to constitutional scrutiny a wide range of juvenile court procedures. *Gault* was preceded, however, by an earlier Washington, D.C. case, *Kent v. United States,* [5] in which the Court, while considering a single procedural issue, set the stage for the substantial reforms of *Gault.*

Kent v. United States

Morris A. Kent was apprehended in 1959, at the age of fourteen, for housebreaking and attempted purse snatching. He was placed on probation by the juvenile court of the District of Columbia, and his record was placed in the social service file. In 1961, after a youth had entered a woman's apartment, taken her wallet, and raped her, police found latent fingerprints which they determined to be those of Kent. Kent, who was then sixteen, was still on probation, but because of his age was subject by the terms of the District of Columbia Juvenile Code to the "exclusive jurisdiction" of the juvenile court. The code did, however, provide for waiver (transfer) to the adult court in certain cases involving older offenders, but only after a "full investigation" had been conducted. Kent's counsel moved to be allowed access to his client's social service file, and for a hearing on the possible waiver of juvenile court jurisdiction. Counsel also filed a psychiatrist's affidavit which recommended that Kent be hospitalized for psychiatric observation. The judge did not rule on these motions, and held no hearing. Instead, he merely stated that after a "full investigation" he was transferring the case to the adult criminal court.

Kent was subsequently indicted by a grand jury and charged with two counts of rape and six of housebreaking. On the rape counts, he was found not guilty by reason of insanity, for which, under District of Columbia law, he would be placed in a mental institution until his sanity was restored. He was found guilty on the other six charges and sentenced to thirty to ninety years in prison, with the time spent in the mental institution to be counted as part of the sentence. Kent's conviction was appealed to the District of Columbia Court of Appeals on the ground that the failure of the juvenile court judge to grant a formal hearing before ordering the transfer to the adult court was a denial of due process. The Court of Appeals affirmed the ruling of the lower court and further appeal was taken to the United States Supreme Court.

Fortas, for the majority, agreed that proceedings in a juvenile court were civil rather than criminal in nature, embodying a rehabilitative rather than punitive philosophy. Nevertheless, he rejected the notion that juvenile defendants were not entitled to procedural rights available to adults accused of crimes in the regular criminal courts. He pointed out that the consequences for a juvenile of being adjudicated a juvenile delinquent, in many cases, differed very little from being convicted as an adult criminal. He cited data indicating the inadequacy of many juvenile courts in relation to personnel, facilities, and expertise, questioned the ability of such courts to function in the *parens patriae* capacity, and the legitimacy of exempting such courts from the constitutional standards applicable to courts which tried adult defendants. On the basis of this reasoning, the Court decided that Kent had been entitled to access to his social service file and to a formal hearing on the question of whether the waiver to the adult court was justified.

The holding of *Kent* was relatively limited, and did not modify either the philosophy or the procedures (with the above noted exception) of the juvenile court. *Kent's* significance is that it was the first time the Court had even considered the procedural problems of the juvenile justice system, and it paved the way for the far more wide-ranging opinions of *In re Gault*

In re Gault

Gerald Gault, age fifteen, was taken into custody by the sheriff of Gila County, Arizona, on June 8, 1964, as a result of a verbal complaint by one Mrs. Cook, a neighbor, who claimed to have received a lewd telephone call. At the time the boy was arrested his mother and father were both at work. No official notice was left to advise them of their son's whereabouts. They learned of his detention from the neighbors. At a hearing before the juvenile judge the following day, neither Gerald's father, who was at work out of the city, nor Mrs. Cook, the complainant, was there. No witness was sworn, no transcript was made, and no memorandum of the substance of the proceedings was prepared. There are conflicting versions of what Gerald said at this hearing, but the weight of the evidence indicated that he had only dialed the number while his friend had made the lewd remarks. Following the hearing, Gerald was returned to the detention home in which he had been confined since his arrest. He was kept there two or three days longer and then, without explanation, released. At 5:00 P.M. on the day of his release the probation officer sent a one-sentence note on plain paper to Mrs. Gault, informing her that on June 15th there would be a further hearing on Gerald's delinquency. At the June 15th hearing, no new information was developed; at no time was the complainant called upon to testify, nor was she given the opportunity to hear Gerald's voice for identification purposes. At the conclusion of the hearing, the judge committed Gerald as a juvenile delinquent to the State Industrial School for the period of his minority, that is, six years. (Had Gerald been eighteen or over, the maximum penalty for his offense would have been a fifty-dollar fine or two months in jail.)

No appeal was permitted by Arizona law in juvenile cases. A petition for a writ of *habeas corpus* was therefore filed with the Supreme Court of Arizona which referred it to the Superior Court for a hearing. In spite of the fact that the juvenile judge was shown to have had almost no basis in fact for his original findings, the Superior Court dismissed the writ. A further appeal was made to the Arizona Supreme Court, in which it was urged that the juvenile code of Arizona was unconstitutional because it did not require parents and children to be notified of specific charges, nor given proper notice of a hearing, nor did it have any provision for appeal. For all these reasons Gerald Gault had been denied his liberty without due process of law. The Arizona Supreme Court denied the appeal. The decision was then appealed to the United States Supreme Court which accepted the case for review.

Justice Fortas, speaking for five members of the Court, noted that while the United States Supreme Court would not, in this case, concern itself with the constitutionality of either pre-judicial or post-adjudicative procedures in juvenile courts, it would concern itself with the procedures questioned by the Gaults.

> A boy is charged with misconduct. The boy is committed to an institution where he may be restrained of liberty for years. It is of no constitutional consequence —and of limited practical meaning—that the institution to which he is committed is called an Industrial School. The fact of the matter is that, however euphemistic the title, a "receiving home" or an "industrial school". . . is an institution of confinement. . . .
>
>   In view of this, it would be extraordinary if our Constitution did not require the procedural regularity and the exercise of care implied in the phrase "due process." . . . Under traditional notions, one would assume that in a case like that of Gerald Gault, where the juvenile appears to have a home, a working mother and father, and an older brother, the Juvenile Judge would have made a careful inquiry and judgment as to the possibility that the boy could be disciplined and dealt with at home. . . . The essential difference between Gerald's case and a normal criminal case is that safeguards available to adults were discarded in Gerald's case. The summary procedure as well as the long commitment were possible because Gerald was fifteen years of age instead of over eighteen.[6]

While the court refused to go so far as to require that all adult procedural safeguards be observed in juvenile cases, it specified certain rights which must be recognized for children as well as adults:

1. Notice of charges.
2. Right to counsel.
3. Right to confrontation and cross-examination.
4. Privilege against self-incrimination.[7]

In the instant case, no notice had been given to Gerald's parents when he was taken into custody, nor had formal notice been given of the dates of the hearings. The parents had not been notified at any time of the specific charges against Gerald. Mrs. Gault testified that she "knew" that she could have had a lawyer, but at no time had any official informed her of this right, nor requested that she make a knowing waiver of this right. The complaining witness was never asked to testify, and therefore could not be cross-examined. While there was conflict as to what admissions Gerald had actually made, at no time had he been informed of his right not to incriminate himself and to remain silent. There was no right of appeal from the findings of a juvenile court in Arizona so no transcript was made of what transpired at the hearings.

The response of the state to these obvious procedural irregularities was simply that since juvenile proceedings are designed to be confidential so as to avoid stigmatizing the child, formal procedures were neither necessary nor desirable. Furthermore, since juvenile procedures are not criminal in nature the constitutionally mandated procedures of the adult criminal trial were not applicable.

The United States Supreme Court rejected all these contentions. It saw no conflict between formal procedures and the goal of rehabilitative therapeutic treatment for the child. It quoted with approval a statement by the President's Crime Commission:

> Fears also have been expressed that the formality lawyers would bring into juvenile court would defeat the therapeutic aims of the court. But informality has no necessary connection with therapy; it is a device that has been used to approach therapy, and it is not the only possible device. It is quite possible that in many instances lawyers, for all their commitment to formality, could do more to further therapy for their clients than can the small, overworked social staffs of the courts.[8]

Furthermore, to label juvenile proceedings noncriminal so as to avoid the need for procedural regularity is at best highly artificial and conceptually dishonest. Any procedure which results in the involuntary confinement of an individual for a lengthy period of time is coercive, no matter how euphemistic the appellation. As a matter of fact, as the Court itself pointed out, there is no assurance in many cases that a juvenile handled by the juvenile courts will remain outside the reach of the adult courts, since in over one-half of the states juvenile delinquents may be transferred to adult penal institutions after an adjudication for delinquency.

PROCEDURAL REFORM: STEP FORWARD OR BACKWARD?

While most criminal justice practitioners would agree that the *Gault* case presents a set of shocking and indefensible facts, the inadequacies of the juvenile justice system are not met by the remedies proposed by the majority opinion in this case. Although the procedural rules that the Court has imposed on the juvenile courts will undoubtedly protect children from the incompetence and neglect found in systems like that of Gila County, the decision does little to resolve the basic contradictions of the juvenile justice system. While it is true that juvenile courts act in a punitive and coercive manner, and therefore children are entitled to formal procedural protection, nevertheless, child wrongdoers are not adult criminals, and the assumptions and procedures of the adult criminal justice system are not always applicable to children.

> The inflexible restrictions that the Constitution . . . made applicable to adversary criminal trials have no inevitable place in the proceedings of those public social agencies known as juvenile or family courts. And to impose the Court's long catalog of requirements upon juvenile proceedings in every area of the country is to invite a long step backwards into the Nineteenth Century. In that era there were no juvenile proceedings, and a child was tried in a conventional criminal court with all the trappings of a conventional criminal trial. So it was that a 12-year-old boy named James Guild was tried in New Jersey for killing Catherine Beakes. A jury found him guilty of murder, and he was sentenced to death by hanging. The sentence was executed. It was all very constitutional.[9]

While Gerald Gault needed and should have had a lawyer, the traditional role of the lawyer in an adversary proceeding is, if possible, to acquit his client. Not every case, however, is a *Gault* case, and not every child should be freed, even if a competent lawyer could secure his release. In the adult criminal proceeding, including the trial, the rules of the game are structured with two ends in view: the fate of the defendant, and the well-being of the community. It is assumed that the greatest good (from the defendant's viewpoint) which the court can confer is the restoration of his previous state of liberty. Neither the goal nor the result of such proceedings is the rehabilitation of an acquitted defendant. In juvenile proceedings, however, the goal is quite different. Here the concern is far more with the future of the child than with the structuring of a style of social and political living. In a sense the juvenile court is like a hospital. To ensure the right of a sick child to avoid treatment would not be productive in terms of serving the child's welfare. In short, the traditional concern of the adult criminal justice system with the welfare of the accused has been whether or not the accused is to retain his liberty. Historically, the concern of juvenile justice has been to help the sick child get well. "The act simply provides how children who ought to be saved may reach the court to be saved"[10]

Thus, while some procedural safeguards are necessary simply because unchecked bureaucracies frequently function inefficiently and even corruptly, the scope and function of these safeguards cannot be quite the same for juveniles as for adults. Where the lines are to be drawn, and how the balance is to be struck, between the protection of the child from inappropriate official action and the need for administrative and judicial flexibility in the rehabilitative treatment of the child is not clear.

It seems probable we cannot have the best of two worlds. If the emphasis is on constitutional rights something of the essential freedom of method and choice which the sound juvenile Judge ought to have is lost; if range be given to that freedom, rights which the law gives to criminal offenders will not be respected. But the danger is that we may lose the child and his potential for good while giving him his constitutional rights.[11]

Despite these problems of striking a balance between procedural rights of the child and his need for protection and rehabilitation, and despite the misgivings expressed in Justice Stewart's dissent in *Gault,* the United States Supreme Court, in 1970, again expanded the rights of juveniles in the *Winship* decision.[12] This case involved a twelve-year-old-boy who was adjudicated a delinquent by the New York Family Court when a "fair preponderance" of evidence indicated that he had taken $112 from a pocketbook. The boy was placed in a training school. An appeal was made to the New York State Court of Appeals on the ground that due process and equal protection of the law required that the same standards of proof for conviction apply in juvenile courts as in adult criminal courts, namely, that guilt must be established "beyound a reasonable doubt" for juveniles rather than merely by a "fair preponderance" of the evidence. The appeal was rejected by a divided Court of Appeals largely on the ground that juvenile courts require greater flexibility in carrying out their special mission, which is different from that of the adult courts. Justice Fuld dissented vigorously, suggesting that "where a twelve-year-old child is charged with an act ... which renders him liable to confinement for as long as six years, then, as a matter of due process, as well as of equal protection, the case against him must be proved beyond a reasonable doubt."[13]

On appeal, the U.S. Supreme Court agreed with Fuld that the due process clause protects the accused against conviction except upon proof beyond a reasonable doubt of every fact necessary to constitute the crime with which he is charged. In the wake of the *Gault* decision, the Court held that the same considerations which protect innocent adults must apply to innocent children. At the same time Justice Brennan, for the majority, denied that such procedural protection would destroy the beneficial aspects of the juvenile process.

Nor will there be any effect on the informality, flexibility, or speed of the hearing at which the factfinding takes place. And the opportunity during the post-adjudicatory or dispositional period for a wide-ranging review of the child's social history and for his individualized treatment will remain unimpaired.[14]

Winship marked the highwater mark of expansion of juvenile procedural rights. A year after the *Winship* decision, in *McKeiver v. Pennsylvania,*[15] the United States Supreme Court held that juveniles do not have a constitutional

right to trial by jury. Justice Blackmun, writing for the majority, acknowledged that while "fond and idealistic hopes" with regard to juvenile courts
had not been realized, if a jury trial were required the juvenile proceedings
would be made into a full adversary process and would put an end to notions
of an "intimate, informal protective proceeding."

The same rationale was in evidence five years later, in 1976, when the Court
turned down a request by the American Civil Liberties Union to decide an
issue on which several states had differed: whether it was permissible for a
juvenile to be adjudicated delinquent on the uncorroborated word of an
accomplice. The adult courts in these jurisdictions required corroboration of
the accomplice's testimony in order to obtain a conviction against an adult
defendant. The case involved a youth named Sammy Joe Chavez who was
adjudicated guilty of delinquency in an armed robbery case in Texas.[16] The
Texas Supreme Court had found the disparity of treatment between juveniles
and adults to be constitutionally permissible. Since *Chavez,* the United States
Supreme Court has not agreed to hear any cases involving procedural rights
for juveniles.*

However, even were the conceptual difficulties of the juvenile justice system to be resolved, and even were we to know where in theory the balance
between protection and administrative flexibility ought to be struck, formi-
dable practical difficulties in the implementation of appropriate standards
remain. The reality of our juvenile justice system is grim. There are in the
United States thousands of Gerald Gaults adjudicated by courts that make a
shabby pretense of rehabilitative handling of the child. Juvenile court judges
are in many cases unqualified and uninterested: one-third lack undergraduate
degrees; ten percent never attended law school; and two-thirds spend less
than one-quarter of their time on juvenile matters. They command less
professional respect from their colleagues than do other judges, and the
juvenile court is not looked upon as a promising or desirable forum for
professional practice. The average juvenile hearing in many localities seems
to be of no more than ten or fifteen minutes duration, and there is a general
scarcity of psychologists, psychiatrists, and clinic facilities. Most jurisdictions
do not have foster homes or group homes available for children who might
do well in a different family setting, so that the range of dispositional alternatives open to most juvenile judges is very limited: outright release, probation,
or institutionalization. Probation supervision, moreover, exists more in theory than in fact. Worst of all perhaps is that conditions in many of the

---

*In *Breed v. Jones,* 421 U.S. 519 (1975), the United States Supreme Court held unanimously
that a youth who had been adjudged delinquent by a juvenile court because he had violated a
criminal statute (robbery) could not then be tried in an adult court. Despite the "civil" label of
convenience attached to the juvenile process, the Court held the youth to have been placed in
jeopardy, and, therefore, he could not be tried again in an adult criminal court in light of the
double jeopardy clause of the Fifth Amendment as applied to the states through the Fourteenth
Amendment.

institutions in which children are confined are not only more custodial than rehabilitative, but are also shockingly inhumane. A well-informed penologist states, "There are things going on, methods of discipline being used in the State training schools of this country that would cause a warden of Alcatraz to lose his job if he used them on his prisoners."[17]

In the face of the reality of a juvenile justice system that conforms very little to the ideals of its proponents, can the courts morally or legally refuse to extend to children the procedural safeguards that will prevent victimization by a system which is fully as punitive as the adult criminal justice system? It may well be that it is not in the best interests of the juvenile offender to be treated like an adult offender, but with mandated procedural safeguards he at least will not have gotten the worst of both possible worlds. Unless the juvenile justice system can be made to resemble the ideal more closely, it is hard to see how the courts can avoid further formalizing procedures.

> While there can be no doubt of the original laudable purpose of juvenile courts, studies and critiques in recent years raise serious questions as to whether actual performance measures well enough against theoretical purpose to make tolerable the immunity of the process from the reach of constitutional guarantees applicable to adults. There is much evidence that some juvenile courts . . . lack the personnel, facilities and techniques to perform adequately as representatives of the State in a *parens patriae* capacity, at least with respect to children charged with law violations. There is evidence, in fact, that there may be grounds for concern that the child receives the worst of both worlds: that he gets neither the protections accorded to adults nor the solicitous care and regenerative treatment postulated for children.[18]

Still another basic problem confronts the juvenile justice system today. The basic assumption underlying the entire system is the notion that children have less capacity for judgment and control than do adults, and, therefore, should not be held responsible in the same way as adults are. Children are also thought to be particularly responsive to rehabilitation efforts. What if neither of these assumptions is true for some children? What should be done with children who, at a very early age, demonstrate a capacity and propensity for extremely violent crime, and despite every effort show no indication of either remorse, or growth towards conformity, or control of violent impulses? Can the procedures of even the best juvenile justice system handle such children with justice to both the child and the community? Within the past decade, there have been increasingly frequent reports of murders, rapes, and vicious assaults committed by children as young as age seven. Many of these youngsters were apprehended, and presented grave problems for the juvenile system, because of a lack of sufficient secure facilities, and because for the older juvenile, the permissible period of confinement is quite short—usually only until age twenty-one. Such children are frequently violent within the institution and present a danger to other inmates. While these youngsters, fortunately, are a very small minority of the entire group of juvenile delinquents, public opinion has been sufficiently aroused as to threaten the therapeutic aspects of the juvenile justice system. Regressive measures, such as the 1978 New York State law lowering the age limit in murder cases to age thirteen for handling in the adult courts (discussed *supra*), are the direct result of the very real problem of public safety that such youths present.

Until recently, the chief problem facing American society was how to make the juvenile courts genuinely rehabilitative instruments using modifications of adult legal safeguards. The obstacle has been and is the lack of resources: qualified judges, detention facilities, foster homes, therapists, and so on. Lacking these resources, the question arose of how legitimate it was to deprive accused youngsters of the procedural protections available to adults. In more recent years, however, still another difficulty has presented itself: how to make the juvenile justice system capable of handling a tiny majority of what may be violent, incorrigible youngsters without destroying the capacity of the system for compassionate, rehabilitative programs for all other troubled children.

Selected Readings

Bloch, Herbert A., and Niederhoffer, Arthur. *The Gang.* New York: Philosophical Library, 1958.

Cloward, Richard A., and Ohlin, Lloyd E. *Delinquency and Opportunity.* New York: Free Press, 1960.

Cohen, Albert K. *Delinquent Boys.* New York: Free Press, 1955.

Haskell, Martin R., and Yablonsky, Lewis. *Juvenile Delinquency.* 2nd ed. Skokie, Ill.: Rand McNally, 1978.

Glueck, Sheldon. *The Problem of Delinquency.* Boston: Houghton Mifflin, 1959.

Lerman, Paul, ed. *Delinquency and Social Policy.* New York: Praeger, 1970.

Matza, David. *Delinquency and Drift.* New York: Wiley, 1964.

Platt, Anthony. *The Child Savers.* Chicago: University of Chicago Press, 1970.

President's Commission on Law Enforcement and Administration of Justice. *Task Force Report: Juvenile Delinquency and Youth Crime.* Washington, D.C.: U.S. Government Printing Office, 1967.

Sellin, Thorsten, and Wolfgang, Marvin E. *The Measurement of Delinquency.* New York: Wiley, 1964.

Notes

1. For a full treatment of the historical background of the juvenile courts as well as the problem of delinquency in America, see Sheldon Glueck, *The Problem of Delinquency* (Boston: Houghton Mifflin, 1959); and Anthony Platt, *The Child Savers* (Chicago: University of Chicago Press, 1970). For a statement on problems of the juvenile justice system, see President's Commission on Law Enforcement and Administration of Justice, *Task Force Report: Juvenile Delinquency and Youth Crime* (Washington, D.C.: U.S. Government Printing Office, 1967).

2. Julian W. Mack, "The Juvenile Court," 23 *Harvard Law Review*, 104 (1909), as quoted in Glueck, p. 324.

3. Kenneth Cruce Smith, "A Profile of Juvenile Court Judges in the United States," *Juvenile Justice*, 25, no. 2 (August, 1974): 27–38.

4. 387 U.S. 1 (1967).

5. 383 U.S. 541 (1966).

6. *In re Gault*, at 27–29.

7. Ibid., at 10.

8. Ibid., at 38, fn. 65.

9. Stewart, J. (dissenting), *In re Gault*, at 79–80.

10. *Commonwealth v. Fisher*, 213 Pa. 48 (1905).

11. *In the Matter of Samuel W.*, 24 N.Y. 2nd 196 (1969), at 202.

12. *In re Winship*, 397 U.S. 358 (1970).

13. *In the Matter of Samuel W.*, at 207.

14. *In re Winship*, at 366.

15. 403 U.S. 528 (1971).

16. *Chavez v. Texas*, 429 U.S. 835 (1976).

17. Quoted in President's Commission on Law Enforcement and Administration of Justice, *Task Force Report: Juvenile Delinquency and Youth Crime* (Washington, D.C.: U.S. Government Printing Office, 1967), p. 8.

18. *Kent v. United States*, at 555–556.

chapter 5

criminal responsibility: insanity

"A society that punishes the sick is not wholly civilized. A society that does not restrain the dangerous madman lacks common sense."
Jerome N. Frank, Introduction to *Murder, Madness and the Law*

Crime under our legal system is more than a physical act: it is an act accompanied by a state of mind. Evil intent, *mens rea,* must motivate the conduct, or no crime has been committed.* Where there is no *mens rea* there is no crime, and if the mind is too diseased to harbor guilty intent, no finding of criminal guilt can be made. Therefore, the insane person who violates criminal law must be handled differently from one who is of sound mind. Historically this distinction has been recognized and has posed few problems in regard to individuals who are obviously and totally out of contact with reality. A continuing problem, however, has been posed by those whose judgment is clouded in some areas but not in all, or who may function imperfectly at one time but not at others. In its less vindictive moods, at least, society has no wish to punish those who truly are not responsible for their acts. At the same time there is always a fear of providing the all too easy alibi of temporary insanity to a malefactor who is not deranged, but malevolent.

While there are variations among the state and federal governments in the method of handling allegedly insane suspects, the way in which such suspects are handled in New York City is probably fairly typical. If a policeman finds a suspect at the scene of a crime who is acting in a bizarre or irrational manner, he will report his observations of the defendant's conduct to the judge at the initial arraignment, which ordinarily will have been held as quickly as possi-

*There are certain exceptions to this general rule. In some *mala prohibita* offenses, such as statutory rape, intent is inferred from the act itself, sometimes even where circumstances contradict the existence of criminal intent.

73

ble after the arrest. If the judge concurs with the policeman's observations, he will remand the prisoner to a city hospital psychiatric prison ward. There the prisoner will be interviewed by psychiatrists, and his mental condition evaluated. These recommendations will be forwarded to the judge who will then decide whether the defendant can stand trial and complete the normal course of legal processing, or whether he should be committed directly to a state hospital for the criminally insane. Should a seemingly rational suspect become irrational at any point between arrest and the completion of his sentence, a similar procedure involving psychiatric recommendation to a judge will be followed, with the exception that a defendant who has already been convicted of a crime and committed to a correctional institution will be sent to a maximum security hospital for insane criminals, rather than to an institution for the criminally insane. In any case, one committed to either type of institution will, in effect, serve an indefinite sentence; that is, he will remain in custody until "cured," even if the length of such custody is longer than the maximum sentence for the offense with which he was, or would have been, charged.

When the psychiatrist evaluates the accused, he does so for the purpose of determining the presence or absence of a mental disorder, a "pathology of the psyche," usually referred to by psychiatrists as a psychosis. The *Psychiatric Dictionary* defines psychosis as

> a major mental disorder of organic or emotional origin in which the individual's ability to think, respond emotionally, remember, communicate, interpret reality, is sufficiently impaired so as to interfere grossly with his capacity to meet the ordinary demands of life ...[1]

In layman's terms, the accused can be said to be out of contact with reality with respect to time, place, and identity. The identification of a psychosis within a given individual is an extremely difficult and complex task, complicated even further by the disagreement among various schools of psychiatry as to which behavior syndromes indicate which, if any, psychosis. To confuse matters even more, the law does not recognize psychosis as a defense in a criminal prosecution. The law talks of insanity (a legal term), rather than of psychosis (a medical term). The relationship between insanity and psychosis is unclear, but essentially where the physician is looking for disease, the law is looking for a status designation indicative of the likely effect of the individual on society. The physician is concerned for the well-being of his patient; the judge is concerned with the well-being of the community.

> The test of insanity as laid down in the law centers about three matters: namely, the knowledge of right and wrong, the existence of delusion, and the presence of an irresistible impulse.... Insanity is purely a legal concept and means irresponsibility, or incapacity.[2]

The judge in a criminal court, then, is faced with the problem of translating medical concepts into legal ones, of using a psychiatrist's evaluation as the basis for a legal finding. This is an enormously difficult task made more difficult by the fact that differences of opinion among psychiatrists force the judge into an essentially subjective evaluation of the situation. The possibilities for error are great. Individuals whose conduct may seem highly irrational and disordered to middle-class observers such as judges may, in fact, be functioning quite rationally in terms of their own particular milieu. In New York State in 1962, one Victor Rosario was released from Matteawan State Hospital for the Criminally Insane, where he had been held for four years essentially because he told a story no middle-class official (including eleven psychiatrists) was willing to believe. Mr. Rosario, who was arrested and charged with assault for kicking and hitting his wife, told the police that his wife's love had been stolen from him by a boarder in their apartment, who had drawn blood from his (the boarder's) arms and drunk it in beer to prove his vigor. Mr. Rosario was sent to Bellevue Hospital for observation, and two psychiatrists who heard his story came to the conclusion that he was paranoid and unable to understand the charges against him. "The doctors told me that if I forgot that story, they might let me go, but the truth is the truth no matter what anyone says," said Mr. Rosario. After four years in a mental hospital, during which time he wrote letters to government officials and drew up six petitions for writs of *habeas corpus* (all of which were ignored by the courts), a lawyer to whom he had been referred believed his story sufficiently to check into it. She found that both Mrs. Rosario and the boarder verified Rosario's story. Rosario was released from the hospital and the assault charges against him dismissed.[3]

On the other hand, there are individuals whose conduct in many areas is rational, well organized, and responsible, sufficiently so to hold a job or to make contracts. Such individuals may, nevertheless, be medically psychotic; their defenses are simply good enough to mask their loss of contact with reality in a particular sphere. For the judge to make an accurate determination or prognostication as to the defendant's future conduct is very difficult, and the consequences of error very serious. Either a sane person may be confined indefinitely with the mentally sick, there to become sick himself, or a sick person may be placed in a correctional institution where rehabilitation is impossible, and his conduct is a source of great difficulty for both prison officials and inmates.

In 1941, during an unsuccessful attempted payroll stickup, Anthony and William Esposito killed two policemen and wounded a third. A taxicab driver who assisted other police in apprehending the Esposito brothers was seriously wounded. The case attracted a great deal of news coverage and one enterprising newspaper reporter tagged the killers as the "Mad Dog" Esposito brothers. The two gunmen were quickly indicted and brought to trial, in spite of the attempts of their lawyers to have the Espositos declared insane and incompetent to stand trial. During the trial, the defense unsuccessfully attempted to convince the jury that the brothers were insane and hence not responsible for their actions. In spite of the fact that the brothers engaged in violent outbursts, urinated, rolled on the floor, "simulated" uncontrolled animal behavior, and made strange noises, the court was convinced that the Espositos were malingering and attempting to escape the consequences of their killings by feigning insane behavior. The jury found both brothers guilty, and the judge, disregarding the pleas of the lawyers, sentenced the Espositos to be executed. Even in the death house their behavior continued to be bizarre, and on occasion they had to be forcibly fed. The Court of Appeals of New York upheld the conviction, the governor ignored pleas for clemency, and both brothers were electrocuted. On autopsy, both brothers were found to be paretic as a consequence of syphilis. There was a good likelihood that the amount of brain damage was sufficient to have caused both brothers to have been in fact psychotic, and probably not responsible for their actions.[4]

The Rosario and Esposito cases illustrate how subjective and culture-bound evaluations of insanity may be, even when made by conscientious and honest judges and psychiatrists. It is to avoid such errors that the law attempts to set objective standards in the form of definitions of insanity and criminal responsibility. Unfortunately, these definitions and the procedures associated with them have to some extent further complicated an already muddled situation.

PRETRIAL INSANITY HEARINGS

The adversary system of criminal justice presupposes a contest between relative equals. At a very minimum the defendant is supposed to be aware of his own self-interest and capable of attempting to preserve it. However, when the mentally incapacitated person is brought before the judge in a pretrial arraignment, he may be unaware of his illness, and have no idea of how best to proceed in his own behalf. It then becomes the obligation of the prosecutor, judge, defense attorney, or next of kin to point out the defendant's condition and ask that the court take appropriate legal action, usually a pretrial hearing. At this point the adversary system is nonexistent as far as the defendant is concerned. He is no longer dealing with opponents but with "friends"—friends who, while active in his behalf, may nevertheless send him away to what may amount to life imprisonment. He may indeed be mentally ill and require indefinite confinement in his own best interests. But what if he is not? Who can speak for him? Only he, himself—and he is presumed to be incompetent. His entire world is populated by enemies in the guise of friends. For such defendants there is no safeguard against the possibility of medical or judicial error. The justification for pretrial sanity hearings relies on the infallibility of judges and psychiatrists. If the competence of the psychiatrist to diagnose the accused's mental state were beyond doubt, and the ability of the judge to translate a medical finding into legal action unquestionable, there would be no problem protecting the defendant's rights. Judges and psychiatrists, unfortunately, are far from infallible, and the pretrial sanity hearing degenerates in some cases to a labelling process wherein the defendant is stigmatized.

The standard test for mental competence to stand trial is whether or not the defendant, *as a result of mental disease, lacks capacity to understand the proceedings against him or to assist in his own defense.* This means that an accused person who is thought to be incompetent generally is clinically examined by a psychiatrist. He is also given a battery of psychological tests by a psychologist, designed to determine whether the defendant has a mental disease. These tests and the clinical examination are not focused solely on whether the accused person knows his name, understands the definition of the crime of which is is accused, recognizes his attorney, and so on, but also, on whether he has a personality disorder or mental defect. While simple questions may be addressed to the accused, he may also be given a Rorschach test, projective drawing tests, and other personality assessment tests, designed to tell the examiner whether or not the defendant suffers from a mental disease which will hinder his capacity to understand the courtroom proceedings and assist in his own defense, even if he appears to the layman to be sane.

Pretrial sanity hearings are held before a judge, and without a jury. They can be held, moreover, over the objection of the defendant, his attorney, or his relatives, since the prosecutor is frequently considered to be a better judge of the defendant's interests than the defense lawyer. If the motion is made by the prosecutor, moreover, and the defendant is adjudged incompetent to stand trial, the state can then incarcerate him in a mental hospital without ever having tried the factual issue of innocence or guilt. (Without suggesting that the pretrial sanity hearing has been used for political purposes in the United States, the potential for its abuse is amply demonstrated by the systematic confinement of dissenters in mental hospitals in the Soviet Union. Those who have displeased the state are given "sanity hearings," are adjudged "insane" and incarcerated.) During the psychiatric examination, the defendant is often pressured to incriminate himself, either as to his guilt or as to his mental condition. The examining psychiatrist, employed by a state hospital or otherwise retained by the government, is perceived by the defendant (often correctly) as an adversary. He is not the patient's doctor in the normal understanding of that term. The defendant may therefore be understandably reluctant to confide to the psychiatrist any information relating to the offense with which he is charged, or to any of his past history, especially in relation to bizarre behavior or previous mental illness. Such uncooperativeness on the subject's part may be interpreted by the psychiatrist as evasiveness, escape from reality, or lack of contact. The defendant is thus in a position where he is damned if he does, and damned if he doesn't: if he speaks freely to the psychiatrist, his statements may be used against him; if he refuses to speak, his silence will be interpreted unfavorably.

Another hurdle encountered by defendants whose sanity is suspect is the prospect of multiple pretrial sanity hearings. If a defendant has been considered incompetent to stand trial and remanded to a mental hospital, he is subject to another pretrial sanity hearing before he can be tried at any later date. Thus, if he is not to serve what amounts to a life sentence, he must at some point be able to convince the state-appointed psychiatrists of his competence to stand trial. Even after he successfully passes the pretrial examination, however, he is not free from the prospect of further examination, because his sanity can again be questioned by the judge or prosecutor, and he can be ordered to submit to further examinations at the trial or sentencing stages. The accused must defend his sanity not once, but as often as the state seeks to question it.

The guidelines to be used by psychiatrists in evaluating the defendant's condition are by no means clear. The data on which the doctor's judgment is based may be scanty or inappropriate. Thomas Szasz, a psychiatrist known for his scathing indictment of the judicial handling of suspected mental incompetents cites the case of Major General Edwin Walker, who was ordered to submit to a pretrial sanity hearing on the recommendation of psychiatrists who had never seen him and who based their judgments on newspaper stories which were later shown to be inaccurate.[5]

In light of the possible miscarriage of justice for an accused individual who cannot satisfy government authorities as to his mental health, Szasz and other critics have suggested substantial modification of the present system. They recommend that the issue of competence to stand trial be separated from consideration of the subject's overall mental condition. Since a judgment of mental illness is, in many cases, either an attempt to reconstruct events which happened in the past, or a prognostication as to the subject's future conduct, such judgments are highly problematical. The critics therefore hold that the state should confine this investigation initially only to the question of whether at the moment of trial the accused is able to understand the nature of the charges against him, and is able to cooperate with an attorney in his own defense. They also look askance at the paternalism underlying and implicit in the state's right to force a sanity hearing on an unwilling defendant "in his own best interest." The defendant himself or his attorney should be the sole determiner of his own best interest unless he is so disoriented and out of touch with reality as to make a trial obviously impossible.

The realities of the criminal justice system are such that in many cases even a mentally ill defendant will be better off pleading guilty to the offense charged and accepting punishment than permitting himself to be labelled insane either before or after trial. It is questionable whether the stigma of insanity is less than the stigma of conviction; certainly, the penalty for a minor offense will be far shorter than the time the accused may expect to spend in an institution for the criminally insane. Even if the accused is subsequently committed civilly to a mental hospital, his future prospects for release are less complicated than if his commitment were criminal. These criticisms suggest that when a sanity hearing is ordered over the objections of the defendant or his attorney, the burden of proof for the justification of such hearings must rest solidly on the state, and the standards for justifying such examinations must be clearly delineated and closely scrutinized. Provision should also be made for quick and inexpensive appellate review of such orders.

THE INSANITY DEFENSE

Defendants who were obviously deranged at the time of the crime present no problems with respect to criminal responsibility. Their mental condition is such that no true *mens rea* can be attributed to them and they must be acquitted by virtue of their insanity. Many defendants whose sanity is questionable, however, display no overtly bizarre behavior. To the casual onlooker, the individual in question may seem calm, well oriented, and rational. Schizophrenics constitute the largest category of the criminally insane, and their behavior is often deceptive.

> Schizophrenics . . . can memorize lists of words, solve problems, and form concepts. . . . They are given complicated intelligence, personality, and concept formation tests, and are expected to understand instructions even though their performance on the tests themselves is likely to be abnormal. They, and psychotics generally, help maintain the hospital by doing work on the grounds, in the wards, and in the kitchens. They publish hospital newspapers and engage in athletics. Where there is a patient government, they take part in it.[6]

If institutionalized mental patients can behave in such an outwardly rational fashion, how can a judge and jury composed of nonpsychiatrically trained laymen make an evaluation of a defendant's claim that he was insane at the time of the commission of the act charged? Somehow a formula must be developed which will permit a distinction to be made between the sane criminal seeking to avoid criminal responsibility for his act, and the seemingly rational but mentally incompetent defendant whose judgment was so impaired that he was not fully responsible for his conduct. It is in this context that the M'Naghten and other rules for determining insanity have evolved.

In 1843, one Daniel M'Naghten, a Scotsman laboring under the delusion that the Pope, the Jesuits, and Sir Robert Peel, Prime Minister of England, were conspiring against him, attempted to shoot Sir Robert, but because he did not know what Peel looked like, shot and killed Peel's secretary Edward

Drummond instead. Eight doctors at the trial testified that M'Naghten really believed in the truth of his delusion. In addition, M'Naghten's conduct at the trial was bizarre and irrational. The presiding judge instructed the jury to bring in a verdict of "not guilty by reason of insanity," and M'Naghten was sent to an institution for the insane. The attack on Peel caused Queen Victoria much uneasiness, coming as it did during a period of economic distress and social unrest and following several abortive attempts at assassination of the Queen herself. There was even suspicion that the killing was part of a plot instigated by the reformers of the Anti-Corn Law League.* The verdict was a disappointment to many, including the Queen herself who protested, "The law may be perfect, but how is it that whenever a case for its application arises, it proves to be of no avail?" As a result of public protest, the fifteen High Court judges were in effect asked to draw up rules applicable to such cases in the future. The judges decided that

> to establish a defense on the ground of insanity, it must be clearly proved that, at the time of committing the act, the party accused was laboring under such a defect of reason, from disease of the mind, as not to know the nature and quality of the act he was doing, or as not to know that what he was doing was wrong.[7]

Further, "he must be considered in the same situation as to responsibility as if the facts with respect to which the delusion exists were real."

In the years since its formulation, the M'Naghten Rule has been subjected to a barrage of criticism. For one thing, M'Naghten himself could not have been acquitted by reason of insanity, using the rule named for him. There was no reason to believe that he did not know that he was killing his victim, or that the act was wrong; nor would his delusion as to the conspiracy, even if true, have justified the killing. The most basic criticism however, is that the concept "disease of the mind" simply does not lend itself to modern psychiat-

---

*A different and provocative view of the M'Naghten case is that of Richard Moran, "Awaiting the Crown's Pleasure: The Case of Daniel M'Naghten," *Criminology*, 15, no. 1 (May, 1977):7–26. Moran argues that far from being insane, M'Naghten was a political radical and an ideological sympathizer with the Chartist movement. Much of his testimony, for example, that relating to his persecution by the Tories, which was considered to be delusional by the judges may, in fact, have been true and the result of harassment of unpopular radicals by the political establishment. The Chartist movement and the reforms it called for, most of which related to the alleviation of conditions of working men and the poor, were an embarrassment and a threat to the Queen and Peel, her Tory Prime Minister. Moran argues that rather than convict M'Naghten for Drummond's murder, which would have enabled him to claim the role of a political martyr, the prosecution decided to stigmatize the defendant by labelling him insane. Up until that time, an individual found to be criminally insane was commonly confined in his own home in the custody of a relative, or in a private, charitable hospital. M'Naghten, however, was committed to Bethlem Hospital, a secure institution, for an indefinite sentence, (the equivalent of a one day to life). He spent the final twenty-two years of his life in confinement, and eventually died of diabetes.

ric diagnosis, and without extensive stretching the language of the formulation hampers the presentation of useful psychiatric testimony to the court.

The word *know*, for example, interpreted narrowly and literally, refers to a kind of cognition absent only in the totally disoriented. A man may know what he is doing in a narrow sense, and yet not appreciate the total impact or consequences of his actions. Similarly, the word *wrong* is difficult to define. Does "wrong" mean moral or legal wrong? If moral wrong, by whose standards? What if the defendant honestly believes that he was commanded by God to kill? Did he think the act was wrong? If "wrong" means legally wrong, this surely is not proof of insanity. Many lawbreakers are ignorant of the law; many others know the law but willfully choose to disregard it. Neither category is necessarily insane.

There is a feeling that the M'Naghten rule is restrictive in that it

reflects an outmoded faculty psychology. It sees thought process as separated into cognitive, emotional, and control components, and classes a man as insane, as having a "defect of reason," only if he suffers from serious cognitive or intellectual impairment. This, the critics argue, is at odds with the "new psychology" which sees man's personality as dynamically integrated and his mental condition as necessarily unsound if any part of its functioning is disordered.[8]

Because of the ambiguities and limitations of the M'Naghten Rule, critics have charged that psychiatrists are impeded in giving meaningful testimony as to the mental condition of the accused. Obviously, a defendant could meet the standards of the M'Naghten test and still be mentally ill in a medical sense, certainly by present standards even if not necessarily by the standards prevalent in 1844. The case of *People v. Horton*[9] illustrates the difficulties the customary judicial interpretation of the M'Naghten Rule creates for the psychiatrist who wishes to testify meaningfully about the mental state of the accused. It also suggests that the rule does not help the jury to understand the components of mental illness, since it was clear that the intelligence and seeming rationality of the accused led the jury to conclude that he could not have been insane.

Norman L. Horton was an eighteen-year-old college student who left his dormitory at about 6:30 in the evening of May 23, 1953, and travelled sixty miles to his home in Chemung County, New York. He entered his father's garage and, taking a hammer and a pair of gloves, "because I knew they would be looking for fingerprints," waited several hours until the light was out in his parents' bedroom, and the whistle of a train due to pass nearby would muffle any noise he might make. When the train whistle sounded, he smashed the pane of glass in the French door, entered the house, and picked up a carving knife in the kitchen. Shoeless and shaking with fright, he crept upstairs to his parents' bedroom. "I kept telling myself," he said, "you have got to do it. It is the only way out. It isn't right but it is just circumstances that led me there and there is no way out." He then plunged the knife into his father's back, fatally wounding him. Leaving the bedroom, he restored the knife to the kitchen, retrieved his shoes, and fled, disposing of the gloves and hammer outdoors. He hitchhiked back to his dormitory, arriving between six and seven in the morning. Shortly afterwards, a message was given him telling him simply that his father had died. His response was, "My father didn't have a heart condition." Horton was later arrested and indicted for murder in the first degree, to which he pleaded not guilty by reason of insanity.

At the trial, the testifying psychiatrist had great difficulty in answering meaningfully the classic question associated with the M'Naghten Rule: "Doctor, in your opinion, did the defendant know the nature and quality of his act, and did he know that it was wrong?" A categoric yes or no answer was required of him by the court.

Defense Attorney
Q. Doctor, did he know what he was doing when he committed those acts?
A. The answer is no. He was psychotic at the time and did not know the nature and quality of his acts. (This answer was stricken out.)

District Attorney
Q. You concede, then, Doctor, that this series of connected activities seemed to be rational?
A. Seemed to be rational just as the case of a paranoid praecox. They are a whole series of connected activities, yet they are a most serious and most malignant form of schizophrenia. Just the ability to rationalize doesn't make it rational. (This answer was stricken out, and the jury instructed to disregard it.)[10]

Horton's insanity defense was rejected by the jury, who obviously had not been able to deduce from the psychiatric testimony the nature of mental illness and how it might manifest itself in the defendant's conduct. The record suggests that the jury had difficulty believing that one intelligent and rational enough to have planned the crime in question could be insane.

Justice Van Voorhis, in his dissent, quoted feelingly from an article by Dr. G. H. Stevenson in the *Canadian Bar Review*:

The psychiatrist's difficulties with the M'Naghten Rules begin with the administration of the oath. He is sworn to tell the whole truth, but the rules, because of their concern only with the intellective aspects of mental function, prevent him from telling the whole truth about the accused's mental condition. If he attempts to tell of the disorganized emotional aspects which may have caused the crime, he may be sharply interrupted by the trial judge and ordered to limit his comments to insanity as defined by the M'Naghten Rules. . . . He is in an impossible position—sworn to tell the whole truth and prevented by the court from telling it.[11]

In an attempt to remedy the inadequacies of the M'Naghten Rule, Judge Bazelon of the United States Court of Appeals in Washington, D.C., in 1954 enunciated the famous "Durham Rule." This held that "an accused is not criminally responsible if his unlawful act was the product of mental disease or mental defect."[12] The court differentiated between mental disease and mental defect in that the former was considered capable of improvement or deterioration, while the latter was considered incapable of change as the result of congenital impairment, injury, or the residual effect of disease.* Only Maine and the Virgin Islands adopted the Durham Rule. Bazelon's decision, however, provoked an enormous amount of discussion and controversy in legal circles and in 1972, in *United States v. Brawner,*[13] the same court rejected the Durham Rule and adopted as its criterion of insanity the rule stated in the Model Penal Code of the American Law Institute (ALI):

> A person is not responsible for criminal conduct if at the time of such conduct as a result of mental disease or defect he lacks substantial capacity to appreciate the wrongfullness of his conduct or to conform his conduct to the requirements of the law.

While both the Durham and ALI rules are concerned with determining whether the criminal conduct involved is a result of mental disease or defect, the ALI rule places emphasis on whether the accused had capacity to appreciate what he had done, rather than on the ability of the psychiatrist to demonstrate a causal relationship between a mental disease (if it is present) and the criminal act. Under the ALI formula, while the psychiatrist may testify as to the presence or absence of mental disease, it is the jury which makes the determination of capacity. Under the *Durham* rule, it was necessary for the psychiatrist to demonstrate not only the presence of mental disease, but a causal relationship between that disease and the act in question. Indeed, in the *Brawner* case itself, there was agreement by the experts that Brawner suffered from a "psychologic brain syndrome associated with a convulsive disorder," but defense and prosecution witnesses disagreed about whether or not there was a causal relation between the mental disorder and the alleged offense.

Judge Bazelon, the author of the original *Durham* decision concurred in *Brawner.* In an article written two years later he commented:

> In the end, after eighteeen years I favored the abandonment of the *Durham* rule because in practice it had failed to take the issue of criminal responsibility away from the experts. Psychiatrists continued to testify to the naked conclusion

*The Durham Rule was not the first judicially suggested alternative to *M'Naghten*. The Pike standard, handed down by the New Hampshire Supreme Court in 1869, was almost identical to *Durham* but had been largely ignored.

instead of providing information about the accused so that the jury could render the ultimate moral judgment about blameworthiness. *Durham* had secured little improvement over M'Naghten.[14]

Another attempt to remedy the deficiencies of the M'Naghten test is the so-called irresistible impulse rule. This rule instructs jurors to acquit the accused if they find that he had a mental disease which made it impossible for him to control his conduct. This new standard seems more in keeping with the concepts of modern psychology because it describes realistically the state in which a mentally disturbed individual might find himself. Recently, however, many lawyers and psychiatrists have become disenchanted with irresistible impulse as a rationale for determining criminal responsibility, because it either adds too little to *M'Naghten,* or too much. On the one hand, if narrowly construed, its meaning is very similar to the usual interpretation of *M'Naghten;* on the other hand, if broadly construed, it sets no viable limits for its application in a criminal case.

Generally whether irresistible impulse is used independently of, or together with *M'Naghten,* the same criticisms may be made of these tests as of earlier ones. The jury still receives no effective guidance as to whether the accused was in such mental condition as to be accorded diminished responsibility under the criminal law. It is extremely difficult for medical experts, especially when there are marked disagreements among them, to translate into usable legal terms a standard capable of being understood and applied by the laymen who sit on the jury. The reality of the situation is that regardless of what instructions are given to the jury, or which test is used, the result is pretty much the same in terms of the verdict.[15]

An experienced trial judge commented to the authors that he has found that regardless of how the judge instructs the jury, each juror tends to decide the insanity issue by asking the question: "Would *this* defendant in his right mind be capable of committing *this* crime?"

Because of the difficulty of giving meaningful guidelines to the jury, and because of the possibilities of injustice inherent in an improperly adjudicated insanity defense, many critics of our judicial proceedings have suggested eliminating the insanity defense *in toto.* * In its place they suggest a factfinding

*The New York State Department of Mental Hygiene, troubled by increasing dissatisfaction with the insanity defense currently in use in New York, identified four alternatives to it: 1) retaining the insanity defense, but converting it to an affirmative defense, that is, giving the defendant the burden of proving the existence of mental disease or defect; 2) a bifurcated trial in which the first stage would determine guilt on the basis of facts relating to the commission of the offense, and the second stage would involve the proper disposition for the defendant in light of his past mental condition; 3) a provision for a "guilty, but mentally ill" verdict, which would result in a sentence to a fixed term of incarceration in a mental institution; and 4) a diminished capacity rule under which, for those crimes requiring the defendant to have acted knowingly or intentionally, the charge would be lowered to a similar offense not requiring such knowledge or intention, but punishable by confinement in a prison rather than in a mental hospital. These alternatives were submitted to the New York State Executive Advisory Commit-

hearing before a judge, with or without a jury, the purpose of which is to determine whether the act in question was committed, and whether the accused did in fact commit the act. Once the determination of fact is made, they suggest that a board composed of possibly a psychiatrist, a psychologist, a sociologist, and a judge dispose of the case in an appropriate manner. Within the confines of such an administrative tribunal, discussion as to the mental condition of the accused could proceed in a more informal and meaningful manner, and an intelligent decision could be reached on the best possible arrangements for the defendant's future.

In *The Crime of Punishment,* Karl Menninger imagines a colloquy between a judge and a psychiatrist in which the psychiatrist points out the irrationalities of the present insanity defense. The judge then asks the psychiatrist for his suggestions for improvement. The psychiatrist replies:

Answer:
I have been waiting for this question, and now I would like to make my main point. Will your Honor indulge me?
Judge:
Proceed.
Answer:
In my opinion, what you should do, what all courts should do, what society should do, is to *exclude all psychiatrists from the courtroom!* Put us all out and make us stay out. After you have tried the case, let us doctors and our assistants examine him and confer together outside the courtroom and render a report to you, which will express our view of the offender—his potentialities, his liabilities, and the possible remedies.

If we doctors cannot agree, let us disagree in private and submit majority and minority reports. That probably will not be necessary; our differences are going to be on minor points. We are not going to raise legal issues like "sanity" and "responsibility" because we are not going to talk legal jargon. Nor should we talk *our* jargon. We should try to say in simple English why we think this man has acted in this way so different from the rest of us, and what we think can be done to change his pattern.[16]

Menninger's suggestion, which has been made by a number of other criminologists and sociologists, is very persuasive. It seems to make very good sense to leave the disposition of difficult cases involving diminished responsibility because of mental impairment to a panel of experts, rather than to a

tee on Sentencing, which, in December 1978, transmitted the report to Governor Carey expressing its disapproval of the diminished capacity rule, the alternative favored by the Department of Mental Hygiene.

At the federal level, S1437, the omnibus proposal to amend the federal code of criminal procedure, included a proposal to abolish the insanity defense. Since S1437 for a variety of reasons failed to pass the House of Representatives, the insanity defense is unlikely to be modified by Congress in the near future. Other proposals to modify or abolish the insanity defense are currently pending in a number of states.

jury composed of uninformed laymen. Surely psychologists, psychiatrists, and sociologists have a better understanding of what makes this defendant "so different from the rest of us," and what to do with him.* The problem is that if one accepts the rationale of expert handling at the administrative level of problem criminal defendants, one cannot stop logically with the mentally impaired. If mental disease makes it impossible for a man to control himself sufficiently to assume full responsibility for his acts, what of sociological disease—poverty, ignorance, alienation, or family disorganization? If schizophrenia entitles a defendant to administrative rather than judicial handling, why doesn't living in a ghetto? Surely, the life of a deprived child is as warping and detrimental to the development of internal controls as mental illness. If the mentally ill are to be judged outside the judicial process, why should not all other defendants who come before the bench damaged, destroyed, or impaired by the society into which they were unwittingly born?

There are indeed many critics of our society who hold that the concept of criminal responsibility is unfair and to some extent meaningless. The law is, of course, an expression of middle-class values, and the administration of criminal justice is weighted in favor of middle-class defendants. To this extent it is true that the ignorant, indigent defendant, like the insane defendant, is frequently given less than a fair shake by the system. But is the answer disposition by an administrative tribunal of experts? At least one noted legal scholar thinks not. Abraham S. Goldstein, provost of Yale University and formerly, dean of Yale Law School, objects to the Menninger type of reform precisely because, logically, it leads to administrative rather than judicial handling of many kinds of defendants. Experts, Goldstein argues, should not handle these cases because the issues being decided in the disposition of criminal defendants are ultimately moral questions, and not technical

*Laymen tend to believe, and psychiatrists encourage laymen to believe, that psychiatrists are possessed of special knowledge and insight which is commonly called "expertise." Bruce J. Ennis, a staff attorney for the New York Civil Liberties Union, and Thomas R. Litwack, an attorney and Associate Professor of Psychology at John Jay College (CUNY), take issue with this assumption in "Psychiatry and the Presumption of Expertise: Flipping Coins in the Courtroom," 62 *California Law Review* 693, May 1974. Ennis and Litwack claim that "based upon our reading of the professional literature, we have concluded that (a) there is no evidence warranting the assumption that psychiatrists can accurately determine who is 'dangerous'; (b) there is little or no evidence that psychiatrists are more 'expert' in making the predictions relative to civil commitment than laymen; (c) 'expert' judgments made by psychiatrists are not sufficiently reliable and valid to justify nonjudicial hospitalization based on such judgments; (d) the constitutional rights of individuals are seriously prejudiced by the admissibility of psychiatric terminology, diagnoses, and predictions, expecially those of 'dangerous' behavior; and therefore, (e) courts should limit testimony by psychiatrists to descriptive statements and should exclude psychiatric diagnoses, judgments, and predictions." The authors claim that psychiatrists' judgments seldom are either reliable (consistent with the judgment of other psychiatrists), or valid (true or accurate). Psychiatrists frequently differ markedly among themselves both as to the diagnosis and prognosis for individual cases. Furthermore, they tend to vastly overpredict possible dangerousness.

ones demanding professional expertise. The judge and the jury, by definition, speak for the community in the setting of moral standards: they are the keepers of the community's conscience.

Menninger himself recognizes this distinction.

> I oppose courtroom appearances [by psychiatrists] because I consider guilt, competence, and responsibility to be moral questions, not medical ones. The judge and jury are the community's representatives in this area. It is for them to make the judgment and apply the sanctions deemed appropriate, not us psychiatrists.*

To ask "What went wrong?" with regard to a defendant instead of "Is he guilty?" is to change completely the relationship of the individual to the law. It is to remove the notion that the individual has a responsibility to society to obey its laws, and to substitute therefor the notion that society has an obligation to the individual to see that he behaves, or at least that it is possible for him to behave, in the manner expected of him. While the latter goal is noble and praiseworthy, it is impossible of achievement both practically and conceptually. Even if we had the resources and political willingness to create a utopia in which no individuals were warped or harmed by their environment, we cannot even agree on what this utopia would look like. To substitute a standard of social responsibility for the individual for the present standard of individual responsibility to society is impractical, dangerous, and conceptually questionable. In the last analysis, the social and political theory underlying a free society presupposes individuals capable of acting with some degree of free will, and not automatons infinitely manipulable by the state. To remove the element of personal responsibility from the criminal law is to cut out the heart of democratic ideology.

> Most fundamentally, eliminating the insanity defense would remove from the criminal law and the public conscience the vitally important distinction between illness and evil, or would tuck it away in an administrative process. . . .
>
> This approach overlooks entirely the place of the concept of responsibility itself in keeping the mechanism in proper running order. That concept is more seriously threatened today than ever before. This is a time of anomie—of men separated from their faiths, their tribes, and their villages—and trying to achieve in a single generation what could not previously be achieved in several. Many achieve all they expect, but huge numbers do not; these vent their frustration in anger, in violence, and in theft. In an effort to patch and mend the tearing social fabric, the state is playing an increasingly paternal role. . . . As this effort gains momentum, there is a very real risk it will bring with it a culture which will not

---

*Menninger, p. 139. Menninger assumes apparently that the judge and jury will still make the final decisions as to the defendant's fate. So they will, but bureaucratic experience suggests that there will be a strong tendency for the judge to defer to the "experts" in these cases, so that the decision will in reality be theirs and not his.

make the individuals within it feel it is important to learn the discipline of moderation and conformity to communal norms.

In such a time, the insanity defense can play a part in reinforcing the sense of obligation or responsibility. Its emphasis on whether an offender is sick or bad helps to keep alive the almost forgotten drama of individual responsibility. . . . It becomes part of a complex of cultural forces that keep alive the moral lessons, and the myths, which are essential to the continued order of society. In short, even if we have misgivings about blaming a particular individual, because he has been shaped long ago by forces he may no longer be able to resist, the concept of "blame" may be necessary.

. . . The concept of "blame" and insanity which is its other side, is one of the ways in which the culture marks out the extremes beyond which nonconformity may not go.[17]

The fact is that the principal importance of the insanity defense is in its conceptual impact on the system. The literature on the subject is voluminous, and it includes work by many of the first-rate scholars in law, sociology, and psychology. The actual incidence of claims of innocence by reason of insanity is statistically minute, however. Most criminal matters are disposed of by guilty pleas, and of the relatively small number that go to jury trial only about 2 percent involve the insanity defense. This means that probably far less than .5 percent of all indictments filed involve pleas of not guilty by virtue of insanity. Thus, the interest in the subject is occasioned far more by its implications for our political ideology than for the defendants involved. This is true for many aspects of the criminal justice system, but is especially marked in this area.

If then, the criticism leveled by Dean Goldstein at Menninger-type reforms in this area is to be taken seriously, what alternatives remain? Goldstein himself suggests several avenues of approach. He argues that the basic flaw in the M'Naghten Rule has not been in its substance but in its application. It has been unreasonably narrowly construed, and there is no basis for the continuation of such judicial interpretation. Judges can easily extend the definition of words like *know* and *wrong* so that they are more meaningful in terms of the determination to be made. The M'Naghten Rule can and should be modified further by statements such as those in the Durham and the irresistible impulse formulations. Steps along these lines have been taken in the Model Penal Code prepared by the American Law Institute (ALI) which suggests that:

1. A person is not responsible for criminal conduct if at the time of such conduct as a result of mental disease or defect he lacked substantial capacity to appreciate the criminality (wrongfulness) of his conduct or to conform to the requirements of the law.
2. As used in this article the terms mental disease or defect do not include an abnormality manifested only by repeated criminal or otherwise anti-social conduct.

Procedural impediments to raising the insanity defense should be reduced, possibly by guidelines such as the McDonald Rule, which places the burden of rebuttal on the state to show that the accused is in fact sane rather than *vice versa,* when evidence as to insanity has been offered by the defense. Above all, the rules of evidence must be sufficiently relaxed to permit psychiatrists to testify in a meaningful way about the mental condition of the accused, so that the kinds of answers demanded in the above-cited Horton case will be avoided. The inclusion of the word "substantial" in the ALI Model Penal Code is an attempt to accomplish this very purpose. The psychiatrist should be permitted to testify fully in terms of his own medical expertise. It is the burden of the judge to translate this testimony into useful legal guidelines for the benefit of the jury.

RELEASING THE INSANITY DEFENDANT

The successful assertion of an insanity defense is seldom a prelude to immediate freedom for the defendant. An accused person who is acquitted by virtue of insanity is almost never set free by the court. To begin with, the insanity defense is usually used only for very serious crimes, such as murder, or violent sexual offenses. When the defendant has been acquitted by virtue of diminished capacity, it means that although he was not responsible, he did, in fact, commit a violent, unlawful act and was, at the time he committed it, a danger to the community. Thus, the question before the court is whether the defendant continues to be dangerous to himself or others, and therefore, should be held in custody, not in a prison, but in a secure mental hospital.

In most jurisdictions, and in almost all cases, the court will remand such a defendant to a mental hospital sufficiently secure to prevent his escape. This commitment, although it is to a secure facility, is civil in nature since the defendant, having been acquitted, is technically not a criminal. Once he is in this facility, the problem for him and for the community is when, and under what circumstances, he may be released. Until fairly recently, it was common practice to confine such defendants almost indefinitely because psychiatrists were reluctant to certify that they would not, in the future, become violent. In more recent years, due in part to a series of lawsuits involving the rights of those held involuntarily in mental hospitals, the courts have become quite solicitous of the rights of all mental patients, both those with a criminal past and those without, and psychiatrists are far more willing to consider them as candidates for release. Indeed, if the patient can no longer benefit from treatment, and there is no strong evidence to suggest the possibility of future violence, then release will be recommended by the medical staff of the institution. Unfortunately, as in the case of parole, while the great majority of such individuals who are recommended for release prove, in fact, to be nonviolent, some released patients do commit violent crimes following their release, and the public understandably becomes concerned. Not only has someone been harmed by the released defendant, but the entire insanity defense and the different handling of the insanity defendant comes to be regarded as illegitimate. If the defendant were so ill that he could not be held responsible and punished for his crime, why is he well enough to be released and escape punishment? When he then commits another crime, the resentment of the public is exacerbated.

There is no simple solution for this dilemma. If all insanity defendants walked around in Napoleon hats or spouted gibberish, the public would not resent acquittal. If all released insanity defendants became model citizens, again the public might forgive their past aberrations and accept their release. But in real life, it is possible for a person to have experienced a period of insanity during which he committed a dreadful act, and from which he may recover fully. To keep such a person incarcerated indefinitely is cruel and unjust. It is also possible for personality disorders to remain latent, and emerge, possibly in the form of violent crime, only under the strains imposed by living in freedom in the community. All release programs embody some element of risk, yet release programs are essential.

The task of separating defendants who are sick from those who are bad is a challenge to a free society. There are no easy answers and no answers which can ignore the role of society itself in creating both sickness and badness. The success of our efforts in this area is, however, one indication of our success as an ongoing social system. As Judge Bazelon said:

> The law is neither a scientific instrument nor an adjunct to any absolute moral doctrine. . . . In the criminal law and the administration of the insanity defense the wisdom of the past, including the free-will postulate, meets modern scientific views, including the postulate of causal determinism. The legal process differs from religion in that . . . it cannot utter moral imperatives. It differs from science in that it cannot choose its experimental subject matter, it cannot plead ignorance and it cannot select its hypotheses freely. A court must resolve all conflicts presented to it, with or without adequate knowledge.[18]

Selected Readings

Arens, Richard. *Insanity Defense.* New York: Philosophical Library, 1974.

Biggs, John, Jr. *The Guilty Mind.* Baltimore: Johns Hopkins Press, 1955.

Bromberg, Walter. *Crime and the Mind.* 2nd ed. Philadelphia: Lippincott, 1965.

Goldstein, Abraham S. *The Insanity Defense.* New Haven: Yale University Press, 1967.

Halleck, Seymour L. *Psychiatry and the Dilemmas of Crime.* New York: Harper & Row, 1967.

Hinsie, Leland E., and Campbell, Robert J. *Psychiatric Dictionary.* 4th ed. New York: Oxford, 1970.

Katz, Jay; Goldstein, Joseph; and, Dershowitz, Alan M. *Psychoanalysis, and the Law.* New York: Free Press, 1967.

Marshall, James. *Law and Psychology in Conflict.* Garden City, N.Y.: Doubleday, 1969.

Menninger, Karl. *The Crime of Punishment.* New York: Viking, 1968.

Morris, Norval, and Hawkins, Gordon. *The Honest Politician's Guide to Crime Control.* Chicago: University of Chicago Press, 1970.

Polier, Justine W. *The Role of Law and the Role of Psychiatry.* Baltimore: Johns Hopkins Press, 1968.

Scheff, Thomas J. *Labeling Madness.* Englewood Cliffs, N.J.: Prentice-Hall, 1975.

Simon, Rita James. *The Jury and the Plea of Insanity.* Boston: Little, Brown, 1966.

Szasz, Thomas S. *Law, Liberty, and Psychiatry.* New York: Macmillan, 1963.

Szasz, Thomas S. *Psychiatric Justice.* New York: Macmillan, 1965.

Szasz, Thomas S. *Psychiatric Slavery.* New York: Free Press, 1978.

Williams, Edward Bennett. *One Man's Freedom.* New York: Atheneum, 1962.

Yochelson, Samuel, and Samenow, Stanton E. *The Criminal Personality, Volume I: A Profile for Change; Volume II: The Change Process.* New York: Aronson, 1977.

Notes

1. *A Psychiatric Glossary.* (Washington, D.C.: American Psychiatric Association, 1969), pp. 80–81.

2. Leland E. Hinsie and Robert J. Campbell, *Psychiatric Dictionary,* 4th ed. (New York: Oxford, 1970), p. 395.

3. Thomas S. Szasz, *Law, Liberty, and Psychiatry* (New York: The Macmillan Company, 1963), pp. 166–168; *New York Times,* September 28, 1962, p. 18.

4. *New York Times,* January 15, 1941, p. 1; March 13, 1942, p. 21.

5. Thomas S. Szasz, *Psychiatric Justice* (New York: The Macmillan Company, 1965), Chapter 6.

6. Abraham S. Goldstein, *The Insanity Defense* (New Haven: Yale University Press, 1967), p. 27.

7. As quoted in David L. Bazelon, "Psychiatrists and the Adversary Process," *Scientific American,* 230, no.6 (June, 1974), p. 19.

8. Goldstein, p. 46.

9. *People v. Horton,* 308 N.Y. 1 (1954).

10. Ibid., at 20, 21.

11. Ibid., at 21.

12. *Durham v. United States,* 214 F.2d 862 (1954), at 874–885.

13. 471 F2d 969 (1972).

14. Bazelon, "Psychiatrists and the Adversary Process."

15. Norval Morris and Gordon Hawkins, *The Honest Politician's Guide to Crime Control* (Chicago: University of Chicago Press, 1970), p. 178.

16. From *The Crime of Punishment* by Karl Menninger, M.D., p. 138. Copyright © 1966, 1968 by Karl Menninger, M.D. All rights reserved. Reprinted by permission of The Viking Press, Inc.

17. Goldstein, pp. 223–224.

18. David L. Bazelon, "The Awesome Decision," *Saturday Evening Post* (January 23, 1960): 56.

chapter **6**

the police

"For the urban poor, the police are those who arrest you."
   Michael Harrington, *The Other America*

"Sed quis custodiet ipsos custodes?" (But who is to guard the guards themselves?)
   Juvenal, *Satires*

To the schoolboy, the policeman is the man who helps him across the street. To the middle-class white, he is the man who gives out traffic tickets, or the man who keeps an eye on his house or store after dark. To the drunk, the policeman is the person who says "Move on"; to the cardiac victim, he is the one who calls the ambulance and gets the patient to the hospital. To the bookie, the cop is the man to watch out for or to pay off; to the potential sucide, he is the man who will crawl out on a ledge to reach him. To the young black in the ghetto he is "The Man," the enemy; to the middle-aged, middle-class black, he is the man too often not there. To the rich man he is a public servant; to the poor he is the face of authority. He is the hero of the St. Patrick's Day parade; he is the scourge of the radical demonstration. To his Irish mother, he is "New York's Finest"; to the Black Panthers and White Weathermen he is "Pig."*

Who is the policeman? What function does he perform? Is he hero or villain? Protector or oppressor? Corrupt or incorruptible? The last bastion of a decadent society or the thin blue line holding back the seas of anarchy?

The perspectives on the police are legion, as are the evaluations of their performance; nor is this a modern phenomenon. The police are obviously a socially necessary institution and have played a role in all modern societies.

---

*In this chapter and for the remainder of the book, the actors in the criminal justice system —police, attorneys, prosecutors, judges, corrections officials, and defendants will generally be referred to as males. Overwhelmingly, the criminal justice system has been, and still largely is, masculine. Until quite recently, for example, almost *no* women were assigned to police patrol duty. The research cited in the police area was done on almost entirely male police departments. Similarly, although women today are beginning to enter the ranks of prosecutors and judges in more substantial numbers, men heavily dominate the scene. Defendants are largely male also. Crime still is a man's business, and a young man's business at that. Thus the pronouns of these chapters are not sexist—only descriptive.

Their utility, however, has not prevented their being a target of criticism. As Arthur Niederhoffer, a foremost student of police systems, has pointed out,

> Between the lines of [Magna Carta] can be deciphered the same problems and complaints about the police: abuse of power, false arrest, oppression, apathy, and their ignorance of, and contempt for the law. . . . And the remedies of that ancient time were no different from those proposed today: recruit better policemen, stiffen the penalties for malfeasance, create a civilian board as an external control upon the police.[1]

The traditional suspicion of the police remained endemic in England up to the time of the creation of the Metropolitan Police Force by Sir Robert Peel in the early nineteenth century, and it is to this distrust that scholars attribute the fact that English "Bobbies" have never been armed. In the United States today few domestic issues have excited as much controversy, or as furious partisanship, as the question of the police and their relationship to the poor, the black, the angry, and the criminal. Essential to any understanding of this problem is an awareness of who, in sociological terms, the police are. It is only after we know who they are that we can talk meaningfully of what they ought to be doing, and how well they are doing it.

WHO ARE THE POLICE?

Whatever their past sociological origins today's policemen, especially in the large cities, are essentially lower-middle-class civil servants. Until recently, there was a widespread feeling among sociologists and others that policemen were a self-selected group, attracted to an authoritarian profession by deep-rooted personality needs. More recent research however, has suggested that policemen, far from representing the "Cossack" stratum in society, are more typically lower-level bureaucrats. The attraction of the policeman's job is less likely to be the power inherent in the night stick than the security inherent in the pension that will be his at the end of twenty years. In New York City today, of all the job opportunities open to high school graduates, the police-man's job ranks as one of the highest in pay, fringe benefits, promotions, and job interest. Study after study of incoming recruits in the New York City Police Academy has shown that the recruits' own perceptions of their reasons for seeking a police job have far more to do with salary, pensions, and working conditions than with any sense of expected psychological fulfillment through the wielding of physical power.* Most authorities conclude that

---

*This is especially true of black recruits. For an interesting study of the attitudes of black policemen, see Nicholas Alex, *Black in Blue: A Study of the Negro Policeman* (New York: Apple-ton-Century-Crofts, 1969), p. xviii: "Black policemen were motivated to enter police work more by the lack of alternative opportunities and by the relative absence of discrimination in civil-service employment than by any positive characteristics to be found in police work itself."

incoming rookie policemen represent a cross section of the American lower-middle and upper-working class,* rather than a self-selected group of potential authoritarians.

> Frustrated elsewhere, our job seeker turns to civil service where there is good pay, security, and decent working conditions. For which positions can be qualify? The obvious choices are jobs in the post office, sanitation, fire, and police departments. His high-school diploma is enough to satisfy entrance conditions. In each case there is a competitive test of roughly equivalent difficulty. But the post office position is federal, and does not pay as well, nor does it have the same early retirement policy as a city job. A sanitation worker does not enjoy as high a status as a fireman or a policeman. A fireman must live indoors with a small group of men and constantly be exposed to fire and smoke. On the other hand, the police position pays very well and offers among its advantages a life outdoors with possibilities of romance and adventure. The police job is an obvious choice for a young man of lower-class background. *It matters little what type of personality he possesses.* [2]

If police recruits as a group do not over-represent authoritarian types, it does not follow, however, that fully trained policemen, socialized into the police system, are equally neutral in regard to authoritarian attitudes. Does the process of training and indoctrination take this rather average group of young men and transform them into the popular stereotype of tough, imperious, night stick-wielding brutes? Are policemen, as distinguished from police recruits, more authoritarian than the general population? As Niederhoffer describes it, they are not, *if one makes allowance for class background.* They may very well be more authoritarian than the population at large but are not more so than the social class, that is, upper-working or lower-middle, from which they are drawn. The concept of authoritarian personality grew out of post-World War II psychological research into the nature of the fascist personality.[3] Some of the variables associated with this type of personality, as labelled by Robert Krug, are:

1. Conventionalism.
2. Cynicism.
3. Aggression.

*Nelson A. Watson and James W. Sterling, in a survey made for the International Association of Chiefs of Police, claim that "the Police Opinion Poll data . . . casts doubt on the accuracy of the view that most policemen are products of lower-middle-class environment.' " The evidence that the authors introduce to support this statement however, is dubious, since they show that "today's police officers have come from the families of craftsmen and foremen, and service workers (including police) in larger proportions than is true for the general adult work force." These occupational groups are customarily subsumed under the heading of lower-middle class or upper-working class. It therefore seems appropriate to continue to describe policemen as belonging largely to these two classes. Nelson A. Watson and James W. Sterling, *Police and Their Opinions* (Washington, D.C.: International Association of Chiefs of Police, 1969), p. 119.

4. Superstition and stereotype.
5. Projectivity.
6. Good versus bad people.[4]

That policemen are conventional is not surprising. If a potential recruit were an unconventional type to begin with, the chances are that the recruitment process, with its emphasis on the personal character investigation of the applicant, would be likely to weed him out. To police administrators, political extremists (of both right and left, but especially of the left) and applicants with poor academic records, documented behavioral problems, or known unconventional sex lives are very much *persona non grata,* as are of course those with prior arrest or conviction records, even from juvenile court. The effect of these recruiting standards is to eliminate from consideration everyone but the individual who has so internalized middle-class values as never to have come into open conflict with school, parental, or legal authority.* One of the difficulties in the use of such standards is that by definition, as it were, most candidates from the lower classes or from different ethnic cultures are, almost automatically in many instances, excluded from the pool of potential policemen. The police force of most large cities is thus largely white and at least second generation American. In recent years great efforts have been made to relax certain of these restrictions (especially those related to prior brushes with the law for minor offenses) for the purpose of recruiting more minority group policemen. These changes have generally met with great resistance and resentment from the men on the force.

Policemen also tend to be cynical, but this too is a byproduct of the police training system; and they probably share their cynicism with others newly inducted into large bureaucratic systems: doctors, lawyers, college professors, and priests. The data suggest that rookies, on the day they enter the police academy, are quite idealistic about the department they are about to join and the police system in general. As they proceed with their training at the academy and are sent out onto the streets, their cynicism increases markedly, to the point where three-quarters of a representative cross section of the force believed that newspapers deliberately and malevolently give an unfavorable

*Although policemen are considered to be conventional, stick-to-the-rules types it was assumed for many years that they had abnormally high rates of divorce and suicide. This aberration in the police personality was attributed to the strains of the job which had a destabilizing effect on police marriages (due to such factors as the rotating shift, limitations on social life, the ever-present danger to the policeman's life, and so on) and to the conflict and need for making quick decisions which his everyday duties entailed. Police experts Arthur and Elaine Niederhoffer, after considerable empirical research, have come to the conclusion that the reputedly high rates of divorce and suicide are largely mythical. They have concluded that the police family is at least as stable as nonpolice families of similar socioeconomic status. Further, data relating to suicide rates of police males are inconclusive, but seem to indicate current rates no higher than those for males throughout the United States generally. Arthur and Elaine Niederhoffer, *The Police Family* (Lexington, Mass.: Lexington Books, 1978).

slant to news concerning police, and prominently play up police misdeeds; three-fifths of the group felt that the average departmental complaint was the result of pressure on superiors from higher authority to give out complaints; almost one-half of the men believed that when the policeman appears at the police department trial room, he will probably be found guilty even when he has a good defense; and almost two-fifths of the sample believed that the majority of special assignments in the police department depend on whom you know, not on merit.[5] This all-pervasive cynicism appears, however, to be a result of realities, or at least that part of reality visible to the recruit from his place in the police hierarchy, rather than the expression of internal psychological stress.

Moreover, police training of necessity teaches recruits to be both aggressive and suspicious. The policeman on his beat is faced with the need to make literally hundreds of decisions during a single tour of duty, and he must frequently take decisive action as a result of those decisions. Indeed, at least one police psychiatrist has testified that the personality factor causing the greatest number of washouts in the police department is the inability of the policeman to make a quick decision and live with it comfortably. A good policeman furthermore must almost by definition be suspicious. In order to prevent crime or detect wrongdoing, he must watch others for signs of unusual, possibly undesirable, behavior. He must, in effect, sit in constant judgment on the behavior of those with whom he comes in contact, and, if he is to be effective, he must be more than usually suspicious.

It would appear then that policemen as a group exhibit many of the characteristics of the authoritarian personality, but so do many people, especially those with similar class backgrounds. It is questionable how much significance these findings have in terms of predicting police performance in a given situation. More relevant perhaps, in determining how police will react towards demonstrators, blacks, rapists, or whatever, is their perception of the world in which they live, and the threat to the things they hold dear that they perceive in various types of conduct.

The policeman is frequently a marginal member of the middle class; that is, he or his family has struggled very hard to rise from a working-class background to the status and financial security of a police position. He has very little margin of safety: should he lose his job he would rapidly sink into the group he so painfully left only recently. Being insecure, he perceives any challenge to the social system, as he knows it, as a threat to his own personal well-being. Attempts to lower civil service standards for the purpose of recruiting minority-group policemen, Supreme Court decisions favorable to criminal defendants, left-wing political agitators, hippies, and homosexuals —all these he sees as dangerous, either to the police or to the social system that makes the police system possible. In this context it is understandable that the most furious anger of the police towards any type of demonstrator was reserved for those university miltants who staged the first wave of campus riots in 1968 and 1969. These children of the upper-middle class, who held in their hands all that the policeman would sell his very soul for, were throwing it contemptuously away to be trampled under the feet of the mob. No wonder the students at Columbia inspired such feelings of outrage! No wonder the policeman sports his little American flag on his uniform and fights for the chance to display it on his patrol car. The policeman, in short, can rarely perceive social change as other than threatening. For this reason he tends to be personally and administratively conservative, and will exhibit his most extreme behavior in those situations where he feels most threatened.*

Police perception of change as a threat applies to change within the police world as well as to change in the outside world. Police attitudes toward the movement for increasing professionalization provide an insight into the nature of these fears. The official police line in regard to professionalization is one of hearty approval. Every police organization, whether of superior officers or patrolmen, every police administrator, every policeman on the beat, will assure the outsider that his dearest wish is to see police work raised to the status of a profession. In some ways this is true. Professionalization will bring, it is expected, an increase in income and a rise in prestige in the eyes of the community, both goals understandably dear to police hearts.

If one probes beneath these surface manifestations of approval, however, one finds far more ambivalence towards professionalization than most policemen normally care to admit. Professionalization generally means raising the educational level of the police force, either through recruitment or through training of men already on the force. Generally, this training is conceived of in terms of college education, particularly in the social sciences and humanities, rather than as additional in-service training in traditional police-type subjects such as patrol, surveillance, or traffic.** To the high school educated

---

*All this is said, of course, in full recognition of the role elected officials play in determining and modifying basic police policy. This role will be discussed in greater detail at the conclusion of this chapter. It is interesting to speculate whether the 1969–1970 incidents involving the killing of Black Panthers by policemen in Chicago were in fact examples of the police taking the law into their own hands because they felt especially threatened. In the Chicago incident there is considerable evidence that the police entered the premises illegally and killed and wounded occupants without proper legal cause. Most policemen consider groups like the Black Panthers to be extremely and imminently dangerous to the social order.

An even more shocking instance of police action taken directly and illegally against a group they perceived as threatening is the Brazilian "Death Squad," made up largely of off-duty policemen, who allegedly assassinate petty criminals. A Brazilian army captain justified this activity, saying "They're ridding society of bad elements—elements that would only be caught and sentenced anyway if our court system worked correctly." *New York Times,* July 21, 1970, p. 1.

**As a response to the pressure for police "professionalization," the federal government, through the Department of Justice's Law Enforcement Education Program, spent more than a quarter of a billion dollars between 1968 and 1978 for the education of police officers at more than 1,000 colleges and universities. The results of this program were severely criticized in a report sponsored by the Police Foundation, an independent organization created by the Ford

man on the force, this emphasis on further training may cause great uneasiness. On the one hand he may feel pressured to go to college himself, a prospect which may fill him with dismay. The mere fact that he did not attend college in the first place suggests that he was less than academically outstanding in his youth, and many police officers enter the force with poor or mediocre high school records. At best, college will mean six to ten years of hard academic drudgery, to be undertaken at the end of a long day's work and in competition with the needs of family, friends, and community organizations. The reward for this education is moreover, in many communities, intangible, since many police departments offer no job credits or pay differential for additional academic training. On the other hand, should the police officer refuse to educate himself further, he must live in fear that one day he will be supplanted, in opportunities for promotion or desirable assignments, by some bright young college-educated rookie or by one of his more industrious colleagues.

Most police officers in the lower ranks are bitterly opposed to schemes for lateral entry, which they see as extremely threatening to their careers. Lateral entry would make it possible for better-educated candidates to be hired at levels above that of patrol officer. In most traditional police systems, everyone enters at the bottom and achieves advancement through credits earned by competitive civil service examinations and seniority. The upper ranks, thus, are reserved for individuals who have served their time on the streets. This prospect, however, is uninviting to young college-trained, career-minded individuals. It is for this reason that suggestions have been made that such people be brought in above the patrol officer level. It has also been suggested that police systems ought to be able to hire from other police systems experienced individuals in the higher ranks, much as universities hire each other's senior professors, or industry hires executives from competing firms. While these proposals have much merit from an objective administrative-management point of view, the patrolman on the beat perceives lateral entry proposals as taking away his all too few opportunities for promotion.

In addition to the unwelcome pressure exerted by the value placed on college education and the fears aroused by the threat of lateral entry, many police officers have a certain distrust for "book knowledge" as opposed to the lessons learned on the streets. This point of view is held by those whose intellect and performance are superior, as well as by those who might be

---

Foundation, and located in Washington, D.C. The report found most police education to have been narrowly focused and technical rather than broad-gauged and conceptual. The report concluded that departments should attempt to recruit educated police officers rather than educate those who were already on the force (*New York Times*, November 30, 1978, p. A20). While the report's criticisms of the quality of higher education offered to the police may be well taken, their suggested solution is probably impractical. The Police Foundation ideal—the police officer whose broad education would qualify him or her for other careers—might very well choose not to enter law enforcement. Thus, if we are to have educated police officers, they will have to attend college while on the job, and efforts should be made to upgrade the quality of the programs offered.

considered mediocre or worse. It is a manifestation of the anti-intellectualism and scorn for the "egghead" that is endemic in American society. While this attitude cuts across class lines, it is probably most prevalent in the social classes from which most policemen are drawn, and it also fits into the construct of the authoritarian personality. Not surprisingly, policemen who have elected to go to college reflect this attitude less strongly than do policemen with equivalent service in the department who have not gone to college. (College-educated policemen also, incidentally, appear to be less authoritarian and less anti-intellectual than civilian college students of the same ethnic and class background.)[6] It is hard to assess precisely the contribution of academic knowledge to the police job. Certainly on-the-street practical experience is a *sine qua non* for successful performance. Education in the liberal arts, and especially in the social sciences, is, however, equally essential to achieve that sense of perspective which helps the policeman to relate to the public he serves, to the offenders with whom he must deal, and to the world of which he is a part.

Professionalism has had some unforeseen consequences for police administration. College education has tended to benefit the upper ranks of the police far more than the lower ranks. The college degree, and even more, the graduate degree, is frequently a decisive factor in top echelon positions which are filled by appointment rather than by competitive civil service examination. At a lower managerial level, even though competitive examination might be necessary for initial appointment, the type of assignment given may be influenced by the educational qualifications of the candidate. For example, a New York City police captain with a college or law degree might be given a far more interesting assignment than a captain without any higher education. While it is true that the same differentiation of assignments can occur in large police departments even at the patrol officer level, proportionately more ranking officers will benefit as compared to patrol officers, simply because there are relatively few choice assignments available to patrol officers.

Further, a college or graduate degree is particularly valuable as police officers near retirement (when they will have achieved their highest rank) because it paves the way for a postretirement career on the professional level. Not only will college educated police officers meet the qualifications for a wider variety of positions, but frequently, because of their education and enhanced social status, they will have made social contacts which make the transition to the nonpolice world easier.

At the lower end of the police spectrum, however, professionalism has done little to meet the needs of working police officers. While it is true that some police departments may give promotional credit and/or salary differentials for advanced education, many departments do not. In any case, the bread and butter issues of salary, fringe benefits, pensions, hours, and working conditions have little to do with education or professionalism, and these are the issues with which the vast majority of lower echelon police officers are concerned. To meet their needs in this area, most of these individuals have become trade unionists, in fact, if not in theory. Many police officers feel some antipathy toward trade unions, partly because they identify unions with left wing politics to which they are generally opposed, and partly because they are resistant to the idea of unionization of public servants. Nevertheless, the economic pressures of an inflationary economy, as well as the example of many other groups, such as teachers and sanitation men who have achieved considerable economic advantages through trade unions, have led the police to convert their police benevolent associations, originally welfare and fraternal organizations, into organizations which are nearly indistinguishable from traditional trade unions.

Unionization has been helped by two factors. First, the widespread fear of crime has led the public to be particularly alarmed at the prospect of police strikes, and indeed, in Montreal where a police strike occurred in 1969, the nightmare of rampant lawlessness in the absence of police patrol came true. Thus, the strike threat has substantially strengthened the police position in collective bargaining negotiations. Second, the process of unionization has been helped inadvertantly by the process of professionalization which tended to replace the quasi-military authoritarianism of the police command structure with a more democratic, participatory, managerial model. Whereas in earlier days police dissidents might have been subjected to summary punishment, the more democratic, college educated police administrator has quite a different role model, and handles his or her staff in line with the style prevalent in industry or the civilian branches of government.

Thus, the net effect of the movement towards professionalization has been to accentuate polarization of the police force between the higher echelons who opt for higher education and professional qualifications, and the lower ranks who have become increasingly militant trade unionists. Whatever problems the unionization of the police present are unlikely to be resolved outside of the general question of the limits of the right of public employees to bargain collectively and to strike. While unionization is a problem that affects the police, it is not distinctively a police problem. Teachers, fire fighters, postal workers, sanitation workers, and even doctors and nurses are turning to unions and the ultimate weapon of the strike as a way of resolving their problems. In this respect, the police are but one group among many. By the same token, the movement towards professionalization is also part of a larger movement to upgrade training and to increase the amount of formal education for a wide variety of occupations and positions. At a time when master's degrees are as commonly sought as were bachelor's degrees a generation ago, there is little reason to suppose that the emphasis on higher education and professional training for the police will wane.

It is in the area of their relationships to the nonpolice world that police officers today express their greatest dissatisfaction.[7] Their most heartfelt complaint is likely to be that the public does not appreciate their efforts on their behalf, does not value their willingness to sacrifice their very lives for the public safety. The ungrateful citizenry is all too willing to criticize the police for rising crime rates or, perhaps contradictorily, for excessive zeal in the performance of their duties. The public is also eternally preoccupied with the subject of police corruption. Although in some ways their status may be rising, in an era of upward mobility police officers feel somehow that they are being left behind.

Police officers today, far from being the authoritarian Cossacks who for amusement growl at children in their spare time, are more likely to be conservative, conforming, well-meaning, minor bureaucrats. They want to believe in the system; they want to do their jobs well; they want to serve the public. For reasons about which they are not quite clear, the statistics seem to show that they are not doing their job well; that the public does not appreciate their efforts; and that they don't know how to go about solving their problems. They may become cynical and suffer from anomie. They are frequently somewhat bitter. They feel themselves to be the ones caught in the middle, between the criminal and the public, between the forces of stability and the forces of change. At the same time they feel isolated, members of a persecuted, misunderstood minority. Only their union gives them some sense of control and independence.

TO ARREST OR NOT: AREAS OF POLICE DISCRETION

It is both impossible and undesirable for the police to enforce equally every law on the books. If they did, we would need a police force of mammoth proportions, and scarcely a citizen would go through the day without official reprimand or arrest. The resources needed in terms of courts and correctional institutions would be of such magnitude as to be almost beyond imagination. Official discretion is obviously called for. In some cases the police will, of course, arrest offenders; in some cases they will warn; and in many more cases they will simply ignore illegal conduct. Wayne LaFave suggests that the decision not to arrest is particularly likely in four categories of offenses: trivial offenses; offenses where the conduct is thought to represent the subculture of a different ethnic or racial group; offenses where the victim refuses to prosecute; and offenses where the victim has also been involved in some kind of illegal conduct.[8]

Trivial offenses are the type of misconduct most frequently ignored by the police. Indeed, nonenforcement of laws relating to petty offenses may be the rule rather than the exception. Minor street arguments, panhandling, public drunkenness, peddling, spitting on the sidewalk, littering, and parking and minor traffic violations are often all handled by warnings, and more frequently are ignored completely by the patrol officer on his or her beat. Normally, outside pressure, in the form of complaints by those who are being annoyed by such violators, will be necessary for the police to take action. Periodic drives against derelicts or drunks in the business areas of large cities are of this nature. Campaigns against certain kinds of parking violations are mounted when street congestion becomes unbearable; tickets rather than warnings are given to motorists when accidents become too frequent. Sometimes the complaint of a single individual is enough to affect the police officer's conduct. A New York City patrol officer recounted an incident where an elderly lady approached him while he was on duty in a public park and demanded to know why he had failed to arrest a panhandler who was soliciting funds nearby. The police officer, who had already observed the panhandler and had decided on a live-and-let-live policy, rather uncomfortably approached the offender and started to speak to him. At that moment, a hippie couple approached and proceeded to berate the officer for harassing a poor man who, after all, was only trying to earn a living. The elderly lady joined in the conversation by scolding the hippie couple for interfering with an officer in pursuit of his duty. At that point, the officer said, "The bum walked one way; I went the other. I left the three of them arguing with each other."

Cultural patterns of subgroups affect police action most notably in the area of personal assaults. The complaint of a middle-class person that she has been the victim of an assault will almost always result in the arrest of the offender if that is physically possible. The lower-class complainant, however, does not evoke the same police response, especially if the assault is a result of a family quarrel or an altercation between friends. This type of police discretion is particularly noticeable in the handling of cases involving either wife beating or rape. Until quite recently, the police tended to avoid making arrests in such cases. Even where, for example, a woman was seriously injured as a result of an assault by her husband, the police, for the most part, treated the incident as a family quarrel to be cooled off or mediated if possible, rather than as a crime.* In many cases, the wife was left defenseless against a husband who knew that he had little more to fear than an admonition or reprimand by the police officer. The police justification for such informal handling was that usually the incident was a family quarrel which both sides would want to forget by the next morning; to arrest the husband was a waste of time because the wife almost invariably refused to press charges. More recently, however,

---

*A technique for handling family disputes, designed to cool off the participants and avert violence, was developed by Morton Bard and Bernard Berkowitz, psychologists for the New York City Police Department. A Family Crisis Unit utilized patrol officers who had been given intensive psychological training and instructions to attempt to resolve family fights before they developed into serious crimes. See Morton Bard and Bernard Berkowitz, "Training Police as Specialists in Family Crisis Intervention," *Community Health Journal* 3 (1967) :315–317.

Bard's work was considered very successful both by the Department and outside observers, and the mediation of family disputes is to be encouraged. Nevertheless, disputes which have already resulted in violence which has led to serious injury must be treated as criminal assaults rather than problems of domestic relations.

at the insistence of women's groups, the police have begun to take severe beatings, at least, more seriously, and felony charges in the criminal courts are beginning to be made against assaultive husbands.

Similarly, the police have tended to handle rape victims (especially lower-class women who appeared to the police to have been sexually permissive) in a perfunctory, rather skeptical manner, and have made the reporting of rape such an unpleasant ordeal for the victim that many rapes have gone unreported. Again, at the insistence of women's groups, rape victims in many jurisdictions are now being handled with more concern and consideration, and are viewed as the victims of a serious crime, rather than as loose women who led on their assaulters. This change in police conduct has been accompanied by a change in many state laws which lowers the standard of proof needed for convicting an assailant charged with rape.

This differential handling by the police presumably stems from the belief that in the context of a particular group, the conduct in question is more acceptable and less deserving of legal sanction than it is for society at large. This restraint on the part of the police is the basis for many of the complaints by blacks of nonenforcement of the law in the ghettos.* Although this pattern of police action is perceived by blacks as racist, it is in reality more likely to be class-based. In the era when the Irish and Italians formed the bulk of the lower class who inhabited the urban slums, precisely the same police nonresponse was evoked when a drunken Irish hodcarrier beat up his wife or brother-in-law or when two Italian laborers cut each other in an affair of honor.

Frequently, when victims appeal to the police for relief against offenders, the relief they seek is not the arrest of the offender. They wish either to have the police make the offender stop doing whatever he or she is doing, or they wish the police to force the offender to make restitution. Small storekeepers, for example, may call on the police to evict troublesome customers or to chase away a crowd of adolescents obstructing the entrance to the establishment. They don't want the offenders arrested, because they don't want to take the time to appear in court as complaining witnesses. Nor are they really interested in seeing the offenders punished. They merely want the annoyance to stop. Similarly, in fraud cases the victims frequently want the threat of arrest to be used to force the swindler to give back that which was stolen. Essentially, such victims are using the police and the district attorney as collectors for bad debts, dishonored checks, and the like. Sometimes victims call the police in a fit of anger and then almost immediately regret their action and refuse to press the complaint. This is most frequently true when the offender is a relative or one with whom the victim has a continuing relationship such as co-worker or neighbor.

*See Chapter 3.

Police frequently are reluctant to take action where the victim has been engaged in conduct that is illegal or embarrassing, either because they feel the victim got his just deserts or because they fear that the victim will be reluctant to cooperate in the prosecution. Men who are tricked out of money which they gave to prostitutes or pimps; individuals who are swindled in get-rich-quick schemes that are patently illegal; victims of assaults which were provoked by actions on the part of the victim himself: all these are typical of cases where the police frequently decline to take action.

Another area in which police discretion is frequently invoked is the handling of juveniles. There is an unusually large number of options open to the police in the disposition of juveniles as compared with other kinds of cases; for example, the police may warn, reprimand, or pick up a child for questioning, may notify parents officially, investigate, and make official notation on the child's record, or refer a child to an appropirate social agency. All of these measures fall short of arrest, which is the ultimate sanction in the hands of the police. Arrest is usually avoided, if possible, because present-day progressive police practice recognizes the importance of labelling: that once the child is officially categorized as a suspected criminal it is hard for him to escape from this category. Some excellent sociological studies have, however, indicated that police discretion not to arrest juveniles is used in fairly predictable ways. Juveniles who act tough and unrepentant or who are dressed in a manner indicative of defiance tend to be dealt with far more severely than the meek, compliant youth, even when the facts confronting the police officer are the same. Black youths, especially those wearing leather jackets, sunglasses, and Afro hairdos, are particularly prone to more severe police reactions. Police tend to be more suspicious of such juveniles, keep them under closer surveillance, and arrest more frequently for conduct that would be handled informally if it occurred among youngsters they found less abrasive.

One officer observing a youth walking along the street, commented that the youth "looks suspicious" and promptly stopped and questioned him. Asked later to explain what aroused his suspicions, the officer explained, "He was a Negro wearing dark glasses at midnight."[9]

The importance of the use of police discretion in juvenile cases is that frequently patterns of police enforcement become a kind of self-fulfilling prophecy in regard to certain groups of youngsters. Because these youths perceive disproportionate suspicion and hostility on the part of the police, they respond with the very kind of conduct—sullenness, sassiness, and defiance—that the police perceive as cues for punitive action. Once arrested, these juveniles are well on their way towards attaining a criminal record and a permanent status on the wrong side of the law. This in turn leads the police to be even more suspicious of other youths of the same type.

Thus it is not unlikely that frequent encounters with police, particularly those involving youths innocent of wrongdoing, will increase the hostility of these juveniles toward law-enforcement personnel. It is also not unlikely that the frequency of such encounters will in time reduce their significance in the eyes of apprehended juveniles, thereby leading these youths to regard them as "routine." Such responses to police encounters, however are those which law-enforcement personnel perceive as indicators of the serious delinquent. They thus serve to vindicate and reinforce officers' prejudices, leading to closer surveillance of Negro districts, more frequent encounters with Negro youths, and so on in a vicious circle. Moreover, the consequences of this chain of events are reflected in police statistics showing a disproportionately high percentage of Negroes among juvenile offenders, thereby providing "objective" justification for concentrating police attention on Negro youths.[10]

Again, while the police are probably harder on black youths than white youths, it is more likely their class status rather than their color which is the operative factor. Lower-class people, black or white, are more likely to be harassed or arrested by the police than middle-class individuals. Middle-class youths of all races who look and act middle-class are treated far more courteously by the police.

LaFave and Piliavin discuss the police decision not to arrest mainly in relation to offences which are not very serious: juvenile delinquency, swindling, traffic violations, and simple assault. By their decision not to arrest, the police are, in reality, informally structuring a system of priorities on the use of their time so as to make the job of law enforcement more practicable given the limited resources usually available to them.* By not arresting indiscriminately, they are conserving their efforts for the containment of more serious offenders.

Another way in which the police utilize the decision not to arrest is in the operation of the informer system.[11] Studies of police departments have shown that it is very common for police officers to extend "protection" to pimps, prostitutes, petty thieves, addicts, small-time pushers, probationers, parolees, ex-convicts, bookies, numbers runners, and the like. This protection takes the form of freedom from arrest or, in some cases, freedom to continue to break the law, in return for which the suspect agrees to inform the police of the activity of more serious criminals of whom he may have knowledge. Prostitutes, for example, may be permitted to ply their trade free from police harassment if they cooperate by reporting to the police information regarding underworld activities that comes their way. Addict-pushers may be allowed

---

*Alexander B. Smith and Bernard Locke, in a survey of police attitudes toward obscenity and pornography laws, indicate that while policemen tend to be outraged by such "filth," enforcement of such laws has low priority. Alexander B. Smith and Bernard Locke, *Response of Police and Prosecutors to Problems in Arrests and Prosecutions for Obscenity and Pornography*, Technical Report of the Commission on Obscenity and Pornography, Vol. 2 (Washington, D.C.: U.S. Government Printing Office, 1970).

to continue their activities in return for tips as to the identity of the whole-salers from whom they make their purchase. Addicts are also used as a source of information as to the disposition of stolen goods. Informants may be rewarded with money as well as freedom from arrest. The police may even undertake physically to protect good informers from the colleagues they have betrayed. While informers may not have absolute immunity from arrest when they are working for the police, they are usually assured that at least the police will attempt to get them the best possible plea bargain that can be arranged, as well as, if need be, advantageous sentences from the court.

The informer system, which rests entirely on the ability of the police not to invoke the full process of the law, is not viewed by law enforcement officials as evidence of police corruption even though the police traffic with known criminals and may go so far as to give lawbreakers money which may be used for further illegal activities. In the police view, the system is essential for effective law enforcement, for without informers, police would lose their lines of communication to the underworld. The London police, for example, bitterly lamented legalization of prostitution because without the tips given to them by the women their efficiency in solving important crimes in the metropolitan London area was seriously impaired. The symbiotic relationship between the police and the petty criminal-turned-informer may, in fact, be so essential to successful law enforcement in our present social system that it should not be eliminated, however unsavory and sordid the details of its operations may be. It is important to recognize however, that it is one mani-festation of the very large amount of discretion residing in the hands of the police force as to *the degree to which the law should be invoked and against whom.* The police can never realistically meet criticism of their activities by saying they are only enforcing the law. The police constantly shape the law through a pattern of *selective enforcement.* They must recognize this reality and meet critics head on by indicating that the pattern of enforcement they have selected is justifiable in terms of agreed-upon societal goals.

POLICE DISCRETION AND POLICE CORRUPTION

It is obvious that police discretion not to invoke the law is greater for those offenses which are considered *malum prohibitum* rather than *malum in se.* Police generally enforce the law fully against murderers, rapists, arsonists; they enforce it much less fully against gamblers, prostitutes, and drug offend-ers. As the previous discussion indicated, nonenforcement may be the result of informal attempts to conserve police resources for more important crimes. Nonenforcement may also be the result of the need for informers. Sometimes, however, nonenforcement is the result of corruption of the police by crimi-nals. Police corruption is the subject of enormous concern, to both practition-ers within the criminal justice system and to the citizenry outside the system,

and periodic exposés of such corruption are so regular as almost to be antici-
pated. There is scarcely a large city in this country which has not had a police
scandal of major proportions. The most significant feature, however, of these
exposés is that the pattern of corruption is virtually the same whatever the
time and whatever the place. Almost always the police are bribed to overlook
offenses that are *malum prohibitum* rather than *malum in se,* especially such
morals offenses as gambling, drug use, and prostitution. It is unusual for the
police to take bribes to overlook murders, rapes, robberies, or burglaries, or,
in the case of the FBI, treason, espionage, or interstate kidnapping.*

The basic reason for the persistence of this pattern of corruption is that the
criminal law does not reflect a true picture of community moral standards[12]
While many people pay lip service to the notion that gambling, prostitution,
homosexuality, and marijuana smoking are evil, a very large minority either
do not think these practices evil, or hypocritically practice in secret what they
publicly disavow. The result is that there is an enormous demand for the
services which numbers runners, drug pushers, and prostitutes supply, a
demand which potential consumers are willing to pay for in cash. Because
these activities are illegal, some of this money is diverted to the police in the
form of bribes. The police, for their part, are tempted by the availability of
easy money, and many of them also share the modal belief of the public that
gambling, prostitution, and marijuana smoking are not so very wrong. The
police reaction to an exposé which indicates that police have been involved
the commission or protection of burglaries is very different from an exposé
which shows police protection of gamblers. While both modes of conduct are
illegal, the former will truly horrify most police officers; the latter will be
greeted with shrugs of the shoulder.

Morals offenses, moreover, frequently have no victim, that is, the victim
is an all too willing participant in the crime.[13] Gamblers do not force bettors
to play the horses, and prostitutes do not seduce their clients with guns. Thus,
there are seldom any complaining witnesses to exert pressure on the police
to enforce the law, nor is there as much risk of exposure of corruption.

This pattern of police corruption has several implications for public policy
makers. It is probable that widespread corruption cannot be eliminated as
long as the criminal law is used as a vehicle for foisting a morality on the
public that the public does not really accept or has outgrown. It may seem
incomprehensible why statutes that do not reflect community standards get
into the statute books in the first place and are so difficult to remove once they
are there. Students of the legislative process know, however, that laws are not
so much the will of the majority as the will of whatever *ad hoc* coalition of
interest groups is able to control the legislature at a given time. Well-organ-

*This is not to say that police have never covered up, or indeed been principals or accessories
to serious crimes, especially those committed by organized mobsters. Nevertheless, the most
serious, widespread, and common type of police graft is that received from pushers, prostitutes,
and bookies.

ized interest groups, moreover, even though they represent a relatively small minority, can effectively veto the repeal of outmoded morals legislation, as witness the success of various religious groups in preventing divorce reform or the legalization of off-track betting. The problem of this type of police corruption must be handled at the level of making our legislatures more truly representative and responsive bodies.

Many segments of the public, moreover, benefit from being able, through bribery, to influence police actions, ranging from the small storekeeper who offers the policeman a free steak or a lunch on the house to act as bouncer or guardian of the premises, to the organized criminals who thus protect their loan-sharking and illegal gambling operations from police raids. A distinction is commonly made between "clean graft" in which the police are paid to do their duty—what they should be doing anyway—and "dirty graft" in which payment is made to overlook criminal activity. Investigations, such as the Knapp investigation in New York City, in 1971, suggest that dirty graft is usually distributed through a complex departmental network using precinct "pads," "bagmen," and a system for sharing the proceeds based on rank and function. This is not always true, however, and individual dishonest police-men have been known to ask for very large bribes on the ground that they had to "share" the money with others—others who were largely mythical.[14]

Whatever form corruption takes, and however it is organized, it is a persis-tent and chronic problem among police departments which affects morale, undercuts administrative control and efficiency, and adversely affects police relations with the community. It is a very complex problem which manifests itself in widely varying ways so that no simple solutions are likely to work. Problems of clean graft are different from problems of dirty graft; organized corruption must be dealt with differently from the "one rotten apple in the barrel." The role that the public plays in benefiting from corruption as well as in acquiescing in the existence of outmoded morals laws is very much a part of the problem.

Corruption in the FBI presents a rather special type of problem. From very early in its history, the bureau quietly, but deliberately, refused to attempt enforcement of drug, gambling, and other morals laws. A perceptive article published some years ago in the *New York Times Magazine* pointed out that until quite recently, the FBI infinitely preferred to expend its resources catch-ing bank robbers and kidnappers (of which there are relatively few in this country) than to become involved in investigating organized crime, the basis for which is the traffic in drugs, prostitutes, and illegal betting.[15] It is only in recent years that the pressure of public opinion forced the FBI to concern itself with types of crime more relevant to the American social scene than the peccadillos of Bonnie-and-Clyde types. J. Edgar Hoover, who was appointed in 1924 as director of the FBI in the wake of the Harding administration Justice Department scandals, succeeded in cleaning up corruption within the FBI. Subsequently, he guarded the public chastity of his agents by keeping

his men free from temptation through ignoring those areas of law enforcement where corruption was predictably most likely to occur. [16]

Towards the end of Hoover's administration, he was forced by pressure
from Congress and the public to permit the bureau to become involved in the
investigation of organized crime, as well as certain types of political activities,
such as civil rights violations. After Hoover's death, the FBI became increasingly politicized. Its acting director, L. Patrick Gray, was unable to withstand
the pressure of the corrupt Nixon administration to use the bureau to cover
up its illegal activities. In the aftermath of the Watergate scandal, shocking
revelations were made of long-standing, persistent, deliberate violations of
the civil rights of individuals in this country by the FBI in relation to wiretapping, searches, and mail covers. Much of this activity was directed against
dissident left wing groups.

The FBI is in an anomalous position since, on the one hand, a police
organization ought to enforce the law without partisan political consideration; and on the other hand, the FBI is a branch of the Department of Justice,
an executive department responsible to the President. While J. Edgar Hoover
was alive, for reasons about which many observers have speculated, he was
sufficiently politically invulnerable to withstand presidential pressure. While
this protected the department from the later Nixon type corruption, it also
made possible Hoover's own brand of corruption: harassment of left wingers,
and failure to become involved in important areas of law enforcement. The
dilemma of how to make the FBI politically responsible without subjecting
it to undesirable narrow partisan pressures is one that Congress is attempting
to solve.

POLITICAL DIRECTION OF POLICE ACTIVITIES

Discretion in law enforcement is exercised at three levels.[17] A patrol officer
decides to warn rather than give a ticket to a speeding motorist; to ignore
rather than arrest a prostitute; to calm rather than bring in an abusive,
drunken husband—all these are examples of discretion exercised at the lowest level of bueaucratic hierarchy.

When a precinct commander orders his men to treat homosexuals with
courtesy and respect; when police administrators decide to saturate a difficult
police precinct with foot police in an attempt to reduce street crime; when the
police commissioner decides that a fourth platoon is needed, the better to
deploy forces during the high-crime hours of the late evening and early
morning—these are exercises in police discretion at the administrative or
command level.

The mayor's office makes the most basic decisions of all in regard to police
policy. The ultimate decision at the mayoral level is, of course, the portion
of the city budget that will go to the police. This determines how many

officers will be available, what kinds of equipment will be purchased, and by determining wage and pension levels, it even influences the kinds of individuals who will enter as recruits. Beyond fiscal policy, however, the mayor's office is the conduit for public opinion as to the kinds of law enforcement the public wants. Does the public want prostitutes chased, arrested, or tolerated? Is the traffic situation serious enough to warrant ten-dollar tickets or a tow-away program? Do the residents of the Upper West Side really need the additional police protection for which they have been clamoring?

On some issues the policy-making process is clear and easy to trace. The impulses of an aroused public opinion are transmitted directly to the mayor, from the mayor to the police commissioner, from the commissioner to his deputies, and so on down the hierarchical ladder to the officer on the beat. When the number of deaths due to heroin overdoses among adolescents mounted sharply in New York City at the end of 1969, great public concern was expressed, especially because the use of heroin appeared to be spreading to middle-class youngsters. Newspapers, clergymen, civic groups, and educators all deplored the situation freely, and as with one voice turned to the mayor and said, in essence, "Do something!" The mayor's response was to turn to the police commissioner and repeat "Do something." The police commissioner turned to his deputies and together they formulated certain departmental narcotics control measures which included, among others, the formation of a special narcotics squad in every precinct in the city focused on the immediate problem of reducing heroin traffic.

The results of this policy were very plain, at least statistically: heroin arrests, for both felonies and misdemeanors, approximately doubled in the first two months of 1970, as compared to the same time period in 1969. At the same time marijuana arrests (felonies and misdemeanors) declined. Superficially these statistics may appear simply to indicate increased heroin abuse and decreased marijuana use. The realities of the situation are, however, quite different, as any experienced observer can testify. By no stretch of the imagination could one suppose that marijuana use and sales had declined, and while heroin traffic may indeed have increased, there is no evidence to indicate an increase of such proportions as to justify the increase in arrests. It is a reasonable assumption that what the statistics actually reflect is the increased concern by the public about a social problem, which was transmitted through the mayor's office to the police department where it was transmuted into a different deployment of police resources. Where formerly narcotics enforcement was mainly the responsibility of the city-wide narcotics bureau, under the new policy additional enforcement personnel was assigned at the precinct level. With the increased number of police officers available, arrests went up sharply. Thus the arrest figure is not necessarily a reflection of the amount of law-breaking occurring; rather it is a reflection of the discretionary enforcement of certain laws, in this case the policy decision to pay increased attention to heroin offenders and less attention to marijuana users. It should be noted that during the very same period that increasing public concern over heroin abuse was being expressed, a markedly more tolerant attitude towards the use of marijuana was manifest, partly because little scientific evidence of the harmfulness of marijuana use had been adduced, and partly because marijuana use was increasing among the "respectable" middle class.[18]

Not all policy making is so clear-cut however. Where an issue is controversial and public response is sharply divided, the cues coming to the mayor's office may be contradictory and ambiguous, and the mayor's response may be either unacceptable or unintelligible to the police department. The policy which then emerges may be quite different from what the mayor intended, and public response may be unpredictable. One of the touchiest issues confronting the Lindsay administration in New York City in the late 1960s was the police handling of street demonstrations. While the public was generally agreed on the need for public order, there was sharp polarization of opinion on the question of how much freedom of action dissenters should be permitted. Where should crowds be permitted to congregate? How much disruption of traffic should be permitted? How should the crowd be contained and controlled? How should disruptive incidents be handled? What level of violence, verbal and physical, should be tolerated? What proportion of the police department's resources should be diverted to the service of demonstrators? How best could crowd-control functions be handled administratively?

The response of the Lindsay administration to these questions reflected the mayor's sympathy for the poor, the black, students, and peace groups who were most aggrieved by Establishment policies during this period. His orders to his police commissioner were intended to provide a police contingent large enough to handle projected crowds with minimal use of direct physical force. Arrests were to be kept to a minimum, and only physically assaultive conduct was to be restrained. The general policy of the special events squad, designed to handle parades, demonstrations, and the like, was to break up disputes and altercations, making arrests only as a last resort or where there had been physical attack on a police officer. This sympathetic administration attitude toward demonstrators was difficult for many police officers to accept. Their personal political preferences often ran counter to those of the demonstrators; they were offended by the noisiness, untidiness, and unconventional appearance of many of the participants; and professionally, they were alarmed at the potential for riot and disorder in the milling and surging of large angry crowds. Because of the complexity of the problem and the disparity of views between the mayor's office and the patrolman on the street, the administrative officials of the police department were forced into an uneasy neutrality between their staff and the mayor's office.

The record shows that the New York City police were remarkably successful in maintaining peace at a time when most of the major cities of the country were devastated by riots. The mayor's policies of nonprovocative, relatively minimal law enforcement towards minority group demonstrators evoked some public and police criticism, but prevailed because they were effective in cooling an overheated situation. In at least two instances, however, the results were not so fortuitous. In 1969, policemen in the City Hall area permitted largely black demonstrators for increased welfare rights to stomp and destroy several parked cars, including a Cadillac belonging to a conservative Republican New York City councilman. A year later in the same City Hall area, the police permitted several hundred helmeted construction workers to disrupt an anti-war demonstration and to physically and severely assault demonstrators, bystanders, and students at a nearby college.

In each case, the stated reason for the inaction of the police was the same: that the police force was inadequate to handle the crowd involved, and therefore could do nothing more than stand its ground and protect City Hall from invasion. While this statement may be accurate, it conceals as much as it reveals. A host of questions remain unanswered. Why was the police force inadequate? On what basis was the determination of the number of officers available in the City Hall area made? Why was provision for reinforcements not made? Were the police as outnumbered as they claimed to be? Were their personal, political preferences in any way involved in their failure to take action? At the time of the incident involving the councilman's car, several police organizations commented bitterly that such violence was the inevitable result of the mayor's permissive policies toward demonstrators. Critics of the police responded by suggesting that the police had deliberately refused to stop the destruction of the car in order to discredit the mayor's policies. At the time of the second incident, even more vigorous charges were made that the police had refused to stop the beatings of students and peace demonstrators by the construction workers because their personal sympathies were entirely with the workmen. It is a fact that almost no arrests were made, although a substantial number of people were injured sufficiently to require hospital treatment. Once again the police line organizations remarked that such incidents were merely the results of the ambiguous and confusing directives on crowd-handling emanating from the mayor's office. They suggested, moreover, that the confrontation had been brought about by the intemperate remarks and misplaced sympathies of the Lindsay administration.[19]

Who, then, makes policy in New York City for the handling of street demonstrations? Certainly, the mayor's office did not intend for either the councilman's car to be stomped or the peace demonstrators to be beaten. Why then did these things happen? Was there simply an honest miscalculation on the part of police administrators as to how many men would be needed to contain the crowds, or was the miscalculation at least in part a result of the ambivalent feeling of police administrators toward official mayoral policy? Was the inaction of the police a response to the reality of the situation or an expression of hostility toward the official policies imposed on the department by "politicians"?

The answers to these questions are impossible to determine. It is evident, however, that while one may conceptually make distinctions in policy making at the various levels of the police system from patrol officer to mayor, in practice the process is not nearly so clear-cut as one might wish. Where an issue is relatively noncontroversial, such as the concern over heroin use, the response may well be straightforward and readily traceable from its inception in public concern to the mayor's office, to police administrators, and ultimately to the lowest levels of the police hierarchy. Where the issue is more controversial, the decision-making process becomes a blur of interactions and *ad hoc* adjustments between many levels of the hierarchy. What the mayor proposes is simply not what the police officer on the street disposes.

One must also note that a distinction should be made between political interference with the police department and political direction of police policies. It is legitimate for police officers to object if an elected official wishes to make his nephew a lieutenant or to award a contract for police cars to his brother-in-law. It is also legitimate for the police to object to instruction by nonprofessionals in the specifics of how to carry out a particular assignment, for example, where units are to be deployed or where reinforcements should be stationed. It is not legitimate, however, for police officers to object to the mayor's telling the police commissioner to make an effort to recruit more blacks and Puerto Ricans, to increase the size of the force (possibly at the expense of wage increases for existing personnel), or to emphasize some areas of law enforcement even at the expense of lesser enforcement in other areas. Police officers, of course, have the right to criticize the mayor's decisions as ill-advised or misguided, but they cannot consider such suggestions as illegitimate. It is the mayor's obligation to control overall policies of the police department in conformity with the wishes of the electorate in much the same way as the president and the civilian secretary of defense control policies of the armed forces. Police organizations frequently express such hostility to this type of political control as leads to the inference that they feel police policy should be made by police officers for society at large. This point of view is wholly unacceptable in a democratic society. Police officials and patrol officers have the right and duty to offer technical advice to elected officials; beyond that they have an obligation to accept and implement policies formulated by those responsible to the voters.

A suggested approach to the problem of political control of police policy is to eliminate as many areas of police discretion as possible through mandating full enforcement of the criminal law as opposed to the *de facto* discretionary enforcement which now exists in almost all jurisdictions. Since it is largely through these selective enforcement decisions that police policy is made, law professors such as Joseph Goldstein of Yale have suggested that, by insisting that all laws be fully enforced, the police will be removed from policy making that is not responsive to the community.

The ultimate answer is that the police should not be delegated discretion not to invoke criminal law. It is recognized, of course, that the exercise of discretion cannot be completely eliminated where human beings are involved.... But nonetheless, outside this margin of ambiguity, the police should operate in an atmosphere which exhorts and commands them to invoke impartially all criminal laws within the bounds of *full enforcement*. If a criminal law is ill-advised, poorly defined, or too costly to enforce, efforts by the police to achieve *full enforcement* should generate pressures for legislative action. Responsibility for the enactment, amendment, and repeal of the criminal laws will not, then, be abandoned to the whim of each police officer or department, but retained where it belongs in a democracy—with elected representatives.[20]

While superficially plausible, this is a naive suggestion. In the first place, it is predicated on the assumption that legislatures will be willing to remove from the statute books obsolete, unenforceable, popularly disregarded morals legislation (such as Sunday blue laws), an assumption which is highly unrealistic politically.

In the second place, even if the deadwood of the criminal code were cut away, the total enforcement of what remains would fantastically overstrain the resources of the criminal justice system.

If each patrolman made an arrest [in the ghetto] in every case where he observed a crime, or had probable cause to believe that a crime had been committed, there would be literally no policemen at all patrolling the precinct. They would all be at the station house or at court on legitimate police duty in connection with the arrest. The station houses, the courts, and the prisons, would be swamped by the sheer magnitude of the numbers of prisoners. Under these conditions is it wise, or possible, to enforce the law to its fullest extent?[21]

In the third place, as the discussion of policy in regard to street demonstrations illustrated, total enforcement of law is, in many cases, a meaningless term. What, for example, would total enforcement of the law in regard to parades mean? Should the same measures be taken in relation to the annual parade of the Sunday school union as to a parade of anti-war protesters? If not, what guidelines should be established, and by whom? How would this guideline-establishing process differ from police department policy making as now instituted in our "nontotal enforcement" police departments?

The police are, in the largest sense, a political organization. They are but one institution in the complex of institutions that we call government, and in a democratic country they, like all other agencies of government, must respond to the shifting currents of public opinion and societal demands. Thomas A. Repetto, in his fine history of the police in America, suggests three theoretical mechanisms for the control of the police: the law, administration, and politics. Both law and administration, however, are in practice subservient to politics. Historically, the police have never had (even if they desired it) the luxury of relying exclusively on "the law" as a guide to department policy making. Aside from the fact that discretion in enforcement, as indicated above, is a pragmatic necessity, the pluralism of American government with its kaleidoscopic, everchanging alliances of pressure groups has made the police subject to irresistible pressures from the dominant group, or groups, in society.

> The American police generally could not look for guidance to the law. Virtually all interest groups consistently ignored it or shaped it for their own purposes. Defense attorneys such as Fallon, Rogers, or Darrow were matched in their excesses by prosecutors like Heney and Jerome and even the highest officials such as Attorneys General Olney and Palmer. Nor was ideology a guide to an individual or group's adherence to the rule of law. . . .
> Almost never was the lesson learned that a worthy end could not be justified by unlawful means. Frequently, the very persons who taught the police to use the questionable techniques were hoist by their own petard.
> As Professor Vern Countryman of the Harvard Law School has observed:
> "The trouble I have is that many people . . . can't get too alarmed about getting informants and surveillants into the Klan. So we tell the law-enforcement agency it's alright. But the law-enforcement agency can't see any difference between the Klan and the Communist Party. They've been told time and again by courts and others that the Communist Party advocates forceable overthrow of the government. If it's justified in one place it's justified in the other. Then, from the law enforcement agency's point of view, there is no real difference between the Communist Party and what they regard as fellow traveller groups sympathetic to the Party.
> It seems to me that when we open the door in one place for all practical purposes, we've opened it across the board. Law enforcement agencies will not make these nice distinctions."[22]

The police are subjected to pressures from the right and from the left. Both as individuals, and as professional guardians of the *status quo,* the police traditionally have been, and still are, more sympathetic to pressures from conservatives than from liberals. Nevertheless, no single elite or group has consistently dominated or controlled police policy. Business elites, social elites, big city political machines, and even street gangs of immigrants and other poor people have influenced the pattern of police action. In recent years, civil libertarians have achieved notable success in restraining and limiting police action against criminal suspects and political dissenters. Largely through litigation at the United States Supreme Court level, the police today operate probably more lawfully than ever before in history, and the safeguards in the Constitution and the Bill of Rights have, in many jurisdictions, become a reality, rather than a polite legal fiction discussed in civics text books and on patriotic occasions.

Flushed by their success, many anti-establishment left wing groups have asserted their right to speech and street demonstrations so inflammatory as to lead immediately to violent action. They have, in effect, claimed First Amendment protection, if not for making a revolution, then at least, a riot. When the police interfere, they are aggrieved and complain of fascistic tendencies on the part of the administration. Yet, their position is illogical and pragmatically unsound, for the basis of civil liberties, in the long run, is the ability of the police to maintain peace in the community—in the constitutional phrase—to insure domestic tranquility. As Reppetto has pointed out in relation to the British police between 1800 and 1900,

> Effective policing provided a climate of law and order permitting abolition of barbarous punishments. More importantly it permitted social and political reforms, since as the fear of mob violence abated greater liberty was extended to proponents of change.[23]
> ... With the rise of the police, transportation and execution for property crimes ceased and imprisonment declined. When Queen Victoria came to the throne in 1837, 43,000 of her subjects were convicts; when she died in 1901, only 6,000 were, despite a doubling of the population. In 1834, two-thirds of convicted burglars received life sentences; by 1886 70 percent got less than one year.[24]

American cities have never achieved the tranquility of British cities. Yet the paradox remains that it is the restraining hand of the police that makes possible freedom and liberty for the community as a whole. This in no way implies that the curbing of police lawlessness by the Warren court was not both salutary and long overdue. It simply means that whatever curbs are placed on the police cannot be so stringent as to interfere with the legitimate function of controlling violence, either of a criminal or a political nature. There is no connection between Cossack police methods and effective crime control, much as some authoritarian policemen would like to think there is. Much police brutality and illegality is, in reality, slipshod law enforcement. As Sir James Fitzjames Stephen once pointed out in relation to the performance of native Indian police officers:

> There is a great deal of laziness in it. It is far pleasanter to sit comfortably in the shade rubbing red pepper into a poor devil's eyes than to go out in the sun hunting up evidence.

Our most unlawful police departments have also frequently been our most incompetent police departments. Nevertheless, the restrictions placed on the police cannot be so constraining as to destroy their ability to maintain order. The police are necessary agents of the state. Properly used in a democracy, they ensure domestic tranquility; improperly used, or uncontrolled, they become subversive of the system they are sworn to uphold.

It would appear that willy-nilly, for better or worse, police policy making is a fact of life that must be accepted by analysts of the criminal justice system. While such policy making cannot be eliminated, it can and should be controlled by the elected officials to whom the police, both on the beat and in administrative capacities, must be subservient. One of the most urgent tasks facing many localities is that of educating the police into an understanding and acceptance of this subservience.

Selected Readings

Adorno, T. W.; Frenkel-Brunswik, Else; Levinson, Daniel J.; and Sanford, R. Nevitt. *The Authoritarian Personality.* New York: Harper & Row, 1950.

Alex, Nicholas. *Black in Blue: A Study of the Negro Policeman.* New York: Appleton, 1969.

American Friends Service Committee. *Struggle for Justice.* New York: Hill & Wang, 1971.

Asch, Sidney H. *Police Authority and the Rights of the Individual.* New York: Arco Books, 1971.

Banton, Michael. *The Policeman in the Community.* New York: Basic Books, 1964.

Bayley, David H., and Mendelsohn, Harold. *Minorities and the Police.* New York: Free Press, 1969.

Bent, Alan Edward. *Politics of Law Enforcement.* Lexington, Mass.: Heath, 1974.

Bordua, David J. *The Police: Six Sociological Essays.* New York: Wiley, 1967.

Chevigny, Paul. *Cops and Rebels.* New York: Pantheon Books, 1972.

Chevigny, Paul. *Police Power: Police Abuses in New York City.* New York: Pantheon Books, 1969.

Cowan, Paul; Egleson, Nick; and Hentoff, Nat. *State Secrets: Police Surveillance in America.* New York: Holt, Rinehart and Winston, 1974.

Goldstein, Herman. *Police Corruption.* Washington, D.C.: Police Foundation, 1975.

Goldstein, Herman. *Policing a Free Society.* Cambridge: Ballinger Publishing Company, 1977.

Janowitz, Morris. *Social Control of Escalated Riots.* Chicago: University of Chicago Center for Policy Study, 1968.

LaFave, Wayne R. *Arrest.* Boston: Little, Brown, 1965.

Manning, Peter K. *Police Work: The Social Organization.* Cambridge: MIT Press, 1977.

National Advisory Commission on Criminal Justice Standards and Goals. *Police.* Washington, D.C.: U.S. Government Printing Office, 1973.

National Advisory Committee on Criminal Justice Standards and Goals. *Organized Crime.* Washington, D.C.: U.S. Government Printing Office, 1976.

Niederhoffer, Arthur. *Behind The Shield.* Garden City, N.Y.: Doubleday, 1967.

Niederhoffer, Arthur, and Blumberg, Abraham S. (ed.) *The Ambivalent Force.* 2nd ed. Holt, Rinehart and Winston, 1976.

Niederhoffer, Arthur, and Niederhoffer, Elaine. *The Police Family.* Lexington, Mass.: Lexington Books, 1978.

Niederhoffer, Arthur, and Smith, Alexander B. *New Directions in Police-Community Relations.* New York: Holt, Rinehart and Winston, 1974.

Reiss, Albert. *The Police and the Public.* New Haven: Yale University Press, 1971.

The Report of the Commission on Obscenity and Pornography. Washington, D.C.: U.S. Government Printing Office, 1970.

Reppetto, Thomas A. *The Blue Parade.* New York: Free Press, 1978.

Richardson, James F. *Urban Police in the U.S.* New York: Kennikat Press, 1974.

Rubinstein, Jonathan. *City Police.* New York: Farrar, Straus, 1973.

Sherman, Lawrence W. and the National Advisory Commission on Higher Education for Police Officers. *The Quality of Police Education.* San Francisco: Jossey-Bass, 1978.

Skolnick, Jerome H. *Justice Without Trial.* New York: Wiley, 1966.

Skolnick, Jerome H., and Gray, Thomas C. *Police in America.* Boston: Little, Brown, 1975.

Stead, Philip John, ed. *Pioneers in Policing.* Montclair, N.J.: Patterson Smith, 1977.

Westley, William A. *Violence and the Police.* Cambridge: MIT Press, 1970.

Wilson, James Q. *Explaining Crime.* New York: McGraw-Hill, 1975.

Notes

1. Arthur Niederhoffer, "Restraint of the Force: A Recurrent Problem," 1 *Connecticut Law Review* 288 (December 1968).

2. Arthur Niederhoffer, *Behind the Shield* (Garden City, N.Y.: Doubleday, 1967), p. 156. Italics added.

3. T. W. Adorno, Else Frenkel-Brunswik, Daniel J. Levinson, and R. Nevitt Sanford, *The Authoritarian Personality* (New York: Harper & Row, 1950).

4. Robert E. Krug, "An Analysis of the F Scale: 1. Item Factor Analysis," *Journal of Social Psychology* 53 (1961): 288, 291.

5. Niederhoffer, *Behind the Shield,* pp. 199–248.

6. Alexander B. Smith, Bernard Locke, and William Walker, "Authoritarianism in College and Non-College Oriented Police," *Journal of Criminal Law, Criminology and Police Science* 58, no. 1 (1967: 128–132; and by the same authors, "Authoritarianism in Police College and Non-Police College Students," 59 *Journal of Criminal Law, Criminology and Police Science* 440 (1968).

7. For comment by police on the negative aspects of their jobs, see Nelson A. Watson and James W. Sterling, *Police and Their Opinions* (Washington, D.C.: International Association of Chiefs of Police, 1969), Chapter 1.

8. Wayne R. LaFave, *Arrest: The Decision to Take a Suspect into Custody* (Boston: Little, Brown, 1965), pp. 102–124.

9. Irving Piliavin and Scott Briar, "Police Encounters with Juveniles," *American Journal of Sociology* 70 (September 1964): 212. This is an excellent study of the interaction between police and juveniles based on observations in the San Francisco-Oakland area.

10. Piliavin and Briar, p. 213.

11. Jerome H. Skolnick, *Justice Without Trial: Law Enforcement in Democratic Society* (New York: Wiley, 1966), Chapters 6 and 7.

12. See Herbert L. Packer, *The Limits of the Criminal Sanction* (Stanford: Stanford University Press, 1968).

13. Edwin M. Schur, *Crimes Without Victims* (Englewood Cliffs, N.J.: Prentice-Hall, 1965).

14. For a good discussion of the corruption problem, see Herman Goldstein, *Policing a Free Society* (Cambridge: Ballinger Publishing Company, 1977), Chapter 8; also Peter K. Manning, *Police Work: The Social Organization of Policing* (Cambridge: MIT Press, 1977), pp. 135–136, 355–356.

15. Tom Wicker, "What Have They Done Since They Shot Dillinger?" *New York Times Magazine,* December 28, 1969, p. 5.

16. For further discussion of the FBI, see Fred J. Cook, *The FBI Nobody Knows* (New York: Macmillan, 1964).

17. Police use of the discretion available to them is covered from several points of view by many social scientists, among them: David J. Bordua, *The Police: Six Sociological Essays* (New York: Wiley 1967); Arthur L. Stinchcombe, "Institutions of Privacy in the Determination of Police Administrative Practice," *American Journal of Sociology* (September 1963): 150–160; and Skolnick, in the work cited above.

18. See discussion, Chapter 2.

19. *New York Times,* May 11, 1970 p. 1; May 12, 1970, p. 18.

20. Joseph Goldstein, "Police Discretion Not to Invoke the Criminal Process: Low-Visibility Decisions in the Administration of Justice," 69 *Yale Law Journal* 586 (March 1960).

21. Arthur Niederhoffer, "The Quantity and Quality of Justice," *The Administration of Justice in America: The 1968–69 E. Paul duPont Lectures on Crime, Delinquency and Corrections* (University of Delaware, 1970), p. 42.

22. Thomas A. Reppetto, *The Blue Parade* (New York: Free Press, 1978), pp. 304–305.

23. Ibid., p. 300.

24. Ibid., p. 21.

lawyers, prosecutors, and judges: bureaucratization of justice

"I should like to have every court begin, I beseech ye in the bowels of Christ, think that we may be mistaken."
> Learned Hand, *Morals in Public Life*, 1951
> (quoting Oliver Cromwell)

"There is no such thing as justice—in or out of court."
> Clarence Darrow, Interview (Chicago, 1936)

For the man in the street, the criminal justice system means the courtroom and its related procedures. It is in the courtroom that the sheep are separated from the goats, the bad from the good, and the label of guilt is finally affixed to one who previously had passed unmarked among his fellows.

The courtroom scene is unquestionably the most dramatic portion of the sequence of events by which justice is administered. In the public mind, truth is discovered through courtroom trial by combat between two equally armed lawyer-gladiators, with the struggle presided over by the judge (as repository of the wisdom of the communty). The adversary model of courtroom procedure is England's contribution to world culture; and, in the United States, not only do the descendants of the original British settlers look upon this model as holy, but the most recent arrival from abroad, not yet English-speaking, still acculturated in the ways of an alien society, seizes upon this model and proclaims it the very symbol of the freedom for which he came to this country.

The picture is an attractive one. For most defendants in most courtrooms in the United States, *it is not true. It is not true, and probably never has been.* In pre-industrial America, the adversary-due process model of criminal justice may have existed in small towns and rural areas which were essentially classless; it may also have existed for some members of the urban upper and middle classes. For all others, and especially the poor, justice frequently was dispensed by vigilantes, lynch mobs, or tyrannical magistrates, if indeed the victim or other members of the community had not already handled the matter informally. Urbanization and industrialization have been accompanied by a vast increase in the number of criminal acts requiring adjudication. At the same time, especially in the last twenty-five years, there has developed an increasing sensitivity to the need for protecting individuals from the vast public and private bureaucracies which structure our complex society. Our response in the criminal justice system has been to provide increasing numbers of courts, judges, prosecutors, and defense attorneys who theoretically function according to the role models of the adversary system, but who in fact have transformed the adversary system into a bureaucratic machine for the handling of presumed malefactors. This transformation has occurred because of the necessity of dealing with vast numbers of defendants in a society that has not allocated (possibly because it cannot) sufficient resources to the criminal justice system to make the dream of Anglo-American justice come true.

PROSECUTORS

The crusading D.A. is an American folk hero. In movies, radio, television, and newspapers, he is the twentieth-century urban equivalent of St. George, Sir Lancelot, and all the other heroic gentlemen who defended goodness and virtue against the dragon of corruption. Not only was a series entitled "Mr. District Attorney" an enormous popular success on radio and television for a good many years, but Thomas E. Dewey, Earl Warren, and Hugo Black, to mention a few out of hundreds, are men whose public reputations were first established as public prosecutors. The position of district attorney, or state's attorney, or attorney general is one of the most frequent jumping-off places for a career in politics and public office.

While the popular image of the prosecutor is that of an avenging angel, strangely enough the role, according to the standards of Anglo-American justice, is not that of inquisitor but of one who sees that justice is done. The prosecutor is supposed to defend the public interest in its largest sense, and as defender he is required to secure the release of any defendant whom he feels is unjustly held. Thus, in the words of the Canon of Ethics of the New York State Bar Association,

The primary duty of a lawyer engaged in public prosecution is not to convict, but to see that justice is done. The suppression of facts and the secreting of witnesses capable of establishing the innocence of the accused is highly reprehensible.[1]

These noble precepts are honored probably more in the breach than in the observance. With some notable exceptions, such as Homer S. Cummings (upon whose exploits the movie *Boomerang* was based),* most prosecutors are interested in a "batting average" of convictions. The boast that he has never lost a case is considered to be worth many votes at election time. While some prosecutors are interested in the position as an end in itself, most look upon the job as a way station on the road to higher office. Frank Hogan, formerly district attorney for New York County, was an exception remarkable for his dedication and devotion to the office he held for almost thirty years. Unlike most other prosecutors he made the district attorneyship the culmination of his career. His office was unusual not only because of his lengthy incumbency but because of his depoliticization of the process whereby the assistant district attorneys were chosen. In most jurisdictions the assistants to the prosecutor (who is usually an elected official) are patronage appointments. These subsidiary positions are rewards to the politically faithful for previous political services rendered. Since salaries are frequently low, and the selection process is dictated by political considerations, many prosecutors' offices suffer from poor quality, part-time, largely uninterested assistants. Hogan's office, on the contrary, became a model for the country because of his continuing battle to upgrade salaries and appoint young lawyers on merit rather than for political reasons, and his insistence on full-time service. This is not to say, of course, that patronage appointments cannot result in dedicated, highly competent assistant prosecutors, only that the patronage problem, compounded by an inadequate salary scale, frequently mitigates against quality appointments.

Prosecutors, like the police, exercise discretion in their enforcement of the law. Whereas the police officer may decide whether or not to arrest, the prosecutor may decide whether or not to prosecute.** For example, in New

---

*The plot of the movie concerned an unpopular drifter who had been charged with the murder of a clergyman, and who was saved from almost certain conviction by the efforts of a public prosecutor who was convinced that the wrong suspect had been arrested.

**In Kings County (Brooklyn, New York), a progressive police practice in most felony arrests is to set up a conference at the station house between the arresting officer, his superior, and an assistant D.A. If the assistant attorney feels there are insufficient grounds for holding the suspect, the case will be dropped and he will not be charged with the crime. (If however, a suspect has been brought into the station house against his will, the motion to dismiss the case will not be made by the district attorney until the initial arraignment. This is to guard against suits for false arrests.) How widespread this kind of station house conference between police and the prosecutor's office in felony cases is, is impossible to say. It would appear to be a useful device, however, for sparing the accused unnecessary time in detention and the courts unnecessary time in considering an improper charge. Similar procedures are used in the other counties of New York City, but in homicide cases only.

York City since 1967, assistant district attorneys have been assigned to the complaint room to supervise the drawing up of complaints against recently arrested suspects. If the assistant district attorney feels there will be no conviction in the case (either misdemeanor or felony,) he will file a form which advises the judge that there is insufficient evidence in the case and asks for a dismissal, a request the judge almost invariably grants. While approximately 3 percent of the cases brought into the complaint room are dismissed as a result of this preliminary screening, the remaining cases which go to court are very rarely dismissed (except when witnesses fail to appear). Even where there is evidence sufficient to sustain the *prima facie* case necessary for the initial arraignment in felony court, if there is a lack of additional corroborative evidence the prosecutor may still recommend dismissal.

The decision not to prosecute can also be made after the initial arraignment. Indictments in felony cases in New York (and other states which use the grand jury) come, of course, from the grand jury rather than from the prosecutor's office. Theoretically, the district attorney presents all cases to the grand jury and leaves the decision as to the filing of the bill to the jurors. In practice, however, the district attorney usually has sufficient influence over the grand jury to get the decision he wants, that is, the jurors return a "true bill" when the district attorney wants to prosecute, and dismiss when the district attorney wants to dismiss.* There are times however, most especially in politically hot cases, when the prosecutor may prefer to be relieved of the responsibility of decision. In those cases he will present his witnesses and evidence in such a neutral manner as to throw the burden of continuing the prosecution on the grand jury. Cases involving political disturbances, well-publicized homicides, and accusations of police brutality are examples of the kinds of cases for which prosecutors prefer to share responsibility with the grand jury.

After the indictment, information, or complaint has been filed against the accused, some district attorneys will feel obliged to prosecute every case. Others however, have a somewhat different view.[2] Some are reluctant to

---

*Ideally, the grand jury is supposed to be a panel of responsible citizens who independently determine whether there is sufficient evidence to warrant proceeding with the prosecution of the accused. In reality, the grand jury is frequently under the control of and completely responsive to the district attorney. This has come about because it is the district attorney who determines the manner of presentation of the case to the grand jury; that is, he decides on the witnesses to be summoned and the evidence to be adduced. Since no defense is presented, and the defendant rarely risks self-incrimination by appearing, it is difficult for the grand jury to do other than that which the district attorney requests. On occasion, grand juries have been known to rebel against prosecutors and judges and proceed independently. The rarity of such occurrences is indicated by the headlines which "runaway grand juries" invariably inspire. On the whole, it is fair to say that district attorneys influence the preliminary pretrial stages of a prosecution through their initial decision whether or not to prosecute and through their control of the indictment process.

Although the grand jury was abolished in England in 1933, it is still used for felonies in all the federal district courts of the United States as well as in many state courts.

press forward in a case where they feel the evidence is weak and an innocent person might be convicted. Some feel that it is morally wrong to prosecute where they have strong doubts as to the guilt of the accused; and some district attorneys, for example, have even been known to go so far as to use polygraph (lie detector) examinations in robbery cases where time has elapsed between the crime and the arrest and there is no corroborating witness. It is true that, by singlehandedly making the decision to terminate a prosecution (judges rarely deny the prosecutor's motion to dismiss), the prosecutor is in effect trying the case by himself, without benefit of judge or jury, and thus short-circuiting the judicial process. On the other hand, such a concerned prosecutor is perhaps doing no more than the standards of his office and the canons of ethics require: defending the public interest by seeing that the guilty are prosecuted but the innocent released.*

Another consideration in the exercise of prosecutorial discretion is the number of cases awaiting prosecution in relation to the prosecutorial (and judicial) staff available to handle them. Many big city prosecutors' offices have found it necessary to perform a kind of triage on felony cases in order to allocate the resources of their offices most advantageously. In New York City, for example, each of the five district attorney's offices has established an Early Case Evaluation Bureau (ECAB) which sorts cases into five categories from "A" to "E". "A" cases are very strong cases: the arrest was proper, the evidence was available and strong, the witnesses are prepared to testify, and so on. These cases are sent to the grand jury immediately following the initial arraignment and bail hearing, usually within forty-eight hours. "B" cases are less strong: some element needed for successful prosecution is not yet in place. These cases may be temporarily set aside, but will probably be presented, ultimately, to the grand jury. "C" cases are weaker yet, and are sent for evaluation to a criminal court judge (similar to a magistrate) to determine whether the case should go to a grand jury at all. "D" cases are weak cases and classified as felonies for plea bargain purposes only. "E" cases are faulty and are set to be dismissed at arraignment. The New York City system of classification is doubtless more formal than that used in many other jurisdictions, but every prosecutor's office which is asked to handle more cases than it has resources to allocate for the purpose must, either formally or informally, set some system of priorities, and this system of priorities is an impor-

---

*LaFave and others have pointed out the racial and class discriminatory patterns underlying the exercise of police discretion in the matter of arrests. If there are similar patterns in the exercise of prosecutors' decisions in the matter of prosecutions, they are more subtle and complex. Probably an important factor underlying the exercise of such discretion is the state of public opinion and the likely repercussions of the decision on the district attorney's political career. Whether there is any marked favoritism toward wealthy and upper-class people, for example, is hard to document. In the Woodward case, cited in Chapter 3, the wealthy defendant was released without indictment; in the Sam Sheppard case, the wealth and prominence of the accused seemed only to whet the determination of the prosecutor to prosecute.

tant element in the decision of whether or not to prosecute a particular case.*

A corollary to the triage of felony cases has been the development of Major Offense Bureaus (MOB). These are bureaus within the prosecutor's office whose purpose is to expedite the prosecution and trial of suspects accused of very serious offenses. Every felony case which comes into the prosecutor's office is scored in relation to seriousness of offense, and the personal history of the accused. Serious crimes, alleged to have been committed by suspects with previous criminal records and histories of violent behavior, score very high. Those cases whose scores exceed a previously determined cutoff point will be handled by MOB. This means a disproportionate allocation of prose-cutorial resources go to these cases so that they can be presented to the grand jury promptly, the evidence and witnesses marshaled as quickly as possible, and the cases brought to trial in short order. Plea bargaining, except to the full indictment, is discouraged, and the most competent assistant district attorneys are assigned to do the trial work. MOB cases have an outstanding conviction record—well over 90 percent, though critics assert that this is due, in large measure, to the fact that MOB selects only those cases in which it is easy to get convictions, (in practice the "A" cases referred to above). The very success of MOB moreover, means that less important or more difficult to prosecute cases are given relatively short shrift because of the dispropor-tionately small amount of time and money allocated to them. While it is desirable that the mugger whose victim was hospitalized be given MOB treatment, it is unfortunate if this is at the cost of permitting the mugger, who only blacked his victim's eyes, to plead to a misdemeanor carrying virtually no punishment.

BAIL

The bail system is the process whereby, for financial consideration, an accused individual is released from custody pending his later appearance in court. The purposes underlying the bail system are first, to permit the defen-dant (who is legally *innocent* until proven guilty) his freedom so that he may continue his normal pursuits, support his family, arrange his affairs, and aid his attorney in the preparation of his defense; and second, to protect the community by insuring his subsequent court appearance through damaging financial penalty if he does not appear.

The bail system originated in England at a time when real property was

*Los Angeles and Detroit do not have the New York city system of triage, but weed out less important and weaker cases through rigorous screening by the prosecutor's office at the com-plaint stage. Whereas in New York City only three percent of felony cases are thrown out in the complaint room, in Los Angeles and Detroit as many as fifty percent of the cases may be dismissed.

frequently the security for the bail bond, the loss of which was extremely serious for the accused. In the United States today the system has lost much of its rationality. Judges frequently set bail for defendants according to the severity of the alleged offense; that is, the bail for armed robbery will normally be higher than the bail for shoplifting. If, however, the defendant is well-to-do he will be able to meet any reasonable bail; if he is poor he may not be able to raise even the most nominal sum. Thus, in terms of protecting the community, money bail determined by the severity of the crime is entirely irrational. It serves only to keep the poor, no matter what their characters, their roots in the community, or their alleged offenses, in jail, while more well-to-do defendants are set free virtually without regard for the consequences in terms of public safety.

Bail, furthermore, has become a commercial enterprise of dubious propriety. In many big city jurisdictions it is customary for defendants to raise bail through the services of a commercial bail-bondsman. The bondsman will provide the bail needed upon receipt of a fee, the amount of which is a percentage of the required bail. This fee is actualy the premium on an insurance policy furnished by a commercial insurance company that undertakes to indemnify the court should the defendant fail to appear at the appointed time. In addition, the bail-bondsman may request (particularly if the defendant is not known to him personally) collateral, in the form of bank accounts, insurance policies, and real estate, for the reimbursement of the insurance company if the defendant forfeits his bail through nonappearance. Defendants who are too poor to pay the premium, or who cannot post acceptable collateral, may be refused by the bail-bondsman. The result of the bail system thus, in the words of former Supreme Court Justice Arthur Goldberg, is that, "at best, it is a system of checkbook justice; at worst, a highly commerciaized racket."[3]

The only legitimate use of the bail system is to insure the presence of the defendant at a future court proceeding. Bail itself is not a punishment or form of restitution for an offense.

> A recognizance of bail, in a criminal case, is taken to secure the due attendance
> of the party accused, to answer the indictment, and to submit to a trial, and the
> judgment of the court thereon. It is not designed as a satisfaction for the offense
> . . . but as a means of compelling the party to submit to the trial and punishment
> which the law ordains for his offense.[4]

It is, however, a common occurrence for judges to use bail to detain in custody defendants whose release is felt to be either dangerous or unpopular. Those accused of capital offenses, for example, are frequently denied bail, or bail is set so high as to be virtually unattainable. The same can be said for those accused of other particularly heinous, violent crimes, such as forcible rape or felonious assault. Similarly, political protesters are frequently held in custody prior to trial because they are unable to meet the bail requirements set by unsympathetic judges. Communist defendants such as Eugene Dennis and Elizabeth Gurley Flynn, who were tried during the 1950s for their preaching of Communist doctrine, could not realistically have been held to be a physical danger to the community; nor were they likely to fail to appear for trial; yet high bail was set for each. Similarly, nonviolent civil rights demonstrators, such as Martin Luther King, Jr., and the thousands of white and black youngsters who joined with him in the many marches he led protesting segregation in the South during the 1960s, could not be considered a physical danger to the communities in which they were arrested; yet they too were forced to post thousands of dollars of bail money before they could be released. It is obvious in these cases that bail was used by the courts to harass and make more difficult the work of political organizations sponsoring protests that were unpopular, either with the courts or with the communities in which the trials were to occur.

It is clear that the use of the bail system as a weapon against political protesters is indefensible in a free society and is simply a manifestation of the weakness of local courts in protecting the constitutional rights of this type of defendant against public pressure. The relationship of the bail system to defendants who are felt to be *dangerous* rather than unpopular (or even subversive) is more ambivalent however. While the community, under our Constitution, has no right to be protected from opinions it deems loathsome, it has a right to protection from those who would murder, rape, or rob. Although it is true that the accused is presumed innocent until his guilt is legally established by a court trial, there are many circumstances in which freeing of the accused may reasonably be thought a danger to the community. The release of a suspect caught committing a violent crime, for example, is properly viewed with trepidation. The bail system, however, provides a very poor mechanism for the handling of such a suspect. To set bail so high as to be unattainable is simply to deny bail and therefore operate outside the context of the system. To set it high enough for an affluent suspect to reach, but too high for the poor man, is to give unjustifiable preferential treatment on the basis of financial means. To set bail low enough for any suspect to reach is, if the suspect is truly dangerous, to deny protection to the community.

In 1835, a man named Lawrence fired two loaded pistols at President Jackson. He missed, and when he was brought up for preliminary examination, Chief Judge Krantz of the District of Columbia Circuit questioned the prisoner and supposed that in view of his very limited economic circumstances, $1,000 bail would be enough, because, "To require larger bail than the prisoner could give would be to require excessive bail."

When the government objected because of the danger to the President's life, Judge Krantz in effect threw up his hands, increased the amount to $1,500 and remarked that if the *ability of the prisoner alone were to be considered, $1,500 was* *too much, but if the atrocity of the offense alone were to be considered, it was too small.* That there is not, then, a single intellectually respectable judicial decision on this problem in the ensuing 129 years is probably a testimonial to the fact that *the riddle is insoluble in the context of the bond system.*[5]

The rising crime rate in the District of Columbia led the Nixon administration, in 1970, to urge passage of legislation permitting "preventive detention" of dangerous suspects. The impetus for a law of this type came from the feeling that recent reforms of District of Columbia bail procedures, whereby the amount of bail was determined by the financial circumstances of the accused rather than the nature of the offense, had led to a sharp rise in violent crimes by suspects who were out on bail. The legislation, enacted in July 1970, provides that prosecutors can, in prescribed cases, request the court to permit pretrial imprisonment of accused persons considered to be dangerous. Such detention would be authorized for suspects meeting stated criteria only after a hearing, to be held shortly after arrest, wherein a high standard of proof of the dangerousness of the accused is required of the prosecution, and the right to counsel and the right of appeal are insured for the defendant. If the court grants the prosecutor's request for the detention of the accused, the date for the trial must be set within sixty days.[6] Proponents of this legislation felt that it would provide a method of holding dangerous suspects without relying on the misuse of the bail system, or the hypocrisy of two standards of justice: one for the poor and one for the rich. Those defendants who were not dangerous would be released on minimal bail; the others would be held for a relatively speedy trial. More defendants would be freed, the jails would be unencumbered, and the community would be protected. Opponents of this system, however, were fearful that the device would be used to harass and detain in custody political opponents of the administration, blacks, and poor people. They suggested that the solution to the problem of the dangerous suspect was a speedy trial. A speedy trial as a practical matter, however, is not always possible, and in at least some cases may even work to the disadvantage of the defendant by not allowing sufficient time to prepare a defense. While many of those detained undoubtedly are blacks (most suspects, like most residents of the District of Columbia, are black), it is also true that the victims of crime in the District of Columbia are predominantly black, and there is evidence that community sentiment in the District is heavily in favor of preventive detention. Ronald Goldfarb, a civil libertarian and probably the outstanding authority in the United States today on the subject of bail, has taken the position that with proper procedural safeguards preventive detention is probably on the whole less unjust to criminal suspects of all kinds, rich and poor, black and white, than the present money bail system.[7]

In respect to defendants whose release does *not* pose a threat to the public safety, the bail system is likewise of dubious value. Again, if the bail is set high enough to be a real deterrent to flight, it may well be beyond the reach of many criminal defendants except the very well-to-do. Thousands upon thousands of those brought into court are literally unable to make *any* bail. For them, unless the system is revised, there is no such thing as pretrial release; for them, the bail system in effect does not exist. For many people, moreover, bail is superfluous because they simply cannot leave and become fugitives from justice. They don't know where to go, how to support themselves when they get there, or who will care for their families while they are gone. Frequently they haven't even the money with which to flee.

Aside from the hardship to individual defendants, the social cost of an unreformed bail system is great. The defendant who is in prison cannot support his family, which then frequently requires public support. When he is released, moreover, even if he is acquitted, his job may be gone and his family may have lost its home through eviction. He himself, may have become embittered, and he certainly will have had undesirable exposure to experienced criminals in the institution in which he was confined. There is a good probability that he may have been subjected to unwanted homosexual advances, or, if he is physically slight, he may even have been raped by fellow inmates. The cost of maintaining him in jail, moreover, is considerable. A large percentage of the inmates in city and county jails are those awaiting trial. Were they to be removed from these facilities, either the cost to the public would be less or, with the same budget, far better services could be provided for those who should not be released or who are serving short term sentences.

In recent years several experiments in bail reform have been successfully mounted. Probably the most publicized was the Vera Foundation's Manhattan Bail Project. The Vera Foundation was founded in March 1961 by Louis Schweitzer, a businessman-philanthropist, as a nonprofit charitable institution to further equal protection of the laws for the indigent through research into neglected aspects of criminal law and procedure. The Manhattan Bail Project was begun in October 1961 in cooperation with the New York University Law School, and was designed to determine whether selected indigent offenders, released without bail, could be relied upon to appear in court when scheduled. Defendants brought into Manhattan's Criminal Court were interviewed by N.Y.U. law students, asked a series of questions, and scored on the basis of their answers. The questions related to the defendant's community ties, residence, family, job, background, prior criminal record, and associations. The information provided was then checked for accuracy by one of the Vera staff, and normally, within an hour, a summary of the findings and a recommendation for disposition of the accused was ready for consideration by the court. Those charged with homicide, most narcotics offenses, and certain sex crimes were not eligible for consideration. The project was very successful. By August 31, 1965, more than thirty-five hundred accused persons had been released on their own recognizance, and of these 98.4 percent returned to court when required. The rate of nonappearance was lower than the 3 percent forfeiture rate of bail bonds. Vera officials believed, moreover, that some cases of nonappearance were due to mishap or misunderstanding rather than willful failure to attend. An interesting sidelight on the effect of pretrial release was that defendants released on bail were subsequently convicted far less often than those not released, even when the backgrounds and offenses of the two groups were similar. Vera kept records on a control group of accused persons whose release had not been recommended although they were eligible by Vera standards. Sixty percent of those recommended by Vera for pretrial release were not convicted, while only 23 percent of the control group were not convicted. Of those in the first group who were found guilty only one in six went to jail; in the control group 90 percent were given jail sentences.

After the feasability of the Manhattan Bail Project had been proved, the New York City Office of Probation took over the management of the program. The change in administration was not successful and the project ultimately came to be run by the Criminal Justice Agency, Inc., a nonprofit, private corporation, some of whose trustees are associated with the Vera Foundation. As the program is currently operated, employees of the agency interview defendants prior to arraignment, and make one of several possible recommendations to the arraigning judge: release on the defendant's own recognizance (ROR) on the basis of *verified* information as to the defendant's roots in the community and the likelihood of his appearing for trial; ROR, but on the basis of *unverified* information given by the defendant; or no recommendation, with bail left entirely to the discretion of the judge. The jump rate for ROR cases recommended for release on the basis of verified information is very low—under 5 percent; it is higher for those cases where the judge releases defendants without the recommendation of the agency. On the whole, the system continues to work reasonably well.

Success of its pilot bail project led Vera to undertake in 1964, a summons project whereby desk officers in precinct station houses screened those arrested in a manner similar to the screening of defendants in the bail project, for the purpose of issuing summonses to appear in court rather than subjecting the accused to the usual arrest and arraignment procedures. The summons procedure is not only a more dignified way of handling the accused; it avoids the disruption caused by an overnight jail stay and the delays attendant on the arraignment process. It also frees the arresting officer from the necessity of spending hours in the station house and in court processing the accused prior to the initial arraignment, and permits the police officer to go back to his or her normal duties. The Manhattan Summons Project, during the two years of its operation under Vera auspices, showed a "jump" rate of 2.6 percent, which compared favorably with the rate for bail jumping.

In July 1967, the Summons Project was taken over by the New York City Police Department and instituted on a city-wide basis. Since then the jump rate has increased to a very unsatisfactory overall rate of 36 percent, with a

50 percent no-show rate for department store shoplifting cases. The marked increase in nonappearance rates is a result of fiscal economies by the police department, which, in an effort to cut down on overtime payments to police officers who must accompany the defendant through the complaint and arraignment stages of the traditional arrest, issues summonses in many inappropriate cases. Had the initial rigorous standards continued to be enforced, the summons project would be far more successful.

It seems clear that the bail system as presently constituted is inefficient, hypocritical, and archaic. Basically, the problem of handling arrested persons before trial should be considered on two levels: for suspects whose release may pose a danger to the community, and for all others. In regard to the latter group, the pattern for reform seems fairly clearly indicated by the successful pilot projects which have been mounted recently. It may even be that bail is meaningless for this latter group of defendants, and the system as we know it may be close to dissolution. For the small group of dangerous defendants, money bail is not the answer either. New methods of handling such persons must be devised, keeping in mind the constitutional rights of the accused as well as the safety of the community.

DEFENSE LAWYERS

Of all the rights claimed for accused persons, the one most accepted by and acceptable to all segments of our society is the right to counsel. Even the most non-civil-libertarian types, who normally view with despair or alarm attempts to "coddle" criminals, will concede that, for the person enmeshed in the toils of the law, the lawyer is a necessity if the outcome of the trial is not to be a mere travesty of justice. While state and local officials may have gotten administrative and budgetary jitters over the prospect of providing thousands of defendants with counsel, few criminal procedure decisions have been as uncontroversial in principle as *Gideon v. Wainwright,* wherein the Court declared,

> Reason and reflection require us to recognize that in our adversary system of criminal justice, any person hailed into court, who is too poor to hire a lawyer, cannot be assured a fair trial unless counsel is provided for him.[8]

The most obvious problem in regard to providing counsel for the accused arises when the accused is indigent. Who will pay for the cost of a lawyer? The response in most jurisdictions has been either a public defender's office (the counterpart of the public prosecutor's office), or services provided by a legal aid society. Unfortunately, many areas of the country have neither legal aid societies nor public defenders, and in those areas indigent defendants must rely on attorneys appointed by the court from the local bar.

Public defenders are paid, of course, from public funds, just as judges and prosecutors are. Legal aid attorneys, however, are usually employees of a legal aid society whose funds traditionally came from private sources (including bar associations). In recent years, however, these funds have been supplemented by grants: on the federal level from poverty program funds, and on state and local levels from general tax funds. Most indigent defendants are thus represented either by public defenders or by legal aid lawyers. A relatively small percentage may also have private attorneys who are appointed by the court, and who generally do not receive compensation except in capital cases. Some defendants, of course, can affort to hire attorneys of their own, and are represented by private counsel. Whereas conceptually the defense attorney is the champion of the accused, whose only concern is the safeguarding of his client's interests, in reality, the relationship is somewhat more ambivalent. In addition to his concern for his client, the defense attorney must also consider his own relationship to the prosecutor, the judge, and even to other court officials. To understand why this is so, one must examine the principal method of disposing of criminal cases in most metropolitan courts today: plea bargaining.

PLEA BARGAINING

In a study of the handling of criminal cases in a major American city, Abraham S. Blumberg, a sociologist-attorney, found that well over 90 percent of felony cases that were processed past the indictment stage were disposed of by guilty pleas on the part of the accused. To put it another way, fewer than 10 percent of those accused of a major crime elected to go to trial. More than nine-tenths pleaded guilty and, in effect, threw themselves on the mercy of the court. In this survey which covered fifteen years (from 1950 to 1964 inclusive), the percentages of those who pleaded guilty ranged from 91.05 percent in 1956, to 94.58 percent in 1961. While this may be a rather high figure (especially for felony indictments), almost every other study of guilty plea practices in the United States confirms the general picture, and it can probably be safely said that fewer than one-third of all those accused of crime will ever go to trial.*

The picture revealed by these statistics is very different from the conceptual model of the adversary system that is normally thought to be the reality of courtroom practice. Instead of each accused standing trial before an impartial judge and jury, with skilled legal counsel who examine the case from

*Abraham S. Blumberg, *Criminal Justice* (New York: New Viewpoints/Franklin Watts, 1967), p. 29. In a nationally televised speech on August 10, 1970, Chief Justice Warren E. Burger stated that 90 percent of all criminal suspects plead guilty and do not stand trial. *New York Times,* August 11, 1970, p. 1. Although Blumberg's statistics are almost 20 years old, and Burger's 10 years old, they are still valid.

different points of view, we find rather that most defendants arrive in the courtroom only to stand before the judge and plead guilty. The differences between the adversary system that is supposed to be and the plea bargaining system that exists in most jurisdictions are great, and are differences in quality, not simply in degree. Why has this change occurred? Why do so many defendants agree to waive their right to trial and content themselves with appearing before the judge for sentencing?

The reasons for the growth of the plea bargaining system are complex, but probably the single most important factor has been the necessity of handling a vast and increasing number of criminal defendants. While statistics purporting to show a rapidly rising crime rate are in many cases of dubious validity, there is no question that the absolute number of crimes is rising and the absolute number of defendants to be processed is also rising. At the same time, the amount of money the public is willing to invest in courts, prosecutors, and jails is not keeping pace with this increase. The result is a court system that is overburdened to the point of near breakdown in some communities.* enormous pressure on the prosecutor, the judge, the defense attorney, and the defendant to handle the case in whatever manner will dispose of it most quickly.

The prosecutor faced with more cases than his staff can handle knows that if he holds out for trial, the trial will be inordinately delayed. If the defendant is in jail awaiting trial, a possibly innocent man may be incarcerated for months, and his family may become destitute and have to be supported at public expense. The defendant, moreover, is taking up jail space of which there is a desperate shortage (which the newspapers frequently comment upon). If the defendant is out on bail pending trial, he may be committing further crimes—a phenomenon on which the mass media also frequently comment. The longer the trial is delayed, furthermore, the harder it is to round up the witnesses and present an effective case. The prosecutor is thus very much disposed towards any acceptable method that will cut down the number of cases awaiting trial. The obvious way out, in most cases, is to accept the offer of a defense attorney to plead his client guilty to an offense less than that charged on the indictment or information; for example, a defendant accused of felonious assault will be willing to plead guilty to simple assault, or one charged with armed robbery will admit attempted robbery. So great are the pressures on a district attorney to bargain pleas

*In January 1968, all civil trials were suspended in Supreme Court in Bronx County, New York, so that all the judges, courtrooms, and facilities could be used to help clear up the backlog of criminal cases awaiting trial in that county. Administrative Board of the Judicial Conference of the State of New York, "Report for the Judicial Year July 1, 1967-June 30, 1968," *Legislative Document* no. 90 (1969): 40–41. For a further discussion of the crisis in the New York City courts, see Alexander B. Smith and Harriet Pollack, "The Courts Stand Indicted in New York City," 68 *Journal of Criminal Law & Criminology* 252 (1977).

rather than bring cases to trial that defense lawyers can at times actually use the threat of going to trial as a weapon against a hard-nosed prosecutor.

The defense attorney may thus find the prosecutor receptive to an offer to bargain a plea. The former is restrained, however, by the necessity of acting responsibly in terms of what the prosecutor requires. The defense attorney cannot risk forcing a plea on a prosecutor which will result in adverse publicity for either the prosecutor or the judge. Clients who are dangerous to themselves or the community must be put away, and pleas bargained accordingly. While superficially this may seem a convenient and efficient way to handle accused persons, it is obvious that it is a shortcircuiting of the entire judicial process, because the determination of guilt has been made, not by judge or jury in open court, but by two lawyers in private conference. The defense attorney, moreover, needs to maintain good relationships with the prosecutor and the judges, since long after his client of the moment has passed from the scene, the defense attorney will be practicing in the same court, and will need the good will of other actors in the system to perform his own roles as efficaciously as possible. It is this almost symbiotic relationship with the prosecutor, the judge, and sometimes even court personnel that makes the relationship of the defense lawyer to his client ambivalent. He cannot devote himself exclusively to the interest of his client if he must also show some concern for the interests of the prosecutor, and even the judge.

The judge too, is co-opted into the system by the pressure resulting from the overload. Although judges routinely question defendants as to whether they have received any consideration in return for their guilty pleas, no matter how vigorous the denial on the part of the accused, the judge knows the truth: that these pleas are the results of deals between the lawyers on both sides. The judge closes his eyes to the obvious and permits the process to go on because he, too, knows that he must clear up the backlog of cases awaiting trial. The trial system itself is moreover so cumbersome in many jurisdictions that, even were the calendars not overloaded, inordinate delays would occur. Cases may be called for trial many times, and each time a continuance may be requested by one side or another. Sometimes witnesses are not present, sometimes counsel is occupied at another trial, and sometimes the defense counsel wishes to give his client more time to raise the fee before proceeding with the trial. Innumerable motions are made and appeals taken from the rulings on those motions. It is sometimes difficult to impanel an acceptable jury. Judges therefore welcome an opportunity to dispose of a case without trial. For the judge who is insecure, incompetent, or inexperienced, moreover, accepting the recommendation of the prosecutor is an easy way to solve many problems and maintain good working relationships with the members of the legal fraternity with whom he is likely to have day-to-day contact.

It is clear that the "grand tradition" judge, the aloof, brooding, charismatic figure in the Old Testament tradition, is hardly a real figure. The reality is the working judge who must be politician, administrator, bureaucrat, and lawyer in order to cope with a crushing calendar of cases. A Metropolitan Court judge might well ask, "Did John Marshall or Oliver Wendell Holmes ever have to clear a calendar like mine?" The Metropolitan Court judge who sits in a court of original jurisdiction, in his role as trial judge, arbiter, sentencer and awarder, cannot avoid the legal, interpersonal, and emotional dynamics of the small group of court regulars and those hangers-on who are inevitably present in a criminal court.[9]

So socialized into the system are many judges that they become angry with a defendant who refuses to avail himself of the opportunity to bargain a plea, and who insists instead on going to trial. It is a rare judge, if indeed there is any, who can avoid a feeling of institutional rejection when confronted with a recalcitrant defendant. Almost all judges become angry at this rejection, either openly or secretly, and express their anger in the form of sentences more severe than would have been dispensed had the defendant pleaded guilty to the same charge.

The willingness of judges to accept prosecutors' recommendations is reenforced by the tendency of judges to associate covertly, and perhaps unconsciously, with the prosecution in criminal cases. This is probably because they see themselves as defenders of the state, and as such tend to be more solicitous of the rights of the community than of the rights of the accused. It is noticeable that judges are far more impartial in their handling of opposing counsel in a civil, rather than a criminal case.

When the charge is a serious crime the judge often drops the facade of objectivity and patience. He frequently excoriates the defense, and the jury as well when they bring in a verdict of "not guilty." So jealous is the judge in pressing for a conviction that his wrath burns the prosecutor who seems to lag in the pursuit. In the Spock conspiracy case Judge Francis J. W. Ford "was heard whispering urgently to his clerk 'Tell that son of a bitch (the prosecutor) to cut it out! He'll blow the case if he keeps this up and get us all in trouble.' "[10]

Once the judge sees himself as the ally of the prosecutor, it is easy for him to reject the adversary model of criminal justice and accept the bureaucratic model. He loses his mediator role and becomes an opponent of the defendant.*

*In fairness it must be said that, at least up to the present, one area in which the judge performs in conformity with the stated role model of a judge is in his relationship to the probation officer assigned to the case. Probation is essentially an institutionalized method for personalizing justice, that is, a formal way of taking into account the individual circumstances and history of each defendant, and tailoring the disposition of the case to fit those circumstances. In spite of heavy caseloads, in the more progressive court systems probation officers have not yet been entirely co-opted by bureaucratic considerations, and perform their jobs *vis-à-vis* defendants with considerable integrity. Judges also, at least in those cases where there are no

DUE PROCESS: THE ADVERSARY MODEL VERSUS THE BUREAUCRATIC MODEL

It is obvious that the reality of our judicial process conforms far more closely to the bureaucratic model than to the adversary ideal. Criminal defendants are adjudicated, not by a trial involving two equally matched lawyer-champions arguing before a neutral judge and jury, but by private negotiations between actors who have at least as much claim on each other as the defendant has on any one of them. The judicial process, in short, is one of bargaining and compromise; it is informal, and indeed exists only through its ability to short-circuit and bypass the prescribed, formal procedures.

The development of the plea bargaining system was not planned. There are no heroes or villains (depending on one's point of view) in this story. The bureaucratic mode of handling most criminal defendants rose from necessity: the necessity of handling with limited public resources vast numbers of accused persons. To make the adversary model a reality would require an almost unimaginable increase in the outlay of tax funds: enough money to re-create for each criminal defendant in our vast megalopoli the unhurried, personal attention that can only exist in small, well-integrated communities. To say that such an increased outlay is unlikely is an understatement. If such funds are to be obtained, an intense struggle by reformers will be necessary, and to succeed in such a struggle they will have to be prepared to answer the obvious question of the economy-minded: What's wrong with the bureaucratic model anyway?

What, if anything, *is* wrong with the bureaucratic model? Isn't it in reality just as good as the adversary ideal that is so hard to effectuate? The plea bargaining system, it must be conceded, works better than many purists would care to admit. Given honest, reasonably conscientious officials and attorneys, it is quite unlikely that a totally innocent person, with no past record, will be wrongfully convicted. The chances of such a miscarriage of justice are probably less under the plea bargaining system than if the accused were forced to appear before a jury of his peers. Further, the informality and flexibility of the system makes it possible for errors to be corrected with a minimum of difficulty at various stages of the process, even occasionally beyond conviction (though before sentence). The defense attorney, prosecutor, or judge who feels that something is wrong in the way that the case is developing, that some bit of evidence does not ring true, that some witness

---

outside pressures, use probation recommendations properly: to individualize sentences in order to achieve whatever beneficial results may be possible. Even a good probation system, however, can be short-circuited by a plea bargain which includes agreement as to the *sentence* to be imposed as well as the charge to which the defendant will plead guilty. This frequently happens in seriously overcrowded courts. In these situations the crucial role of the probation officer has been eliminated.

is not what he appears to be, can easily and quickly call an informal conference of the participants in the case to convey his disquiet. This would be far more difficult if formal adversary procedures were adhered to. The plea bargaining system is also economical in terms of both time and money. This economy is, of course, its supreme virtue, and its virtual *raison d'être*. While this may not provide conceptual justification, it is of enormous practical importance because it is quite possible that our society cannot afford the outlay of time and money needed to create an adversary system for the overwhelming number of accused persons our present laws and criminal justice system produce.

However, the plea bargaining system cannot be looked upon with complacency. Despite its very considerable virtues, it has inherent within itself some very dangerous defects. For one thing, it is more vulnerable to corruption at the hands of dishonest, incompetent, or lax participants than is the adversary system. The very informality and secrecy of the procedures and the negotiations out of court lend themselves to questionable arrangements which may be adverse to the interests of both defendant and society at large.

Even, however, assuming the honesty and competence of the actors, the plea bargaining system has serious drawbacks. While it is true that a totally innocent person with no previous record may benefit from the system, an accused with a previous criminal record is almost certain to be harmed. There are few persons in prison who are totally innocent; there are many who are innocent of the specific crime for which they were convicted, but who are or were guilty of something else. The defense attorney considers that a client's past criminal record impairs his (the attorney's) bargaining power *vis-à-vis* the district attorney. This is particularly true if the client has a record, not only of past convictions, but of arrests which did not lead to conviction due to considerations such as lack of evidence. In such a case, the defense attorney will in all likelihood feel (probably correctly) that the district attorney will not settle for anything less than a plea of guilty to some charge somewhat less than that in the indictment, complaint, or information. The result is that any defendant with a questionable past record is going to be pleaded guilty by his attorney, even if he is innocent of the specific charge against him. In a true adversary system, in which evidence of the specific charge would be needed for conviction, he might be found not guilty; in the plea bargaining system he will surely plead guilty to something. A member of the Fortune Society* with a long criminal record recently recounted an occasion when he wished to face trial for the crime with which he was charged, but his attorney (who was privately retained by the defendant's family) threatened to withdraw from the case unless the accused agreed to bargain a guilty plea. When the defendant protested, the lawyer explained that, should the client go to trial and be convicted, he could be sentenced to sixty years in prison. Such

*A group of ex-convicts organized for self-help.

a sentence would not only be hard on the defendant, the lawyer explained, but would be bad for his own reputation as a defense attorney.[11]

The plea bargaining system, while it may under-protect certain kinds of criminal defendants, may also over-protect others, thus denying society the protection it ought to have against some dangerous criminals. In a large city, the pressure of moving the cases of thousands of defendants is so great that frequently district attorneys are virtually forced to accept pleas of guilty to charges far less than the offense in question warrants. Murder is reduced to manslaughter, rape is reduced to simple assault, and burglary is reduced to unlawful entry. Minimal punishment is sometimes dispensed by the judge in accordance with a previously struck bargain. The bitter comments by police officers about revolving-door justice, where arrested persons plead guilty, are sentenced, and are out on the street again repeating their nefarious crimes, stem partly from the practice of accepting very much reduced guilty pleas and imposing perfunctory sentences.

This kind of overprotection of criminals and underprotection of the community is frequently blamed on the judges who accept inappropriately lenient pleas to serious charges, but a closer analysis of the situation reveals that the dynamics are far more complex. The following analysis of the New York City courts suggests some of the factors involved, and while the numbers are specific to New York City, the overall picture is probably relevant to every large city in the country. The disastrous state of the New York City courts is caused not by the personal failings of the judges, but by numbers: the number of cases compared to the number of courts and related facilities which are available to handle them.

The arithmetic is simple. From 1952 to 1974 the total number of regular, housing and transit police officers in New York City increased from 19,450 to 36,574, or approximately 88 percent. During the same period of time the number of judges sitting in the misdemeanor and felony courts rose from 91 to 190, or approximately 108 percent. While the number of police and the number of judges increased in roughly similar proportion, the number of felony arrests rose from 16,957 to 101,748: a 500 percent increase. Another way of saying this is to note that in 1952 every police officer statistically made .89 felony arrests; in 1974, each officer was responsible for 2.8 felony arrests. The felony workload of the criminal courts thus increased six-fold at the same time that the number of judges available to cope with the workload barely doubled.

This disparity between the number of judges and the number of potential cases would by itself be sufficient to seriously overload the courts. The situation is, unfortunately, further compounded by the fact that a felony trial in 1974 is a far different procedure from the felony trial of 1952. Due in large part to a series of Supreme Court rulings which extended rights to indigent defendants which had previously been exercised only by the well-to-do, felony trial procedure has become substantially more complex and time-consuming. Even in 1952, all felony defendants in New York State were represented by counsel, but the role of the defense attorney has changed markedly since then. Pursuant to the Supreme Court's decisions in *Miranda v. Arizona, United States v. Wade,* and *Terry v. Ohio,* defense attorneys can and do challenge the admissibility of confessions, eye witness identifications, the legality of arrests and attendant searches, and the propriety of many types of police procedures. In previous years, neither assigned counsel nor Legal Aid attorneys had the resources or the appellate court encouragement to under-take such activities. Today they have both. The result is that felony court judges in 1974 sat an average of seven working days longer than in 1952, but they handled only 14.8 trials each as compared to 23.3 trials in 1952, a decrease of 33 percent.

These statistics lead to only one conclusion: the number of cases to be handled has increased faster than the resources available to handle them. In the last twenty years, there has been ever-increasing pressure on criminal court judges in New York City to clear their calendars and keep their case-loads current. This pressure has been increased by public awareness of the civil liberties problems of lengthy pretrial detentions and by the overcrowd-ing of remand facilities such as Riker's Island and the Tombs. Given this pressure, it is understandable that plea bargaining, as a short-cut to the disposition of cases, has been and continues to be used to excess.[12]

The New York City situation is such that a threat by the Legal Aid Society, which handles 70 percent of the criminal cases in the New York City criminal courts, to take these cases to trial is enough to bring the toughest district attorney to the bargaining table in a chastened mood. With the court calen-dars crammed to the point of chaos, the thought of any substantial proportion of the Legal Aid cases going to trial is so horrifying that other considerations pale by comparison. This does not mean to say, of course, that any hardened criminal can get a minimal sentence by simply demanding a trial. Many defense attorneys will cooperate with the prosecutor in seeing that "bad men" are sent away for a long time. While in one sense this may be reassuring to the public, it is at the same time a clear indication of how, under the plea bargaining system, the determination of guilt is removed from the hands of the judge and the jury to the hands of the "defense" attorney and prosecu-tor.[13]

Serious as these criticisms of the plea bargaining system are, they are perhaps not as great as a drawback which is apparent to very few defendants, attorneys, or public officials. The bureaucratic model of criminal justice has an adverse social effect on society not only because it may harm individuals caught up in the system, but because it has a stultifying effect on the law itself. The very essence of the bureaucratic system is that each member performs the task assigned to him and works harmoniously with other mem-bers of the system. Each actor, as they say, goes along to get along. Every one plays ball with everyone else, and so the ball game goes on. But therein lies the difficulty: there is no one on either team to stand back and say, "Is this what we should be doing? Is this the game we ought to be playing?" In short, everyone is concerned with procedure, no one with the nature of the law itself. Everyone concentrates on what to do with a particular defendant under the system as it currently operates. No one has time or motivation to wonder whether the system itself may not need change.

Oliver Wendell Holmes said that the law grows in response to "the felt necessities" of the time. A meaningful system of law is a dynamic system, one which changes as society changes. The plea bargaining system tends to make static what should be dynamic, to blunt those felt necessities. The criminal law cannot change or respond as long as those who participate in the ad-judicatory process are concerned primarily with not rocking the boat, that is, disposing of the accused in such a way as to cause the least possible disruption to the system.

The naive observer may, at this point, protest, "But the criminal law has changed! It is changing so rapidly that the courts are in a state of chaos and confusion. Never have criminals had so many rights. Why, look at *Miranda* and *Escobedo!*" Our naive friend is quite correct. The criminal law *is* changing rapidly, and at the very same time the adjudicatory process has become increasingly bureaucratized. The point is, however, that these changes in the criminal law have not been brought about by the normal actors in the plea bargaining system. They have been brought about by outsiders. These out-siders have acted as mavericks, goads, sometimes even thorns in the flesh. They have forced the system, often painfully, to reexamine the rules by which it operates.

Who are these outsiders? Most frequently they are attorneys for civil liberties or legal defender groups whose interest in a particular case is cen-tered on the law itself rather than on the needs of a particular client. A great proportion of recent defendants whose cases have established significant precedents relating to a change in the criminal law have been represented by attorneys affiliated with the Legal Aid Society, the NAACP Legal Defense Fund, or the ACLU. Many others have been represented by court-appointed attorneys who have volunteered their services to the court primarily because of their ideological interest in the law itself. These attorneys tend to see justice not only in procedural terms but in substantive terms as well.

Consider, for example, the role of Clyde W. Woody who represented Aguilar in *Aguilar v. Texas.* The defendant had been arrested on an affidavit from police officers which simply stated that they had "reliable information" from a credible person that narcotics were kept in Aguilar's home. No further information was given to the magistrate issuing the search warrant as to the nature of either the informant or the source of his information. Woody commented:

It was necessary to fully apprise the Court of Criminal Appeals as well as the trial courts of the State of Texas of the real meaning of the Fourth and Fifth Amendments of the Constitution of the United States. In my opinion the Courts of this state, as well as the citizens of the State of Texas, were the victims of a fraud being perpetrated under the guise of law enforcement. The function of the arrest and search warrant in Texas prior to Aguilar had been utilized as a writ of assistance which in my opinion would bring discredit and lawlessness to the Courts and cause the citizens to lose respect for the Constitution as well as the Judiciary. It was obvious that the executive branch in Texas had already succeeded in bringing discredit upon themselves.

In a similar vein, Gretchen White Oberman (then a Legal Aid attorney), discussed *Sibron v. New York,* a case involving the New York State "stop and frisk" law which lowered the standards for police searches and seizures of suspected persons.

The Legal Aid Society is assigned to hundreds and thousands of cases at the trial level and this was one of the many. The trial attorney saw the legal potential and asked Mr. Finkel of the Appeals Bureau to handle it personally on appeal. . . . Mr. Finkel had it in the Appellate Term and the New York Court of Appeals. I had handled *People v. Rivera,* the first stop and frisk case in the New York Court of Appeals a couple of years before and Mr. Finkel, knowing my commitment to the privacy principle of the Fourth Amendment asked me to collaborate with him on the jurisdictional statement to the Supreme Court, and on the brief and argument when the case was taken by the Court for review.

Our work together was a true labor of love. We believed every word we wrote in the brief and every statement we made orally before the Court. I would have done the same thing without salary from the Society because I believed that the issue involved was important to the law and ultimately to the entire social fabric of the country.[14]

Similarly, Miranda's attorney Victor M. Earle III, claimed not that his client was handled badly by the police, but that the "good" handling of prisoners was basically unfair. Attorneys who make claims such as these must be outsiders. No working system can tolerate the disruption caused by their iconoclasm.

Not many attorneys have the temerity (or even the inclination) to play the role of gadfly. The system is not kind to those who do play such a role, and in fact many criminal lawyers have been punished for defending a client by attacking the system. In a recent study of courtroom behavior, Niederhoffer and Smith point out that small-time criminal lawyers, "the courtroom regulars," can commit minor transgressions against the propriety of the courtroom and established courtroom procedures with impunity.[15] At worst they will be subjected to a reprimand by the judge. Outstanding criminal lawyers such as Clarence Darrow, Samuel Leibowitz, F. Lee Bailey, Melvin Belli, Jake Ehrlich, and William Fallon, on the other hand, have all been in serious trouble stemming from their courtroom defense of a client. Clarence Darrow and William Fallon, for example, were tried for subornation of perjury; others were threatened with disbarment. Though these attorneys were probably less ideologically oriented than legal defender organization attorneys, their relationship to the system was the same: they were outsiders. By refusing to take a plea and forcing the case to trial, they were fighting the system. They bargained with neither the court nor the district attorney, and once their independence of the system had been established, their transgressions could not be forgiven as they might have been for those who played in the regular ball game. While legal defender lawyers probably suffer less direct punishment, those who are outstandingly aggressive in support of particular clients, for example, William Kunstler defending the Chicago Seven or northern attorneys defending civil rights clients in southern courtrooms, find themselves punished in such ways as citations for contempt of court.

The plea bargaining system is the reality of criminal adjudication in the big cities of the United States, and despite its obvious imperfections, it works reasonably well to process the multitude of criminal defendants brought before the courts each year. It is fortunate that it works as well as it does, because the likelihood of creating or recreating a true adversary system consonant with the ideals of Anglo-American jurisprudence is slim indeed, given the present political complexion of our government and the prevailing ordering of priorities on the use of public funds.

Certainly for good or for ill, the United States Supreme Court has sustained every challenge to the validity of the plea bargaining system. Two cases came to the Court in the early 1970s. In *McMann v. Richardson*, [16] Richardson had been indicted for first degree murder and initially pleaded not guilty. He subsequently withdrew his plea and pleaded guilty to second degree murder, for which offense he was sentenced to 30 years to life. After fruitless attempts at collateral relief in the state courts he petitioned the federal court for a writ of *habeas corpus,* arguing that his guilty plea was the product of a confession coerced by a police beating and poor advice from his assigned counsel who, after a ten minute conference, advised Richardson to plead guilty and suggested that the matter of the coerced confession be brought up at *habeas corpus* hearings after conviction. The Court of Appeals for the Second Circuit granted the request for *habeas corpus* on the ground that a guilty plea waives pretrial irregularities only if the plea is voluntary, but Richardson's plea resulting from an involuntary confession was not voluntary. On appeal, the United States Supreme Court reversed the Court of Appeals decision, holding that the guilty plea was voluntary even if the confession was not, and was intelligently made even if the advice given by the lawyer was mistaken.

A year later, the Court decided *North Carolina v. Alford.* [17] Alford had been indicted for first degree murder, an offense punishable by death unless the jury recommended life imprisonment. Under North Carolina law, however, if the defendant pleaded guilty (as opposed to being found guilty after trial) the penalty could be no more than life imprisonment. The case against Alford was very strong, and in light of the evidence against him, Alford's attorney recommended a plea of guilty to murder in the second degree which Alford then entered, at the same time protesting before the judge that he was innocent and was pleading guilty only because of his fear of execution.

> ... Before the plea was finally accepted by the trial court, the court heard the sworn testimony of a police officer who summarized the State's case. Two other witnesses besides Alford were also heard. Although there was no eyewitness to the crime, the testimony indicated that shortly before the killing Alford took his gun from his house, stated his intention to kill the victim, and returned home with the declaration that he had carried out the killing. After the summary presentation of the State's case, Alford took the stand and testified that he had not committed the murder but that he was pleading guilty because he faced the threat of the death penalty if he did not do so.[2]
>
> [2]After giving his version of the events of the night of the murder, Alford stated:
> "I pleaded guilty on second degree murder because they said there is too much evidence, but I ain't shot no man, but I take the fault for the other man. We never had an argument in our life and I just pleaded guilty because they said if I didn't they would gas me for it, and that is all."
> In response to questions from his attorney, Alford affirmed that he had consulted several times with his attorney and with members of his family and had been informed of his rights if he chose to plead not guilty.Alford then reaffirmed his decision to plead guilty to second-degree murder:
> "Q. [by Alford's attorney]. And you authorized me to tender a plea of guilty to second degree murder before the court?
> "A. Yes, sir.
> "Q. And in doing that, that you have again affirmed your decision on that point?
> "A. Well, I'm still pleading that you all got me to plead guilty. I plead the other way, circumstantial evidence; that the jury will prosecute me on—on the second. You told me to plead guilty, right. I don't—I'm not guilty but I plead guilty."[18]

Alford's guilty plea was accepted by the trial judge who, in view of Alford's long criminal record, sentenced him to thirty years in prison, the maximum penalty for murder in the second degree. Alford then applied to the Court of Appeals for the Fourth Circuit for a writ of *habeas corpus* on the ground that his plea was involuntary—the product of fear of the death penalty and coercion by his lawyer. The Fourth Circuit granted *habeas corpus* but, on appeal to the United States Supreme Court by North Carolina, the Court, in a 6–3 decision, reversed. The standard, said the Court, for voluntariness was not whether the defendant was motivated by fear of the death penalty, but whether the plea represented a willing and intelligent choice of the courses of action open to the defendant. In Alford's case, because he had competent counsel, the choice had been freely and knowingly made. The Court went on to deal with the question of whether a judge may accept a guilty plea accompanied by protestations of innocence, and concluded that such a plea is acceptable. Justice White, who wrote the majority opinion, drew an analogy between the guilty plea unaccompanied by an admission of guilt, and *nolo contendere* cases where the defendant does not expressly admit guilt, but accepts the right of the court to punish him. There may be reasons, as where the defendant desires to avoid an insanity plea, for a plea of guilty without an admission of guilt.

The net effect of both *McMann* and *Alford* was to bind defendants absolutely to the terms of the bargain they had made at the time they pleaded guilty. The Court found the circumstances of neither *McMann,* where the evidence against the defendant had been produced by an illegal beating, nor *Alford,* where the defendant protested his innocence, sufficiently compelling to modify the terms of the bargain. Not only was the plea bargain to be upheld, at almost any cost, as one dissenter charged, but the bargain was equally binding on the prosecution. In *Santobello v. New York,* [19] which was decided shortly after *Alford,* Santobello, a gambler, had been indicted on two felony gambling counts and had agreed to plead guilty to one lesser gambling count, the maximum penalty for which was one year in prison. In return, the prosecutor agreed to make no recommendation for sentence. Several months passed between the agreement and the actual day of sentencing, during which time both a new judge and a new prosecutor had entered the case. The new prosecutor recommended that Santobello be given a one year sentence and the judge accepted the recommendation. Santobello protested that the terms of the plea bargain had been violated and he appealed on the ground that the state's failure to stick to the agreement had denied him due process. The United States Supreme Court agreed, holding that while there is no absolute right for a defendant to have his guilty plea accepted, once the state has entered into a plea bargain, the promises made by the state must be fulfilled. The case was remanded to the New York courts for such relief as they wished to give: performance of the bargain or permission to Santobello to withdraw his guilty plea and plead anew to the original felony charges.

Six years after *Santobello* the Court reaffirmed its willingness to uphold plea bargains, regardless of coercive pressures on the defendant prior to the plea. In *Bordenkircher v. Hayes,* [20] a Kentucky man was indicted for forging an $88 check, and the prosecutor promised a less than maximum sentence if the accused would plead guilty rather than go to trial. If the defendant insisted on a trial, the prosecutor warned that he would seek a second indictment against the accused as an habitual offender based on two previous felony convictions. Hayes, the accused, insisted on a trial, was found guilty of forgery, and then given a life term as an habitual offender, as opposed to the five-year sentence the prosecutor had promised to recommend if Hayes had plea bargained. When the case reached the United States Supreme Court on appeal, a narrow five man majority held that Hayes had not been denied due process. While the majority conceded that "to punish a person because he had done what the law plainly allows him to do is a due process violation of the most basic sort," nevertheless, this standard did not apply to Hayes and the plea bargaining situation because he was free to accept or reject any offer made him. Four justices dissented arguing that the prosecutor had acted vindictively with the admitted purpose of discouraging, and then penalizing, the defendant's exercise of his constitutional rights.

Less than one year later, the Court again upheld the sanctity of the plea bargain and the permissibility of pressure by the state on the defendant. By a 6–3 vote, with Justices Stevens, Brennan, and Marshall dissenting, the Court held that a New Jersey statute did not violate the constitutional rights of murder defendants by mandating life sentences for those convicted of first degree murder after a jury trial, but permitting a judge to impose a sentence of thirty years if the defendant pleaded guilty before trial. In some respects, the issues in this case, *Corbitt v. New Jersey*,[21] were similar to those in *Alford* where the defendant pleaded guilty rather than face the possibility of execution. New Jersey had no capital punishment statute; nevertheless, the mandatory life sentence created a similar type of pressure on the defendant, with the lesser thirty-year sentence acting as an inducement to plead guilty.

In the eight years since *McMann,* the United States Supreme Court has never deviated from its policy of sustaining plea bargaining agreements, despite factual situations which, in the opinion of the dissenters at least, indicated unfair use of the coercive power of prosecutors and judges against defendants. Despite the strong protests of the liberals on the bench, plea bargaining has been sustained against all challenges, possibly because it is so essential to the functioning of the large urban courts that chaos would ensue were the Court to undermine its foundation. If plea bargains could be successfully appealed, not only would they be harder to negotiate at the pretrial stage (because of the increased bargaining power of the defendant) but the appellate court calendars would be inundated as well. Plea bargaining reduces congestion not only in the trial courts, but a firm plea bargain also forecloses the entire appellate process, and eliminates from the appellate courts a potentially large number of criminal appeals. Thus, the naturally conservative bent of the Burger court has been reenforced by a healthy fear of the disastrous impact on the court system of successful challenges to the plea bargaining system.

It is very difficult even to suggest reforms that would lead toward the realization of the adversary system, which unquestionably is a superior system for the handling of accused persons in a democracy. The likelihood of sufficient men, money, and time to handle each defendant as he should be handled in the name of justice and liberty seems almost hopelessly remote. Perhaps this is simply another way of saying that a free, open society that creates so many criminal defendants cannot perform as a free, open society should, at least insofar as these most unfortunate of its citizens are concerned.

Perhaps the answer is that a successful democratic society must find ways to reduce the number of those accused of crime. Perhaps we make too many modes of conduct criminal; perhaps we warp too many personalities so that they become enemies of society instead of builders of the social order. Perhaps we must think, not in terms of tinkering with the criminal justice system, but in terms of the basic, needed reforms, both in the law as a device for social control and in the larger institutions of society itself, so that fewer individuals will come to be regarded as criminally deviant. It is totally unrealistic to think of providing adversary system treatment for all offenders, ranging from those who go through stop lights, to alcoholics, to marijuana-smoking students, to pugnacious husbands, to burglars, muggers, rapists, and murderers. It may conceivably be feasible to provide such handling for those who commit serious *malum in se* crimes of violence or potential violence. Other ways need to be found for handling other types of defendants. Are their offenses really so antisocial that they need be labelled criminal? Can their conduct be corrected without sanctions of such seriousness that they must be dispensed by a court rather than an administrative agency? Certainly no simple, short range solutions will resolve the dilemma in which our courts find themselves: desiring to do justice to each individual, and at the same time to protect society with resources that are not only inadequate but which can in no foreseeable way be made adequate for the job that needs to be done.[22]

Selected Readings

Auerbach, Jerold. *Unequal Justice.* New York: Oxford, 1976.

Blumberg, Abraham S. *Criminal Justice.* New York: New Viewpoints/Franklin Watts, 1967.

Casper, Jonathan D. *Lawyers Before the Warren Court.* Urbana, Ill.: University of Illinois Press, 1972.

Goldfarb, Ronald. *Ransom.* New York: Harper & Row, 1965.

Hughes, Graham. *The Conscience of the Courts.* Garden City, N.Y.: Anchor Press, 1975.

Jacob, Herbert. *Justice in America.* Boston: Little, Brown, 1972.

James, Howard. *Crisis in the Courts.* New York: McKay, 1977.

Murphy, Walter F., and Pritchett, C. Herman. *Courts, Judges, and Politics.* 2nd ed. New York: Random House, 1974.

Rosenthal, Douglas E. *Lawyer and Client: Who's in Charge?* New York: Russell Sage, 1974.

Schur, Edwin M. *Crimes Without Victims.* Englewood Cliffs, N.J.: Prentice-Hall, 1965.

Schwartz, Richard D., and Skolnick, Jerome H. *Society and the Legal Order.* New York: Basic Books, 1970.

Simon, Rita James, ed. *The Sociology of Law: Interdisciplinary Readings.* San Francisco: Chandler, 1968.

Notes

1. New York State Bar Association, *Canons of Professional Ethics; Canons of Judicial Ethics,* adopted January 1909, amended January 1963 (Brooklyn: Edward Thompson Company), p. 13.

(These canons of ethics have been superseded by the Code of Professional Responsibility as promulgated by the American Bar Association in August, 1969, and adopted by the New York State Bar Association as of January 1, 1970. The quoted portion is substantially the same in the newer version, Section DR 7-103 of the New York State Judiciary Law.)

2. The information concerning the activities of district attorneys in the New York area was gathered from informal conversations with present and former assistant district attorneys. See also David S. Worgen and Monrad G. Paulsen, "The Position of the Prosecutor in a Criminal Case," *The Practical Lawyer* 7, no. 7 (November 1961): 44–58.

3. Arthur J. Goldberg, "Foreword" to Ronald Goldfarb, *Ransom* (New York: Harper & Row, 1965), p. ix.

4. *Ex parte Milburn,* 34 U.S. 704 (1835), as quoted in Goldfarb, p. 10.

5. Caleb Foote, as quoted in Goldfarb, pp. 13–14. Italics added.

6. P.L. 91–358 District of Columbia Court Reform Act, July 29, 1970.

7. For a full discussion of bail and preventive detention problems, see Goldfarb, *Ransom,* and Goldfarb, "A Brief for Preventive Detention," *The New York Times Magazine,* March 1, 1970, p. 28.

8. 372 U.S. 335 (1963), at 344.

9. Abraham S. Blumberg, *Criminal Justice.* (New York: New Viewpoints/Franklin Watts, 1967), pp 122–123.

10. Arthur Niederhoffer and Alexander B. Smith, "Power and Personality in the Courtroom: The Trial of the Chicago 7," 3 *Connecticut Law Review* 233, (Winter 1970–1971) at 240.

11. Statement made by Chuck Briganski, a member of the Fortune Society, Brooklyn College, July 21, 1970.

12. Alexander B. Smith and Harriet Pollack, "The Courts Stand Indicted in New York City," 68 *Journal of Criminal Law & Criminology* 253 (1977).

13. Blumberg, pp. 92–94.

14. Alexander B. Smith and Harriet Pollack, *Some Sins Are Not Crimes* (New York: New Viewpoints/Franklin Watts, 1975), pp. 185–186.

15. Niederhoffer and Smith, p. 240.

16. *McMann v. Richardson,* 397 U.S. 759 (1970).

17. *North Carolina v. Alford,* 400 U.S. 25 (1970).

18. Ibid., at 28.

19. 404 U.S. 257 (1971).

20. 434 U.S. 357 (1978).

21. 439 U.S. 212 (1978).

22. For a somewhat different approach to the problem of reform of the criminal justice system, see Herbert L. Packer, "Two Models of the Criminal Process," 113 *University of Pennsylvania Law Review* 1 (November, 1964). For a discussion of the labelling of modes of conduct as criminal, see Edwin M. Schur, *Crimes Without Victims* (Englewood Cliffs, N.J.: Prentice-Hall, 1965).

chapter **8**

the rights
of the accused

"We must never forget that it is a *constitution* we are expounding."

   John Marshall, *McCulloch v. Maryland* (1819)

"We are under a Constitution, but the Constitution is what the judges say it is."

   Charles Evans Hughes, Speech at Elmira, New York (1907)

"The history of liberty has largely been the history of the observance of procedural safeguards."

   Felix Frankfurter, *McNabb v. United States* (1943)

"A policeman's affidavit should not be judged as an entry in an essay contest."

   Abe Fortas dissenting, *Spinelli v. United States* (1969)

THE SUPREME COURT AND THE AMERICAN SYSTEM

If the adversary system is England's contribution to jurisprudence, the United States Supreme Court is strictly an American contribution. The Constitution, which was adopted in 1789, established a high court with power to sit in judgment on and reverse the actions of both national and state legislatures—or at least so John Marshall said. Article III provides for a court called a Supreme Court in which "the judicial power of the United States shall be vested," and whose jurisdiction will "extend to all cases, in Law and Equity arising under this Constitution, the Laws of the United States, and Treaties made . . . under their Authority." In this brief, ambiguous section the founding fathers set up an institution which has had enormous influence on the shape of American law and society.

Whether those who drew up the Constitution meant for the Court to have the power of judicial review, that is, the power to sit in judgment on legislative (especially congressional) acts, is a question about which historians have argued heatedly since 1803. Nor is it clear whether, if the Supreme Court were intended to have such power, the electorate who voted to ratify the Constitution understood this to be the case. In any event, in 1803, in deciding the

149

politically explosive case of *Marbury v. Madison,* John Marshall announced that the Supreme Court did indeed have not only the power, but the duty of reviewing such acts of Congress as were relevant to the cases under litigation and determining whether those acts were in conformity with the Constitution. Having thus confidently asserted its power, the Supreme Court then very prudently refrained from exercising that power *vis-à-vis* Congress for the next half-century, until the disaster of *Dred Scott* on the eve of the Civil War.

Whatever the merits of the historical arguments, judicial review is today a *fait accompli* and an accepted part of American government. The Supreme Court can hear cases brought to it from the highest state courts, as well as from the intermediate federal appellate courts. It hears a very limited (largely insignicant) number of cases on original jurisdiction, and a similarly small number of cases from lower state courts.[1] While the rules of jurisdiction and procedure which have evolved since the *Marbury* decision are fairly complex, two features are significant. In the first place, the Court can speak *only in the process of deciding a case. It does not render advisory opinions.* This means that if the Court has something to say, it must wait until a suitable vehicle in case form happens to present itself. It also means that if any individual or group in the United States wishes to elicit from the Court an authoritative statement or definition of constitutional rights, it may approach the Court only by litigating a suitable case. In short, no matter how brilliant, how wise, how urgent the opinions of the justices may be, they will remain forever unheard and unsaid unless a case presents itself wherein these thoughts may be appropriately included. No law, no matter how outrageous or how patently contrary to the Constitution, is unconstitutional until the justices declare it to be unconstitutional; and they cannot so declare it until it is challenged by a case or controversy which the procedural rules of the Court permit it to hear.

Secondly, the caseload of the Court is almost entirely discretionary; that is, the Court has the power, in over 90 percent of cases requesting review, to decide which ones it wishes to hear. Furthermore, the number of cases that the Court hears is miniscule compared to the number of cases it *could* theroretically hear, and is a small fraction of even those cases requesting a hearing. For most litigants, thus, the Supreme Court as a court of last resort does not, in reality, exist. The Court itself recognizes that its function is far more subtle and complex than that of the ordinary appellate court. As Justice Frankfurter once said, "After all, this is the Nation's ultimate judicial tribunal, not a super-legal-aid bureau."[2] The Court, in deciding which cases to hear, is not primarily motivated by the justice or injustice of the lower court's verdict, or by the fate of the defendant should the review not be granted.*

---

*There is evidence, however, that the justices heartily dislike, and hesitate to reject cases involving capital punishment where the defendant will be executed in the absence of Supreme Court action. See for example, Barrett Prettyman, Jr., "The Electric-Chair Case," in C. Herman Pritchett and Alan F. Westin, ed., *The Third Branch of Government* (New York: Harcourt, 1963), pp. 83–117.

Its chief motivation is presumably that the question to be decided is of national significance. The Court's formal rules of procedure provide some guidance: for example, cases must arise under the laws or Constitution of the United States and present a federal question for decision; litigants must have suffered a personal injury or damage in order to have standing to sue and must have exhausted all previous remedies. In the last analysis, however, the rules of procedure are only guidelines to be more or less flexibly applied; the Court hears what it thinks is important for the Court to hear, and the definition of "importance," like the definition "national significance," is determined by the justices themselves.

While the members of the Court make the final determination as to which cases will be heard in a given term, it is worth noting that almost all the important cases decided by the Court (especially in recent years) have been shaped to some extent by judicial pressure groups. In *Griswold v. Connecticut* (the Connecticut birth control case) for example, the appellant Griswold was the director of the Planned Parenthood League of Connecticut, and the allegedly illegal acts charged were committed at her direction while acting in her official capacity; PPLC retained the attorneys who defended her and paid for the entire course of litigation; Planned Parenthood of America, of which PPLC was an affiliate, also entered a brief *amicus curiae* at the Supreme Court level. The *Griswold* case, in short, would not have reached the Court for adjudication except for the activities of a group which (at least at that point in its history) existed in large part specifically for the purpose of challenging restrictive legislation in the courts.

Griswold and Planned Parenthood is perhaps an extreme example, but dozens of others come to mind. The American Jewish Congress has been involved in almost all cases where church-state relations have been challenged; the NAACP has been active in segregation cases; and the ACLU has argued in scores of civil liberties cases. Pressure group involvement can take many forms, but probably the most frequent is the presentation of an *amicus curiae* brief at the U.S. Supreme Court level, or the providing of counsel or money to defray expenses at any level of the case. Sometimes a group may provide the litigants (as in *Griswold*) or even witnesses. Although the ACLU and the NAACP are currently the most active and well-known judicial pressure groups, not all such judicial pressure groups represent liberal points of view. Many conservative groups on occasion provide either counsel, financing, or *amicus curiae* briefs for cases in which they are interested. Administrative officials, moreover, frequently band together and act in a manner very similar to the ACLU; for example, in the *Miranda* case, the attorneys general of many states filed briefs *amicus curiae* in opposition to the position taken by the ACLU briefs *amicus curiae*.

Thus, the contribution of judicial pressure groups (whether permanent or *ad hoc*) is to shape the caseload of the Court by making it possible for certain cases to reach the highest appellate levels, and to influence the thinking of the justices themselves by the arguments made before the Court. Even private attorneys sometimes play a role similar to that of a pressure group, as did, for example, Abe Fortas in his appearance for Clarence Gideon, in *Gideon v. Wainwright.* [3]

In 1963, one Clarence Gideon, a drifter with a long criminal record, was convicted in Panama City, Florida, of breaking and entering a poolroom, a felony offense. Gideon, an indigent, had requested court-appointed counsel to represent him at the trial. The request was denied, since Florida law provided court-appointed counsel for indigents in capital cases only. After his conviction, and while confined in the state penitentiary, Gideon appealed, first to the Florida courts (which denied him relief), and then *in forma pauperis* * to the U.S. Supreme Court, on the ground that the failure of the state to provide him with counsel was a denial of his due process rights.

The Supreme Court not only agreed to hear the case on its merits, but appointed Abe Fortas (later Justice Fortas), of the prestigious Washington firm of Arnold, Fortas and Porter, as counsel for Gideon.

In appointing Fortas, the Court was no doubt looking for a competent attorney to represent Gideon; Fortas, in accepting the appointment, was, to be sure, motivated by his desire to help an unfortunate prisoner. It is impossible however, to read Anthony Lewis's splendid study of this case without becoming aware of the fact that at least as important as the concern for Gideon as a man *was the concern, on the part of both the Court and Mr. Fortas, with the state of the criminal law.* [4] The Court was essentially looking for a lawyer good enough to reevaluate the old precedents relating to the right to counsel; Fortas, for his part, was interested in reshaping an area of constitutional law in a manner he thought desirable.

Fortas' role in the Gideon case was very different from the customary role of a lawyer in a criminal case. To begin with, it was unusual for an attorney like Fortas to become involved in a criminal case. Criminal lawyers, for the most part, are not part of the legal elite. (Judge Samuel S. Liebowitz recalled his decision to specialize in criminal law. His dean at Cornell Law School received the news with the same horror a medical school dean might have displayed to a student wishing to specialize in abortions.) Most Ivy League law students aspire to Wall Street or Washington, D.C. firms that specialize in corporate law. Fortas was a member of just such a firm, yet he had appeared on behalf of criminal defendants even though such appearances did not relate in any way to the customary business of his firm or to the area of his usual practice.

Fortas entered the case, moreover, at the appellate, rather than at the trial level, and had relatively little personal contact with his client. Indeed, Fortas never saw Gideon during the entire appeal, nor did he have a financial

*The procedural rules of the United States Supreme Court permit prisoners who are poor and without access to a lawyer to file an appeal in whatever way they can. Appeals have been received and heard from men who have written in pencil on grocery bags and lined note paper —misspelled and ungrammatical, but decipherable.

relationship with Gideon, inasmuch as his services were donated. A more significant difference was that Fortas was not concerned with questions relating to Gideon's guilt or innocence. Gideon, like most defendants in criminal procedure cases before the Supreme Court was almost certainly guilty in fact. Fortas' concern was the *law* of the situation—whether the conviction had been obtained fairly and in accordance with the law. The actions of the state were far more significant than those of defendants.

Questions of law are extremely important. As dangerous to society as an unchecked murderer or rapist may be, his threat to the community is much less fearsome than the threat of unlawful use of power by the state. If the agencies to which we extend the right to use force against individual citizens —police, courts, and corrections officials—do not use their powers properly, our personal liberties are in serious jeopardy. Questions of law are also significant because their solutions provide precedents. A conviction or acquittal has no bearing on future cases, since each was determined by a set of unique facts. But a question, say, of whether the police acted properly has great bearing on future cases. Police action is normally dictated by guidelines for official policy drawn from previous cases. Thus, lawyers who address themselves to questions of law look to the future as well as the present.

Fortas, in this case, though he acted as an individual, did precisely what attorneys affiliated with organized judicial pressure groups do: he discussed the state of the law from a previously determined ideological vantage point. The function of the judicial pressure group or the ideologically motivated attorney is to introduce arguments relating to value systems—the preference for one set of norms over another. To phrase the matter somewhat differently, they argue the case in its political and philosophical context. Those unacquainted with the true role of the U.S. Supreme Court are frequently horrified that such considerations should be introduced. They conceive of the judicial decision-making role in technical terms—as the finding of justice in the law books in a manner analagous to the finding of a good recipe for chocolate cake in a cookbook. But not only is it not nefarious for ideology to enter into Supreme Court arguments, it is vital that such considerations appear. Supreme Court decisions are essays in law, but law conceived in its broadest sense—as the basis on which society rests. In this context, law is almost synonymous with political philosophy. It is healthy and essential that adversaries representing different ideological points of view appear before the Court, because it is from such interchanges that the shape of the law is slowly changed to meet the changing needs of society.

In the last thirty-five years, a large proportion of the major decisions of the United States Supreme Court have been concerned with individual rights. This is probably a reflection of increasing social concern over bureaucratization, centralization, and other institutional changes in our mass society that threaten the uniqueness and integrity of the individual. These decisions have been made in many fields: the rights of blacks to equal treatment in education, transportation, and voting; the rights to freedom of speech and press, and equality before the law for the politically and sexually unorthodox; and the rights of suspects and defendants in criminal cases. It is important to note that concern for criminal defendants is simply part of the larger picture of concern for the rights for all individuals of whatever status and capacity. Concern for criminals is not evidence of weakness in society or of over-permissive attitudes toward evil and violence. It is, instead, merely another manifestation of the struggle to preserve the sanctity of the individual and his personality from the dehumanizing effects of over-mechanization and subordination to senseless technology.

The interest of the United States Supreme Court in the rights of the criminal defendant has gained momentum in the last twenty years. While criminal procedure decisions have been handed down from time to time throughout the entire history of the Court, since World War II their number has been increasing, and in the last two decades they have formed a significant part of the Court's caseload. The earliest decisions in this area attracted little public attention; more recent ones, particularly in the area of confessions and the right to counsel, have been quite controversial and have attracted attention from the public at large, as well as from those directly involved in the law enforcement field. A large number of these decisions have been concerned with the legality of various kinds of police procedures, such as how and under what circumstances the police may arrest a suspect, or search him or his home; whether wiretapping or electronic eavesdropping is permissible; how rigorously the police may question a suspect for the purposes of obtaining incriminating information; how voluntary a "voluntary" confession must be; and when a suspect is entitled to confer with counsel. While police procedure probably constitutes the largest single category of criminal procedure decisions made by the Supreme Court, several other important issues have also been of concern: the conglomeration of rights that ensure a fair trial, such as the right to a jury selected without social or racial prejudice; the right to be free from excessive prejudicial publicity; the right to reasonable bail; the right not to be placed in double jeopardy; and the right not to be subjected to cruel and unusual punishment. All of the cases in the above areas considered by the United States Supreme Court have raised new questions even while they have settled others. Basically, these cases, while seemingly concerned with the technicalities of criminal procedure, are really concerned with the kind of world we wish to live in. The questions that are left unanswered relate not only to the way this world will look, but whether such a world is even possible to achieve.

SEARCH AND SEIZURE

The restriction on the right of the police to arrest is the hallmark of a free society. The basic condition for freedom, as far as any individual is concerned, is that he cannot legally be seized in an arbitrary or capricious manner at the discretion or whim of any government official. It is customary to refer to the writ of *habeas corpus*, the "Great Writ," as the guarantor of personal freedom in a democracy. The reference is correct; but it should be noted that *habeas corpus* is merely a method of remedying wrongful administrative action. The writ of *habeas corpus* is a challenge to an arrest or other detention which has already occurred and which may have been illegal. The statutory and constitutional standards for the making of an arrest are of crucial importance because they prevent police action which may be very harmful to the individual. Furthermore, by establishing a standard for legal action, they make it possible to obtain *habeas corpus* relief from other kinds of action.

No other constitutionally guaranteed personal rights are meaningful in the absence of strict controls on the right of the police to arrest. To say that the individual enjoys freedom of speech or freedom of religion when he or she may be arbitarily arrested for exercising either freedom is a contradiction in terms. In the United States, historically, purely political arrests have been relatively infrequent, at least as compared to the vast numbers of arrests that have been made for criminal activity.* It is very important, nevertheless, that stringent controls be maintained over the right to arrest, for at least three reasons: (1) the Constitution exists for criminal suspects just as much as for any other individuals, and it is important that their rights be protected; (2) erosion of rights in one area leads to erosion of rights in other areas, and the protection of the criminal suspect's rights is essential for the protection of other people's rights; and (3) many activities which are political in nature, such as street assemblies, picketing, and mass demonstrations of all kinds, also fall afoul of the criminal law, and it is essential for political freedom that standards for the enforcement of the criminal law be strict and evenhanded.

The Fourth Amendment of the United States Constitution is the source of constitutional protection from arbitrary arrest.

> The right of the people to be secure in their persons, houses, papers, and effects, against unreasonable searches and seizures, shall not be violated, and no warrants shall issue, but upon probable cause, supported by oath or affirmation, and particularly describing the place to be searched, and the persons or things to be seized.

As interpreted by the courts, the standard for a legal arrest is "probable cause." Probable cause has no precise definition but has been described as something more than mere suspicion and something less than "beyond a reasonable doubt." The policeman, therefore, can arrest only if he has suffi-

---

*If strikebreaking and the resultant arrests are considered political arrests, then political arrests were not, in the past, such a rare phenomenon. Historically, the police were used very frequently, at least up until World War II, as strikebreakers.

cient reliable information to establish a fair degree of certainty that a particular individual has committed an offense warranting an arrest. Similarly, he may search either a suspect or the premises to which a suspect has had access only on the basis of probable cause, rather than on mere suspicion or a hunch; and when he does search he may normally do so only for certain categories of evidence: the instrumentalities of a crime, the fruits of a crime, or contraband (that which it is illegal to possess, such as heroin or policy slips).

Searches and seizures may be made either with or without a warrant. A warrant is an order issued by a magistrate who in effect certifies as to the soundness of the police officer's judgment that probable cause exists. If time and circumstances permit, warrants must be obtained prior to arrests or searches. Frequently, however, the fleeing of a criminal caught in the act or the threat that important evidence will be destroyed will necessitate on-the-spot police action. Such proceedings without benefit of warrant are legal, providing the police officer had probable cause for his actions.

The Constitution forbids unreasonable searches and seizures, but it does not define the term "unreasonable." The courts have held, however, that at a very minimum, an *illegal* search is unreasonable, hence unconstitutional. Theoretically, the police are thus deterred from making any but legal searches and seizures. Practice, unfortunately, does not conform with theory. The police have made in the past, and continue to make at present, thousands of illegal arrests and searches each year. The justification offered for this illegal activity varies with individual cases, but the chief reason is probably that, in the opinion of the officer, the act was necessary in order for him to fulfill his function of maintaining law and order. In the practice of his profession the police officer acquires an expertise which leads him to look upon certain kinds of people in certain circumstances as suspects and to take action against them. The fact that his standards for action vary from the legal standards established by the courts does not deter him, because in his eyes, his standards are both more relevant and more binding than the court's standards which, after all, were established by a judge who likely had never walked a beat. Where there has been a particularly nasty rape, for example, and the victim describes her attacker in general terms, it makes sense to many police officers to round up everyone in the immediate area who looks anything like the assailant. This may or may not result in the arrest of the real culprit; it positively *will* result in the arrest and detention of many entirely innocent people. The courts, presumably, weigh the claims of the community for security from rapists against the need of individuals for freedom from arbitrary arrest. The police officer, however, is not a social scientist, nor does he ordinarily wax philosophical. His job is to find criminals, and he frequently goes about it in the most direct way he knows.

Another reason for the frequency of illegal arrests and procedures in this country is that police forces often see themselves as the agents of the most politically powerful groups in the community—the Establishment. And while they treat members of these groups with respect and even deference, they may treat politically impotent individuals, such as blacks, hippies, petty criminals, homosexuals, and drug users, with contempt or brutality. The illegality of police methods can sometimes be attributed to corruption within the police force. This is less frequent, however, than illegality resulting from the distortions of the police role due to faulty perception of its function and place in society.

It is unfortunate but true that American law enforcement, especially at the local level, has in the past been notorious for the frequency with which police officials utilized illegal methods. Much of this illegality was associated with the attempt to enforce vice laws that were widely disobeyed by the public. At the turn of the century bordellos and gambling houses existed at the sufferance of the police who, for a fee, tolerated such activities. Elected officials generally winked at such corruption for which they, in turn, received a share of the proceeds. When a reform administration was elected, usually after the eruption of some particularly sordid scandal, illegal activities in the poorer parts of the town would stop for a while. More rarely, the better class houses of prostitution and betting parlors would be affected, but inevitably, the demand by the public for the services provided by prostitutes and gamblers, and the rich source of revenue available to the police and the politicians, led to a reopening of the vice establishments and a repeat of the cycle. During the 1920s, prohibition added a new dimension, with illegal saloons and bootleggers providing new sources of illegal money. Still later, public alarm over the increasing popularity of heroin and other drugs created a situation where drug traffic took the place of the former illegal liquor trade. The net result was that it was impossible for most urban police forces to remain honest, and the dishonesty stemming from the taking of graft spilled over into the area of enforcement of laws unrelated to vice. The policeman who operated in a *milieu* where he saw crime ignored for a fee, could hardly be expected to be meticulous about the rights of criminal suspects when he was called upon to enforce the ordinary criminal laws relating to serious *malum in se* crimes. The police frequently took the law into their own hands and operated in the way that seemed easiest and best to them.

While police corruption appears to be much less prevalent today than it was at the turn of the century when cities, such as Chicago and San Francisco, were wide open, there are still episodes of police lawlessness that are reminiscent of the very worst kinds of law enforcement. Consider for example, the operations of the Office of Drug Abuse Law Enforcement (ODALE):

On the night of April 23, 1973, Herbert Joseph Giglotto, a hardworking boilermaker, and his wife, Louise, were sleeping soundly in their suburban house in Collinsville, Illinois. Suddenly, and without warning, armed men broke into their house and rushed up the stairs to the Giglottos' bedroom. Giglotto later recalled, "I got out of bed; I took about three steps, looked down the hall and I [saw] men running up the hall dressed like hippies with pistols, yelling and screeching. I turned to my wife. 'God, honey, we're dead.' " The night intruders threw Giglotto down on his bed and tied his hands behind his back. Holding a loaded gun at his head, one of the men pointed to his wife and asked, "Who is that bitch lying there?" Giglotto begged the raiders, "Before you shoot her, before you do anything, check my identification, because I know you're in the wrong place." The men refused to allow the terrified couple to move from the bed or put on any clothes while they proceeded to search the residence. As books were swept from shelves and clothes were ripped from hangers, one man said, "You're going to die unless you tell us where the stuff is." Then the intrusion ended as suddenly as it began when the leader of the raiders concluded, "We made a mistake."

The night raiders who terrorized the Giglottos that April night were members of a new federal organization called the Office of Drug Abuse Law Enforcement (ODALE). On the same evening in Collinsville, another group of raiders from ODALE kicked in the door of the home of Donald and Virgina Askew, on the north side of town. Virginia Askew, who was then crippled from a back injury, fainted as the men rushed into the frame house. While she lay on the floor, agents kept her husband, Donald, an operator of a local gas station, from going to her aid. Another agent kept their sixteen-year-old son, Michael, from telephoning for help by pointing a rifle at him. After the house was searched, the agents admitted they had made another mistake and disappeared. (Virginia Askew the next day was rushed to a mental hospital for emergency psychiatric therapy).[5]

These ODALE incidents were reported only because the agents had mistakenly broken into the wrong homes. They are perhaps atypical today, but in the not too distant past, such police practices were not uncommon, particularly against southern blacks, or unpopular ethnic or political groups.

It is against this historical background that the criminal procedure decisions of the United States Supreme Court, were made. Earl Warren, chief justice during the period when most of these decisions were made, had been, for seventeen years, a prosecutor in California, during which time he was a first hand observer of police operations. The opinion he wrote for the Court in *Miranda* is hardly flattering to the police, and hints at more than theoretical knowledge of how local police actually function. Critics of the Warren court's criminal procedure decisions have pointed out that the British courts are far less restrictive of their police. The comparison is flawed. The record of the British police in relation to lawful law enforcement is very different from that of their American counterparts.

The exclusionary rule was developed by the courts specifically to restrain the lawlessness of the police. In 1914, for the first time, the United States Supreme Court ruled that evidence seized in an illegal search could not be used in federal courts.* The purpose of this ruling was obvious: to deter

*Weeks v. United States, 232 U.S. 383 (1914). Weeks excluded illegal evidence only if seized by *federal* agents. Illegal evidence seized by state law enforcement could be turned over to federal agents and was admissible in federal courts. This so-called silver platter doctrine was declared unconstitutional by the United States Supreme Court in Elkins v. United States, 364 U.S. 206 (1960), which held that no matter who seized the evidence, if the seizure was illegal, its use in federal court was not permitted.

federal agents from making illegal searches by removing the incentive, that is, by forbidding the use of the seized evidence in obtaining a conviction. Thus, since 1914, no convictions have been obtained in federal courts on the basis of illegally seized evidence. Federal agents have continued, however, to make some illegal searches and seizures. The evidence thus obtained has either been used for the purpose of obtaining leads or informers, or, when appropriate, has been turned over to state law enforcement officials for use in the state courts.

Contrary to federal practice, up until 1950 relatively few states employed an exclusionary rule to deter police lawlessness. In 1949, police in Colorado illegally broke into the office of one Wolf, a physician who was suspected of being an abortionist. They seized his appointment book, which was subsequently used to obtain Wolf's conviction in state court. Wolf appealed on the ground that the use of illegal evidence by the state to obtain a conviction denied him due process of law and thus contravened the Fourteenth Amendment. Essentially, Wolf's claim was that for the state to break the law in order to convict him was basically unfair. A majority of the Supreme Court, in a decision written by Felix Frankfurter, agreed that an illegal search was contrary to the concept of "ordered liberty" and fell within the protection offered by the Fourteenth Amendment, but that the exclusionary rule was not *per se* required of the states. If the states chose to use the exclusionary rule as a method of disciplining their police forces they were free to do so, but there was no constitutional requirement for them to follow the federal practice adopted in the *Weeks* case. Frankfurter pointed out that, as of 1949, only seventeen states were in agreement with the *Weeks* doctrine.[6]

The force of Frankfurter's reasoning was considerably weakened when, three years later, he wrote a somewhat contradictory opinion in *Rochin v. California.*[7] Rochin was a suspected narcotics dealer whose house the police entered illegally. When they entered, they found Rochin in his bedroom, partially dressed, sitting on his bed where his wife was lying. On the night table were two capsules which Rochin seized and swallowed upon seeing the officers. Assuming that the capsules contained illegal narcotics, the police grabbed the suspect, rushed him off to the hospital, and had his stomach pumped. The recovered evidence was used to obtain a conviction. Rochin appealed on the same grounds as Wolf: that the state's use of illegally seized evidence was a violation of the Fourteenth Amendment. This time Frankfurter agreed, not only that the search was a violation of the Fourteenth Amendment, but that the fruits of the search could not be used in court. The police-directed stomach pumping, Frankfurter said, was conduct that shocked the conscience.

Wolf and Rochin, taken together, present a confusing picture. The use of illegally seized evidence was clearly a violation of the Fourteenth Amendment and the evidence could—or could not—be used in state courts to obtain a conviction. The confusion was further compounded when the court held, in *Irvine v. California*[8] that evidence obtained by *repeated* illegal entries by the police into the premises of the accused was admissible for purposes of obtaining a conviction. There seemed to be very little rhyme or reason behind these declarations of admissibility or nonadmissibility, except perhaps the use of physical force on the defendant. Even this rationale was not clear, since the Court upheld a conviction based on the blood samples, drawn without consent from the accused, to prove his intoxication.*

There was, moreover, considerable protest both within and outside the United States Supreme Court against the notion that the states were free to do what was forbidden to the federal government. Many commentators felt that standards of due process must be comparable for state and federal authorities; that is, what is sauce for the goose must be sauce for the gander. The dissenters in the *Wolf* case, moreover, protested that to hold a search illegal but not apply the exclusionary rule was ridiculous, because the exclusionary rule was what made the Fourth and Fourteenth Amendment guarantees against illegal seizures a reality. After several years of confusion and heated controversy, the Court finally resolved the issue in the *Mapp* case[9] by declaring unconstitutional the use of illegally seized evidence in state courts.

Dolree Mapp was a Cleveland woman whose home was entered by the police acting on the basis of a tip that Miss Mapp was hiding a fugitive and/or a large amount of policy paraphernalia in her two-story home. When the officers initially demanded entry, Miss Mapp, after telephoning her lawyer, refused to admit them without a search warrant. Three hours later the police reappeared and forcibly entered the premises. When Miss Mapp demanded to see their warrant, a paper was held up by one of the officers. She snatched the paper and placed it in her bosom, whence it was immediately forcibly retrieved by a police officer who then handcuffed her. In the course of the ensuing search, neither the policy slips nor the fugitive was found. Some obscene literature was discovered in a basement trunk, and on the basis of this evidence Miss Mapp was subsequently tried and convicted of the crime of possession of obscene literature. On appeal, the Supreme Court held that her conviction must be set aside because the requirements of the Fourth Amendment, as incorporated in the Fourteenth, make unconstitutional the use of illegally seized evidence. The Court specifically required the states to apply the exclusionary rule to illegally seized evidence. In *Mapp,* the majority apparently bought the argument of the dissenters in *Wolf:* that the exclusionary rule was the only effective method of deterring police lawlessness and effectuating constitutional guarantees. The Court also noted that, by 1961, more than one half of the states had adopted the exclusionary rule.

Breithaupt v. Abram, 352 U.S. 432 (1957). In all fairness it should be noted that the blood sample was drawn by appropriate medical personnel from an unconscious (and therefore unprotesting) patient. It is conceivable that had the defendant kicked, screamed, or otherwise struggled, or had the sample been taken by police rather than physicians, the decision of the Court might have been otherwise.

While the *Mapp* decision put an end to confusion over the admissibility of illegally seized evidence, it did not, unfortunately, end the problem of illegal law enforcement. Critics claimed that only some of the worst excesses and the more blatant disregard of the procedural niceties were curbed, but other procedures of dubious legality continued unchecked, such as the time-hallowed police custom of indiscriminately stopping and searching "suspicious" people on the street. The police argued that to perform their function of maintaining the peace through preventing crime, they must be permitted to stop and question individuals who look or act "wrong," and they held that the professional expertise gained from years of on-the-street observation gave them a rational basis for such judgment. Others charged that to give the police such wide discretion in the matter of on-the-street stops might expose everyone who was either unconventional or disliked by the police to harassment.

In 1968, three cases came to the U.S. Supreme Court questioning the constitutionality of such on-the-spot searches and questioning. *Terry v. Ohio*[10] involved a suspect who was stopped and searched by an experienced police officer who had observed the suspect apparently "casing" a store for robbery. *Sibron v. New York*[11] concerned a patrolman who questioned, and then reached into the pocket of a man whom he had observed over a period of eight hours to be in conversation with known drug addicts. In *Peters v. New York*[12] the suspect was collared and searched by an off-duty veteran policeman who saw Peters prowling around his (the policeman's) apartment house hallway. In each of these cases incriminating evidence was found: Terry had a gun, Sibron had heroin, and Peters had burglar's tools. Each defendant moved to suppress the incriminating evidence on the grounds that the police in each case had not had probable cause to make either the stop or the search.

In deciding these cases the Court was faced with a number of difficulties, some conceptual and some practical. If the Court were to declare that under certain circumstances policemen need not have probable cause in order to conduct a stop and search, then how much meaning would be left in *Mapp v. Ohio?* If probable cause was not to be the clear-cut constitutional standard for legality in searches and seizures, what standard would take its place? On the other hand, if the Court were to insist on a far higher standard for action than the police had traditionally observed regarding on-the-street stops and searches, would, or even could, the police obey such a decision? Were the police, in fact, correct in maintaining that a more flexible standard for street questioning was essential for proper law enforcement?

The Court decided that an on-the-street stop for brief questioning accompanied by a superficial search or patting down of external clothing was something less than a full-scale arrest and search in the constitutional meaning of those terms, and therefore could be conducted on grounds somewhat less than the traditional probable cause. In *Terry,* the Court felt that the policeman's expertise, acquired through thirty-four years on the job, invested his decision to stop and search Terry with sufficient reasonableness to pass constitutional muster. In *Peters,* the Court split on the question of whether the patrolman had probable cause, or only reasonable suspicion as a justification for his search and seizure of the suspect.* All the justices agreed, however, that the search under the circumstances was not unreasonable. In *Sibron,* however, the Court agreed with the defendant's contention that the policeman had insufficient grounds for his search of Sibron's pocket. The state had justified the patrolman's search on the ground that an experienced officer could logically have deduced from Sibron's lengthy conversation with known addicts that Sibron was selling drugs, since only selling and the negotiations connected with such sales would have required such protracted interaction. The Court rejected this argument and held that the officer had no reasonable grounds for the search.

Very few working police officers would agree with the Court's finding in *Sibron,* and many police officers will see the police action in this case to be fully as reasonable as the police action in *Terry* or *Peters.* This suggests that something more than reasonableness or unreasonableness underlies the divergent result in *Sibron. Terry* and *Peters* were concerned with crimes of violence or potential violence; *Sibron,* however, involved infraction of a morals law. It may be that in balancing the equities, that is, the need of the community for protection against the right of the individual to be free from police harassment, the Court was willing to tip the balance in favor of community protection only where violent crime was concerned, especially in cases where the policeman had reason to fear for his own safety. In *Sibron,* however, the alleged offense was not a violent one, and traditionally it has been in the area of the enforcement of morals legislation that the greatest amount of police harassment of suspects has occurred. In the eyes of the Court, thus, *Sibron* may have appeared to be a case where neither the community nor the policeman was endangered by a *violent* criminal suspect, and the alleged offense was of such nature that an unchecked police force might resort to considerable illegal harassment of suspects. The Court therefore tipped the balance in favor of the defendant, apparently concluding that Sibron was more likely to need protection from the police than the community from Sibron.

To the criticism that in *Terry* and *Peters* the Court was backing away from the *Mapp* decision, Justice Warren responded,

> Street encounters between citizens and police officers are incredibly rich in diversity.... Encounters are initiated by the police for a wide variety of purposes, some of which are wholly unrelated to a desire to prosecute for crime. Doubtless

---

*"It is difficult to conceive of stronger grounds for an arrest short of actual eyewitness observation of criminal activity." Warren, C. J., *Peters v. New York,* at 66. "I do not think that Officer Lasky had anything close to probable cause to arrest Peters." Harlan, J., (concurring), at 74. Truth is in the eye of the beholder.

some "field interrogation" conduct violates the Fourth Amendment. But a stern refusal by this Court to condone such activity does not render it responsive to the exclusionary rule ... it is powerless to deter invasions of constitutionally guaranteed rights where the police either have no interest in prosecuting or are willing to forego successful prosecution in the interest of serving some other goal.[13]

The Court said, in short, that no purpose would be served by too slavish an adherence to the excusionary rule since the exclusionary rule only deterred the police *to the extent that the police wished to carry a case to the courts for prosecution.*

There are many reasons why a policeman may arrest or search other than a desire to prosecute the offender for a crime. The most important of these, perhaps, is that often when a policeman detains a minor offender, he is not so much interested in arresting him as in obtaining him as an informant. Once incriminating evidence is found, it matters little to the suspect that the search was illegal: the path of least resistance is to purchase freedom by supplying the police with information on more important criminals. Even in important cases, moreover, where prosecution rather than information is the controlling consideration, the finding of contraband, for example, inevitably shifts the balance of forces against the suspect. Courts tend to rationalize the legality of police behavior when the results in terms of evidence prove the police to have been correct in their original suspicions. The norms of police organization also put pressure on the police to confiscate harmful objects such as narcotics or weapons, so that even if prosecution fails, the policeman feels that at least he has protected the community to the extent of removing dangerous commodities from circulation. For all these reasons, the exclusionary rule is only a partially effective deterrent to illegal police action, and the *Terry, Peters,* and *Sibron* decisions are not so much a backing-away from *Mapp* as a recognition of the realities and necessities of police procedure.[14]

Other Warren court decisions continued the Court's tendency to approve dubious police procedures which, however, led to obtaining hard objective evidence of the guilt of the accused. In *Davis v. Mississippi,*[15] a 1969 case, the Court indicated that even a dragnet fingerprinting campaign might be permissible if the police had prior permission from a judge. The Court had earlier also permitted the use of evidence of a robber's clothing—"mere evidence" —as opposed to the usual fruits of the crime, instrumentalities of a crime, or contraband.[16] The Court, during this period, also lowered the standards for the use of wiretap evidence and nontestimonial evidence, such as blood and urine samples drawn from the body of the accused. (The use of body fluids as evidence presents Fifth Amendment as well as Fourth Amendment problems. At least one justice—Black—consistently held that if a man's conversation cannot be used to convict him, then neither can his blood, urine, or exhaled breath. Black's concept of *self*-incrimination extended to the flesh as well as the spirit.)

For five years after *Terry, Peters,* and *Sibron,* very few decisions were made by the United States Supreme Court in the area of procedurally defective searches and seizures. In 1973, however, the Court headed by Chief Justice Burger, handed down three decisions, *Cupp v. Murphy,*[17] *Schneckloth v. Bustamonte*[18] and *U.S. v. Robinson,*[19] all of which continued the Warren court policy of permitting the police moderate deviations from procedural norms for the purpose of producing nontestimonial evidence of the suspect's guilt. The decision in *Robinson,* moreover, seemed to eliminate the distinctions the Warren court was willing to recognize in *Sibron.* While all three cases were decided in favor of the police by a majority of the Court, in *Cupp,* Justices Douglas and Brennan dissented, and in *Schneckloth* and *Robinson,* Justices Douglas, Brennan, and Marshall dissented.

In *Cupp v. Murphy,* the estranged wife of Daniel Murphy was found at home, dead from strangulation, with abrasions and lacerations on her throat. Murphy voluntarily appeared at the police station accompanied by his attorney. When the police observed a dark spot on Murphy's finger they asked whether they could take a sample of scrapings from his fingernails. Murphy refused, but the police nevertheless, took samples that turned out to contain bits of blood, skin, and fabric from the victim's nightgown. This evidence, introduced at the trial, resulted in Murphy's conviction. On appeal, the United States Supreme Court sustained the conviction on the ground that the police had had probable cause to arrest Murphy, and therefore, even though no arrest had in fact been made, the search was nevertheless reasonable especially since the evidence might have been destroyed had the search been delayed.

In *Schneckloth v. Bustamonte,* a California police officer, while on routine patrol at 2:40 A.M. stopped a car operating with a burned out headlight and license plate light. Of the six occupants of the car, only one had identification, and the driver could not produce an operator's license. Two additional police officers then arrived, and when the officer asked whether he could search the car, one of the men said, "Sure, go ahead," and even helped by opening the trunk and glove compartment. Under the left rear seat the police found three checks previously stolen from a car wash. Arrests were made, and at the trial the defendant moved to suppress the evidence on the ground that while consent is one of the specifically established exceptions to the probable cause requirement for a search, consent had not been established inasmuch as no showing was made that the suspect knew he had a right to refuse the officer's request. The defendant was convicted, and on appeal the United States Supreme Court sustained the conviction, accepting the state's argument that the defendants, though poor and uneducated, and alone on a road with three armed police officers in the early hours of the morning could reasonably be supposed to be capable of knowing and exercising their right to refuse to permit a police search of their car.

United States v. Robinson was a Washington, D.C. case stemming from the arrest of Willie Robinson at 11 P.M. in an automobile which the police had reason to believe was being driven without Robinson's having an operator's license. In fact, Robinson was driving with a revoked permit, an offense for which District of Columbia law permits a full scale arrest. Robinson was arrested, taken to the station house and searched. In a cigarette package, the police found 14 capsules of heroin. Robinson moved to suppress the evidence on the ground that custodial arrest for a traffic offense was unnecessary and unusual and constituted insufficient legal ground for a complete search. The police also had had no right to open and look inside the cigarette package in Robinson's possession, which could simply have been removed from him. Both the trial court, and ultimately the United Supreme Court disagreed, accepting the counter-arguments of the state: the full-scale arrest was permissible under the statute and therefore was legal. Further, when the police assumed custody of the suspect, they assumed total responsibility for him and therefore needed total control. Such control necessitated a complete search, including a detailed inventory of the suspect's possessions so that he might have his property returned at the proper time.

In all three of these 1973 search and seizure cases, the Burger court denied the claims of defendants, denials which were probably justified from a technical legal point of view. In *Cupp,* the facts strongly suggested probable cause to arrest, and therefore to search, and the fact that the search was made prior to the arrest, was not necessarily significant. In *Schneckloth,* though there was a question as to whether the consent given was truly informed, to have required the police to prove that the defendant knew he had a right to refuse, might in the real world have eliminated the possiblity of any consent searches whatever, since a defendant, after the fact, could simply claim that his consent was uninformed. In *Robinson,* however unusual an arrest for a traffic offense might have been, it was clearly permissible under the statute, and once the defendant was in custody, the police were obliged in the name of safety, to search him thoroughly. Nevertheless, the three cases taken together created the impression that the Burger court was not only continuing the pattern of the Warren court—lowering procedural standards for the police in the interest of obtaining reliable evidence of guilt—but was encouraging the police to make questionable arrests and searches on increasingly technical grounds.[20] This impression was heightened in 1976 by two more decisions in this area: *U.S. v. Watson*[21] and *U.S. v. Martinez-Fuerte.*[22] *Watson,* a rather complex case, involved an informer who told United States postal authorities that Watson had stolen credit cards in his possession. An arrest was made, and the cards were found, (though in Watson's car rather than on his person). The legal problem was that the arrest and search were *warrantless,* even though the authorities had had ample time and grounds to obtain a warrant. *Martinez-Fuerte* involved an arrest of illegal aliens who were found in a routine stop of the defendant's car by customs officials at a check point north of the Mexican border. While customs officials do not need probable cause to stop cars at the border, the question in this case was whether they could stop cars and question occupants routinely *inside* the border. (Because of the physical difficulty of patrolling the entire United States-Mexican border, check points have been established well within the United States where side roads leading from Mexico converge with main United States routes). The Burger court decided both cases in favor of the government, and went on to decide a third case which further restricted the rights of defendants. In *Stone v. Powell,*[23] the Court in a 7–2 decision, ruled that where a state has provided an opportunity of fully and fairly litigating a Fourth Amendment claim of illegal search or seizure, a state prisoner may not be granted *habeas corpus* access to the federal courts for purposes of litigating that claim. The Court, in effect, was removing itself (at least in Fourth Amendment cases) as an overseer of the administration of justice in the states, provided that the state courts made provision for determining whether searches and seizures met constitutional standards.

In 1978, the United States Supreme Court further narrowed the scope of the exclusionary rule. In *Rakas v. Illinois*[24] the Court held, in a 5–4 decision, that an occupant of a car had no right to challenge the illegal search of the car which had produced evidence subsequently used to convict him of a crime. Rakas had been a passenger in a car which was searched illegally by the police. The search produced a sawed-off rifle and a box of rifle shells which did not belong to Rakas, but which were used as evidence in his trial for robbery. Prior to the *Rakas* case, the law gave any occupant of a car the right to challenge the fruit of an unconstitutional search. The Court restricted this right to the owner of the car on the ground that only the owner had a "legitimate expectation of privacy" in the premises being searched. Although both Justice Rehnquist who wrote for the majority, and Justice Powell who wrote a concurring opinion indicated that the ruling might not apply to homes where the expectation of privacy is higher than in a car, the dissenters argued that the majority was protecting property and not people and inviting the "police to engage in patently unreasonable searches every time an automobile contains more than one occupant."

The Burger court clearly does not like the exclusionary rule. Like Cardozo, they deplore letting the criminal go free because the constable has blundered. Some members of the Court, the Chief Justice in particular, have indicated their feeling that communities are paying too heavy a price in loss of security for holding the police to what they see as excessively high technical standards. Yet, the Court has not overruled *Mapp.* For all its defects, and for all the attempts to modify it, the exclusionary rule still stands. The lessons of history have not been lost even on such conservatives as the Burger court majority. The police excesses that *Mapp* was designed to curb were neither minor nor technical, but gross and flagrant. If police performance and legality have improved markedly in recent years, the much abused exclusionary rule must be given a good part of the credit.

WIRETAPPING AND ELECTRONIC EAVESDROPPING

In considering the constitutionality of government wiretapping and electronic eavesdropping, the basic problem is that the authors of the Constitution were not acquainted with telephone taps or electronic microphones. The Constitution talks of invasions of privacy in terms of unreasonable searches and seizures, referring obviously to physical entries by police officials into private premises. With the advent of modern electronic devices, snooping without physical penetration of the premises became a reality, and the question immediately arose whether a search for evidence via a tapped wire, or by means of an electronic listening device, was a search within the meaning of the Fourth Amendment. In *Olmstead v. United States*,[25] a case involving wiretapped evidence against a bootlegger, Chief Justice Taft, writing for a majority of the United States Supreme Court, held that a wiretap was not a search within the meaning of the Fourth Amendment, since there was no seizure of a tangible object, and since the evidence in question was obtained through the sense of hearing rather than by the usual physical act of searching. Four justices dissented vigorously, including Brandeis who protested that the intent of the founding fathers was obviously to protect the right of privacy—the right to be let alone—and that the Fourth Amendment must, therefore, be interpreted broadly enough to handle problems stemming from technological advances. Holmes was repelled by the "dirtiness" inherent in wiretapping and the unattractive role that governmental officials were forced to play.

We have to choose, and for my part I think it is a less evil that some criminals should escape than that the government should play an ignoble part.[26]

Six years later, the question of whether a wiretap was a search within the meaning of the Fourth Amendment was mooted when Congress passed the Federal Communications Act, Section 605 of which provides:

No person not being authorized by the sender shall intercept any communication and divulge or publish the existence, contents, substance, purport, effect, or meaning of any such communication to any person.

The courts subsequently interpreted this passage as applicable to both state and federal agents as well as private persons, and to messages both within the state or between two states.[27] While the average English-speaking layman might thus conclude that wiretapping was made illegal for everyone all over the United States, the United States Department of Justice and the Federal Bureau of Investigation read Section 605 and came to the conclusion that unauthorized interception of telephone messages was permitted *if no divulgence takes place*. Moreover, divulgence in the Department's lexicon was interpreted to forbid publication or use in evidence but to permit use by agents in the preparation of cases for prosecution (that is, as leads). As a result of this somewhat unusual interpretation of Section 605, federal agents continued to employ wiretapping as a method of gathering evidence in federal cases. In 1939, the United States Supreme Court held that neither interception nor divulgence was permissible, and that even leads developed from wiretaps could not be used in federal courts.[28] State agents however, continued to wiretap despite Section 605, and in 1952, in *Schwartz v. Texas,*[29] the United States Supreme Court held that while Section 605 forbade such state action, the state courts were nevertheless not constitutionally compelled to exclude such illegally gathered evidence. Five years later this decision was modified slightly in *Benanti v. United States,*[30] when Chief Justice Warren held that the federal courts must exclude wiretap evidence illegally gathered by state agents, even if there was no collusion between the two sets of law enforcement officials. (Left undecided was the question of whether such evidence could be used in state courts.)

In a very real sense, however, the *Nardone, Benanti,* and *Schwartz* decisions were irrelevant, since both the United States Department of Justice and most of the states continued their operations in total disregard of what the United States Supreme Court had to say. The United States Department of Justice has ordered wiretaps from 1931 to the present time, with the exception of a brief interval in 1941, and has justified this practice by the idiosyncratic interpretation of Section 605 cited above. To criticisms that the Department ought not to be doing what the Supreme Court has so plainly said was illegal, the Department response has been a bland statement that it wiretaps only when "national security" is involved. The United States Supreme Court has been so ineffective in curbing wiretapping that some states passed laws specifically permitting what the federal law prohibits.

> The best known of these state laws is that of New York, which authorizes the state courts to issue orders which permit the tapping of wires for a specified length of time. . . . The Supreme Court of the United States held in 1957 that every New York policeman who taps a wire under one of these orders and subsequently repeats what he has heard is guilty of a federal crime. But, despite the Supreme Court's clear statement that this is a federal crime, New York courts continue to issue wiretap orders, New York police continue to tap wires and to testify in court and the Department of Justice continues to look the other way.[31]

No one today knows how many illegal wiretaps were ordered in the past by state and federal officials, but it is clear that the occasional official figures issued far understated the real numbers, and there is evidence that thousands of wiretaps were authorized annually by law enforcement officials, and in addition, thousands of unauthorized, totally illegal wiretaps were placed by private individuals. To complicate matters even more, the use of electronic devices such as hidden microphones ("bugs") or parabolic receivers, became increasingly popular in contrast to the older method of physical intrusion on telephone wires. For a long time, electronic eavesdropping where there was no physical trespass was covered neither by Section 605 nor the Fourth Amendment,[32] and as a result, eavesdropping by anyone, including private persons, was legal under federal law and in all but seven states until 1968. In six of these seven states, moreover, eavesdropping was legal if done by authorized persons on court order.

In an attempt to remedy the more obvious abuses inherent in this state of statutory and constitutional anarchy, the United States Supreme Court struggled for years to restrict electronic eavesdropping practices without going back to the ultimate constitutional question which had been decided so unsatisfactorily in *Olmstead:* Was eavesdropping by a government official on a private individual's conversation a prohibited search within the meaning of the Fourth Amendment? To avoid upsetting the *Olmstead* decision the Court went so far (in *Silverman v. United States*)[33] as to assert that sticking a spike microphone into a party wall a short distance until it made contact with a heating duct in a house was a physical trespass forbidden by the Fourth Amendment, even though the physical penetration of the microphone into the defendant's premises was miniscule.

The Court also developed the principle that an unauthorized disclosure of a confidential communication is permissible if the disclosure is made by or with the consent of one of the parties to the conversation. In *On Lee v. United States,*[34] an undercover agent of the Federal Narcotics Bureau entered the defendant's premises with the latter's consent and, while conversing with him, elicited several incriminating statements. The narcotics agent had on his person an electronic transmitter which conveyed On Lee's statements to another agent outside the premises. Similarly, in *Lopez v. United States,*[35] an Internal Revenue agent who falsely represented himself as willing to accept a bribe, instead recorded Lopez's illegal offer on a pocket tape recorder. In both cases the Court reasoned that when the defendants made their incriminating statements to parties who subsequently turned out to be undercover agents, they assumed a risk that the other party to the conversation might not be trustworthy. The rationale was a kind of *caveat emptor* policy with relation to conversations. Thus, when James Hoffa made incriminating statements to an undercover government informer who had entered Hoffa's hotel suite under false pretenses, the Court held that Hoffa should not have been so naive as to trust the informer. The majority of the Court felt that the evidence had been obtained not by an invasion of Hoffa's privacy, but rather because of Hoffa's misplaced confidence in the undercover agent.

> The argument is that Partin's failure to disclose his role as a government informer vitiated the consent that the petitioner gave to Partin's repeated entries into [Hoffa's hotel] suite, and that by listening to the petitioner's statements Partin conducted an illegal "search" for verbal evidence....
> Where the argument falls is in its misapprehension of the fundamental nature

and scope of Fourth Amendment protection. What the Fourth Amendment protects is the security a man relies upon when he places himself or his property
within a constitutionally protected area, be it his home or his office or his
automobile. . . .

Partin was in the suite by invitation, and every conversation which he heard
was either directed to him or knowingly carried on in his presence. The petitioner, in a word, was not relying on the security of the hotel room: he was
relying upon his misplaced confidence that Partin would not reveal his wrongdoing. . . .

Neither this Court or any member of it has ever expressed the view that the
Fourth Amendment protects a wrongdoer's misplaced belief that a person to
whom he voluntarily confides his wrongdoing will not reveal it.[36]

Despite the earnest efforts of the Court to avoid reevaluating *Olmstead,* the
question of whether information obtained by eavesdropping or wiretapping
was therefore obtained by an unconstitutional search simply would not go
away. Finally, in 1967, in *Berger v. New York,* [37] the Court overruled *Olmstead*
by holding that conversations are protected by the Fourth Amendment, and
an eavesdrop is a constitutionally impermissible search. Berger was convicted
of conspiracy to bribe the chairman of the New York State Liquor Authority
on evidence obtained by a series of wiretaps placed by the district attorney
of New York County. The wiretaps were placed pursuant to a New York State
law, which authorized certain administrative officials to request a court order
for a wiretap if there were reasonable ground to believe that evidence of a
crime might thus be obtained. The persons to be eavesdropped on and the
telephone number involved had to be specified, and the order was effective
for only two months unless renewed. Berger appealed his conviction by
challenging the constitutionality of the New York State statute under the
Fourth Amendment. The Court reversed Berger's conviction on the ground
that the sweep of the New York statute was far too broad. To pass constitutional muster, reasonable ground would have to be the equivalent of probable
cause, and the crime, the place to be searched, and the conversations to be
seized would also have to be specified.

The *Berger* decision freed Berger, at least temporarily, but it clearly opened
the door to the legalization of wiretapping and electronic eavesdropping.
While the decision did much to end the absurdities and strained interpretations forced on the Court by the *Olmstead* decision, nevertheless, by bringing
conversations under the protection of the Fourth Amendment, the Court
paradoxically opened the door to legalized electronic surveillance. The Court
defined its position even more clearly in *Katz v. United States,* [38] decided
shortly after *Berger.* Katz was convicted of transmitting betting information
in violation of federal law, on the basis of evidence obtained from an FBI bug
of a public telephone. Once again, the conviction of the defendant was
reversed because of procedural irregularities. (In this case, although the FBI
had had sufficient grounds for the search, and had carefully limited the scope

of its surveillance, no proper warrant had been obtained.) At the same time, the Court clearly indicated that electronic eavesdropping is constitutionally permissible under restrictions similar to those required for traditional searches.

In 1968, Congress, taking advantage of the broad hints dropped by the Court in *Berger* and *Katz,* enacted, as Title III of the Omnibus Crime Control and Safe Streets Act, a series of regulations establishing guidelines for legal wiretapping and eavesdropping. The Act is quite complex, but the substance of it tries to create as close a parallel as possible with the traditional restrictions on the usual kinds of physical searches and seizures; that is, the person and place to be searched must be specified, the application must be made by an administrative official to a judge, and the evidence procured may be used only for specific purposes.

Although *Berger, Katz,* and Title III have made contributions towards bringing order into the chaos of the wiretapping and eavesdropping field, confusion, constitutional and otherwise, is still the order of the day. The establishment of legal guidelines has probably not ended the prevalent police custom of illegally tapping and snooping electronically, nor has it ended the totally unauthorized, completely illegal use of eavesdropping by private individuals. Worse yet, the legal guidelines established in Title III have so many loopholes that it is questionable whether any effective control over law enforcement officials has been established at all. For one thing, there cannot be any advance notice to the subject that his premises are about to be searched, as there is when the warrant is produced in a conventional search. For another, although Title III requires the termination of a tap after thirty days (unless an extension is obtained from the court), how can such termination be enforced and/or verified? Is overhearing a conversation a search or a seizure, or both? If a conversation is heard, but not used, is it a seizure, or merely a search? Can there be such a thing as an overheard conversation that is not used? How can a defendant protect himself against a tape that has been tampered with? What controls are there over the police to ensure that the tape recording introduced into evidence is accurate and intact? Is a tap which is conducted over a period of time a single intrusion into the suspect's privacy, or a series of intrusions? If it is a series of intrusions, can it be legally justified on the basis of only one showing of cause? What about the rights of innocent third persons who may be party to the conversations under surveillance? Are not the rights of such persons infringed far more than would be the case in a traditional search?

The inadequacies of Title III were perhaps most glaringly revealed, however, in the national security field. The Act provided for eavesdropping without a warrant for 48 hours in cases involving either national security or organized crime. (After 48 hours the search could be continued only after a warrant had been obtained from a court.) The definition of the terms "national security" and "organized crime" was left largely to administrative discretion however, and most serious of all, the loose wording of the Act encouraged the Nixon administration to claim and exercise investigatory powers unprecedented in American history. This claim was finally challenged in *United States v. United States District Court,*[39] a case involving right-wing political extremists charged with conspiring to destroy government property. In seeking evidence against the defendants, the government had tapped their telephones without a court order, relying on Section (3) of Title III which stated that none of the Act's requirements shall

> ... limit the constitutional power of the President to take [necessary measures to protect] against the overthrow of the Government by force or other unlawful means, or against any other clear and present danger to the structure or existence of the Government.

The Justice Department, headed by Attorney General John Mitchell, argued that in national security matters, the President had an inherent right to protect the nation that was not limited by the customary requirements of the Fourth Amendment; that the President could order electronic surveillance at any time of any person if he, in his uncorroborated judgment, felt national security was endangered. The United States Supreme Court unanimously disagreed, finding that the section of Title III relied upon did no more than declare that Title III did not "legislate with respect to national security surveillance." The government, (in this case, the executive branch), most assuredly was bound by the standards of the Fourth Amendment—in domestic security cases even more than in others—since such cases presented even greater jeopardy to constitutionally protected speech. In somewhat offended tones, the Court rejected the Justice Department's contention that only the executive branch was capable of handling the problems presented by political extremists.

> We cannot accept the Government's argument that internal security matters are too subtle and complex for judicial evaluation. Courts regularly deal with the most difficult issues of our society. There is no reason to believe that federal judges will be insensitive to or uncomprehending of the issues involved in domestic security cases. Certainly courts can recognize that domestic security surveillance involves different considerations from the surveillance of "ordinary crime." If the threat is too subtle or complex for our senior law enforcement officers to convey its significance to a court, one may question whether there is probable cause for surveillance.
>   Nor do we believe prior judicial approval will fracture the secrecy essential to official intelligence gathering. The investigation of criminal activity has long involved imparting sensitive information to judicial officers who have respected the confidentialities involved. Judges may be counted upon to be especially conscious of security requirements in national security cases. . . .[40]

The *District Court* case was followed closely by the Watergate scandal and the forced resignation of President Nixon. Since then, no president has asserted his claim to unspecified inherent powers in the area of national security. With the revelation of decades of shocking illegal activities by the FBI and CIA,* a major effort by the Carter administration has been to draw up legislation which will prevent abuse of the intelligence gathering and law enforcement powers of the government. A bill was introduced in May, 1977, which would extend and strengthen the warrant requirement for electronic surveillance in national security cases and which specifically did not recognize the inherent power of the President to authorize such activity outside the provisions of the bill.[41] This bill, along with several other similar measures are, as of this writing, still under consideration.

Wiretapping, as Justice Holmes said so long ago, is a dirty business. It is probably impossible to conduct a wiretap without violating the civil liberties of the defendant, and the opportunities for lawless police work, harassment, and invasion of privacy are almost unlimited. It is a procedure which raises the hackles of every civil libertarian, but which traditionally has been defended as an efficacious tool in law enforcement which police and prosecutors have maintained they could not dispense with, and should not be asked to give up. Recently, however, critics have suggested that not only is wiretapping "dirty" and dangerous to civil liberties, but it is also far less effective in the fight against crime and subversion than its defenders would have the public believe. Herman Schwartz, Professor of Law at the State University of New York at Buffalo, maintains that wiretapping has had only a very limited impact on organized crime, and none at all on street crime.[42] From the time of the enactment of Title III in 1968 to 1976, federal and state governments installed 5,495 legal taps or bugs and listened in on 3.6 million conversations between 282,429 people for law enforcement purposes, not including hundreds of thousands of people eavesdropped upon ostensibly for national security purposes. Of those place under surveillance, over half were suspected of illegal gambling activities, and one-quarter of dealing in drugs. In 1975 and 1976, over 80 percent of the taps were on small time gamblers and drug peddlers. These taps, moreover, were costly: $11,000 for the average gambling tap, $20,000 for a drug tap, exclusive of the cost of police, prosecutors', and judges' time in preparing and processing the applications.

The breakdown shows that in only 7 percent of the federal cases, none of which involved major crimes, were there convictions for other federal crimes. On the state level, the classic example is that of Special Prosecutor Maurice Nadjari of New York who installed a tap that "operated for almost three months, overheard 123 people in 625 conversations, cost at least $110,000 . . . and never produced a single arrest."[43]

*Government records indicate that the FBI illegally spied on the Socialist Worker's party for well over 30 years, monitoring their mail, wiretapping, bugging, and burglarizing their offices!

Schwartz also suggests that legislative attempts to prevent indiscriminate eavesdropping in national security cases by strict enforcement of the warrant and "probable case" requirements are futile. In reviewing the operations under Title III, he found that while the applications for authorizing wiretaps had to show "probable cause," in the period from 1969 through 1976 only 15 out of 5,563 applications for wiretaps were rejected in both federal and state courts. As long as permission to eavesdrop can be granted in cases where no *criminal* activity is suspected, abuses are likely to persist. It should be noted, moreover, that in the last few years under two Congresses and two Administrations, no one has been able to make a case that noncriminal standards for intelligence eavesdropping are essential for national security. Both Secretary of Defense Harold Brown and CIA Director Stansfield Turner have stated that their respective agencies could function within the Fourth Amendment and that the departure from the Fourth Amendment protections was "principally an FBI requirement."

No happy or simple solution suggests itself at this point to the problems raised by wiretapping. Perhaps the best that can be hoped for is a political culture and climate of public opinion that frowns upon police harassment of individuals and unnecessary intrustions into their private lives. Technology is not an unmixed blessing.

CONFESSIONS AND THE RIGHT TO COUNSEL

In 1649, John Lilburn, on trial for treason, refused to answer questions, saying, "I am upon Christ's terms, when Pilate asked him whether he was the Son of God, and adjured him to tell him whether he was or no; he replied, 'Thou sayest it.' So say I: thou, Mr. Prideaux, sayest it, they are my books. But prove it." The right not to be forced to testify against oneself is historically very old. Talmudic law, a compilation of ancient Hebrew legal dicta, practices, and precendents predating the Christian Era, records the maxim *ein adam meissim atsmo rasha,* a man cannot represent himself as evil.[44] The same notion appears in the Common Law a thousand years later as *nemo tenetur seipsum accusare,* no one is obliged to testify against himself. The principle reappears in the Canon Law of the Catholic Church, and in the Fifth Amendment of the United States Constitution.

The idea that individuals should not be forced to incriminate themselves in a criminal investigation no doubt arose in reaction to the inquisitorial practices of governmental authorities seeking to root out treason, heresy, subversion, or whatever offense or mode of thought seemed most threatening to the *status quo* of the time. Whether the issue involved Catholics rooting out apostate Protestants, Protestants searching for heretical Catholics, the Spanish Inquisition looking for Jews and disbelievers, or the Stuart kings investigating political opponents—whatever the issue historically, investigators and prosecutors have used physical torture to elicit confessions from hapless defendants. It was in reaction to this type of proceeding that the notion of a right against self-incrimination developed. It was the memory of what had gone before that led the founding fathers to incorporate into the Fifth Amendment the phrase "nor shall any person be compelled in any criminal case to be a witness against himself." As Chief Judge Calvert Magruder once said, "Our forefathers, when they wrote this provision into the Fifth Amendment of the Constitution, had in mind a lot of history which has been largely forgotten today."[45]

Traditionally, the U.S. Supreme Court has excluded physically coerced confessions on the ground that such confessions might very well be unreliable or untrue because of the duress used against defendants to produce them. *Brown v. Mississippi,*[46] in 1936, was the first Fourteenth Amendment due process confession case decided by the United States Supreme Court. The conviction of the defendant was reversed when the record was found to indicate that the deputy who had presided over the beating of the defendants conceded that one of them had been whipped, but "not too much for a Negro; not as much as I would have done if it were left to me." The Court, rejecting the law officer's evaluation of black psychology, decided that even a slipshod whipping might make the resulting confession unreliable, and therefore inadmissible. In 1944, the Court rejected a confession obtained after thirty-six hours of continuous interrogation of the defendant by the police.[47] The exclusion of such confessions was, at least in part, an attempt by the Court to discipline lawless police officers by refusing them the convictions they had worked to obtain.

As the quality of police work improved in the years after World War II, the use of severe physical torture by the police declined, at least insofar as cases seeking Supreme Court review were concerned. More recent cases have concerned the use of psychological, rather than physical, pressure on defendants. In *Spano v. New York*[48] the accused was questioned for eight hours by six police officers in relays and was told falsely that the job and welfare of a friend who was a rookie cop depended on his confession. He was also refused contact with his lawyer. The Court reversed Spano's conviction by holding his confession inadmissible because involuntary, but a reading of the majority opinion shows that the Court was moving away from the old unreliability rationale to a new rationale of fairness. There was not sufficient physical force used against Spano to warrant the conclusion that his confession was untrue; but the use of such a confession was repugnant to the Court because it was obviously not a voluntary statement.

> The abhorrence of society to the use of involuntary confessions does not turn alone on their inherent untrustworthiness. It also turns on the deep-rooted feeling that the police must obey the law while enforcing the law; that in the end life and liberty can be as much endangered from illegal methods used to convict those thought to be criminals as from the actual criminals themselves.[49]

In *Spano,* the Court was adding a new dimension to the old unreliability standard: the importance of the state and its agents observing the decencies of civilized behavior. Even if a defendant's confession is reliable and can be independently verified, it must not be used if the defendant was coerced, psychologically or otherwise, into making it. Though this fairness rationale may be new in terms of Supreme Court jurisprudence, it probably hews more closely to the thinking of the old Talmudists than does the unreliability standard, in that the purpose of the old Talmudic law was primarily the preservation of the dignity and integrity of the defendant as a human being. As Dean Erwin Griswold of Harvard (formerly Solicitor General of the United States) has said,

> We do not make even the most hardened criminal sign his own death warrant, or dig his own grave, or pull the lever that springs the trap on which he stands. We have through the course of history developed a considerable feeling of the dignity and intrinsic importance of the individual man. Even the evil man is a human being.[50]

The state, in short, may convict and punish a defendant, but it must not force him to condemn himself out of his own mouth. The current interpretation of the self-incrimination clause of the Fifth Amendment thus enhances a constellation of values: lawful law enforcement, the reliability of evidence used for conviction, and the preservation of the dignity of the accused.

The exclusion of coerced confessions, like the exclusion of illegally seized evidence, is an only partly effective sanction against undesirable police and prosecutorial practices. Unless all confessions are to be eliminated, there is no means of excluding the confession which results from the fear induced in the defendant by the very circumstances surrounding the process of arrest and arraignment. Only the most experienced and hardened criminal can fail to be terrified when surrounded by armed policemen in a strange and forbidding environment, cut off from communication with friends and family, and faced with an accusation which, if proved, may lead to severe punishment. Even the most secure defendant feels panic and bewilderment. Under these circumstances, any questioning by the police is threatening, and any statement by the accused, especially if he is not completely aware of his legal rights, is not really a voluntary statement given with consent based on knowledge. An example of this is the case of Danny Escobedo.[51]

On the night of January 19, 1960, Escobedo's brother-in-law was fatally shot. At 2:30 A.M., Danny was arrested without a warrant and questioned. He made no statement to the police, and was released fourteen and one half hours later, after a lawyer retained by his family had secured a writ of *habeas corpus.* Because of the testimony of one DiGerlando, another suspect who had fingered Danny for the murder, Danny and his sister, the widow of the deceased, were arrested and taken to police headquarters. With his hands handcuffed behind his back, as Danny later testified without contradiction, the "detectives said they had us pretty well, up pretty tight, and we might as well admit to this crime," to which Danny replied, "I'm sorry but I would like to have advice from my lawyer." His request was denied, even after the lawyer arrived and requested permission to see his client.

Escobedo was questioned for several hours, handcuffed and standing up. Finally, a Spanish-speaking police officer suggested to him that, if he pinned the murder on DiGerlando, he could be released. Escobedo, in a face-to-face confrontation with DiGerlando, accused the latter, saying, "I didn't shoot Manuel, you did it." By his statement, Escobedo for the first time admitted some knowledge of the crime, and also acknowledged complicity, an admission which, under Illinois law, is as damaging as firing the fatal shot. On the basis of this and other statements made by Escobedo, he was ultimately convicted. At no point during his questioning had anyone advised him of his right to remain silent, and it was apparent that he was unaware of the legal implications of his statement accusing DiGerlando. His conviction was appealed to the United States Supreme Court on the ground that the police denial of his request to speak to his lawyer made the statements elicited in the subsequent statement inadmissible, because the defendant had, in effect, been denied his right not to incriminate himself. The United States Supreme Court agreed, saying that where

> the investigation is no longer a general inquiry into an unsolved crime but has begun to focus on a particular suspect, the suspect has been taken into police custody, the police carry out a process of interrogations that lends itself to eliciting incriminating statements, the suspect has requested and been denied an opportunity to consult with his lawyer, and the police have not effectively warned him of his absolute constitutional right to remain silent, the accused has been denied "the Assistance of Counsel" in violation of the Sixth Amendment to the Constitution as "made obligatory upon the States by the Fourteenth Amendment," *Gideon v. Wainwright,* and that no statement elicited by the police during the interrogation may be used against him at a criminal trial.[52]

While the Court based its decision on Escobedo's Sixth Amendment right to counsel, the real thrust of the decision was to protect the defendant's *Fifth Amendment right not to incriminate himself.* What the Court was saying, in effect, was that to make the right against self-incrimination a reality for a suspect detained in police custody, the services of an attorney are essential; that most accused persons are too scared, too ignorant, too flustered, and too bewildered to utilize effectively the protection offered by the Fifth Amendment without the support and advice of an attorney trained in the law. The decisions rendered in *Miranda* and its companion cases* two years later add

---

Miranda v. Arizona, Vignera v. New York, Westover v. United States, and *California v. Stewart,* 384 U.S. 436. Miranda was charged with rape, Vignera, Westover, and Stewart with robbery. In each case, the accused was questioned for several hours while in custody. While some of the defendants had been informed of some of their legal rights, none had been effectively informed of either his right to remain silent, or his right to have a lawyer present during questioning. No evidence of physical coercion was introduced, but in *Miranda,* there was some evidence that the "confession" was in police language rather than Miranda's own words. In each case, there was probably sufficient independent evidence for conviction without the use of a confession.

very little conceptually to Escobedo. They simply set down in fairly explicit form the guidelines for lawful police procedure: that a suspect must be warned of his right to remain silent; that he must be told of his right to consult with a lawyer, and have his lawyer with him during interrogation; that if the suspect indicates that he wishes counsel, questioning must stop until counsel is present; and that if the accused is without funds to obtain a lawyer, a lawyer will be appointed for him.

Very few people aware of the realities of police procedure will disagree with the Court on the need for counsel if the accused is to be effectively protected in his right to silence.* The *Escobedo* and *Miranda* decisions have nevertheless created a tremendous furor in law enforcement circles, largely on the ground that the presence of counsel will so inhibit the responses of the accused as to virtually forestall any possibility of a confession or even of information helpful to the police in their investigation. The police, in short, are afraid that if suspects are protected from having to answer questions relating to the crime, investigations will be so hamstrung that the solution of crimes will become impossible.

While it is impossible to determine accurately how damaging *Miranda* and *Escobedo* have been to the police and prosecutorial processes, such evidence as has been gathered by studies of police practices in the years since *Miranda* (1966) indicates that there is not too much factual basis for these fears.[53] For one thing, suspects frequently feel a strong need to talk to the police, either as a form of emotional catharsis, or because of a desire to explain away seemingly incriminating evidence or circumstances. Many suspects, even when warned, could not grasp the significance of what they were told, or in any event could not apply what they were told to the situation at hand. Furthermore the police, even when they gave the required warnings, implied by their tone of voice, or by the selection of the words used, that the warnings were a routine formality and of no great consequence. They encouraged suspects to disregard the warnings and proceed with their statements. In a fair number of cases the police simply ignored the *Miranda* requirements entirely and failed to issue any warning to the suspects. Several conclusions can be drawn from these studies. One could argue that the statistics showing little change in the pre- and post-*Miranda* rate of convictions in selected precincts were due to the nonimplementation of *Miranda* by the police, but there is

*John Griffiths and Richard E. Ayres, "A Postscript to the Miranda Project: Interrogation of Draft Protesters," 77 *Yale Law Journal* 300 (1967). The authors report the results of a study of twenty-one Yale faculty, staff members, and students who were interviewed in their homes by FBI agents in connection with their having turned in their draft cards as a gesture of protest against the Viet Nam War. The authors found that even where the suspects were highly educated, articulate, reasonably mature, and strongly motivated individuals who were questioned *in their own homes* by experienced, professional FBI men, the suspects were unable to understand and make effective use of their constitutional rights. The authors found that nervousness "decidedly impaired their judgment and behavior, and that questioning did not cease even when they stated that they did not wish to answer any further questions."

also considerable data to suggest that: first, suspects talk even when warned (and possibly even after consultation with counsel); and second, that confessions are not always crucial in obtaining convictions.[54]

Despite the lack of evidence that *Miranda* warnings are adversely affecting police and prosecutorial functions, public opinion generally is still hostile to the concept of protecting the rights of the suspect in custody largely because many people attribute the increase in crime to the fact that the courts are too "soft" on criminals.[55] When the Burger court acquired a majority of conservative justices, many critics of the criminal justice system hoped and expected that *Miranda* (along with *Mapp*) would be overturned. Although the Chief Justice himself is apparently in favor of such a move, that has not yet happened, and the advent of the more liberal Carter administration makes it less likely to occur in the future when Carter appointees take their place on the Court.

Miranda has, however, been modified to some extent, principally in four cases decided by the Court since 1970: *Harris v. New York,*[56] *Oregon v. Hass,*[57] *Michigan v. Moseley,*[58] and *Oregon v. Mathiason,*[59] In *Harris v. New York,* the Court, in a 5–4 decision, held that a statement given to the police by an unwarned suspect, while not admissible as part of the prosecution's case, might be brought in as part of the cross-examination of the defendant, should he elect to testify in his own behalf. (The defense, however, presumably could then introduce the circumstances under which the statement was obtained). The Court reaffirmed this line of reasoning four years later in *Oregon v. Hass* which involved a suspect who had been taken into custody and given *Miranda* warnings. The suspect, Hass, indicated to the police that he would like to telephone his lawyer, but was told he could not do so until he reached the police station. Before reaching the station house, Hass made incriminating statements, which, while not used by the prosecutor as part of the state's case, were used to impeach Hass' credibility when he took the stand in his own defense. The United States Supreme Court, *per* Justice Blackmun, affirmed the conviction. Brennan, joined by Marshall dissented, protesting that

> ... after today's decision, if an individual states that he wants an attorney, police interrogation will doubtless now be vigorously pressed to obtain statements before the attorney arrives. . . .[60]

Some months later, the Court considered *Michigan v. Mosely,* a case involving a robbery suspect who, after having been given *Miranda* warnings at the time of his arrest, exercised his right to remain silent. Mosely was then placed in a cell, where, two hours later, a police officer, after again giving him *Miranda* warnings, proceeded to question him about an unrelated holdup murder. This time Mosely neither asked for a lawyer nor indicated that he wished to remain silent. He made several incriminating statements which were subsequently used to convict him. On appeal, the United States Supreme Court in a 7–2 decision affirmed the conviction, holding that while *Miranda* required that interrogation must cease when the suspect indicates he wishes to remain silent, it did not forbid a second interrogation directed toward an unrelated crime. Again Brennan and Marshall dissented sharply.

> ... Today's decision ... virtually empties *Miranda* of principle, for plainly [it] encourages police asked to cease interrogation to continue the suspect's detention until the police station's coercive atmosphere does its work and the suspect responds to resumed questioning. . . .[61]

Two years later, the Court once again narrowed the scope of *Miranda*. In *Oregon v. Mathiason* a parolee was called into a police station, but was not told that he was a suspect or that he was under arrest. The police falsely told him that his fingerprints had been found at the scene of a burglary, where-upon Mathiason confessed. At his trial his attorney attempted, unsuccess-fully, to suppress the confession because the defendant had not been properly given his *Miranda* warnings. The trial court admitted the confession which led to Mathiason's conviction. On appeal, the United States Supreme Court sustained the conviction, 6–3, on the ground that *Miranda* applied only to suspects who were in custody. Since Mathiason had not been formally ar-rested, he was not in custody, despite the fact that in the real world, most people (and parolees *a fortiori*) consider a request to appear at a police station an order, and a restraint on their liberty.

The *Mathiason* decision led some observers to predict that the Burger court would shortly overturn *Miranda,* but only two months later, the Court, over the vigorous protests of the Chief Justice, and in a case involving a particu-larly revolting crime, reaffirmed its adherence to the basic *Miranda* holding that a suspect in custody must be protected from unwittingly incriminating himself. In *Brewer v. Williams,* [62] Williams, the defendant, on the advice of counsel, surrendered to the Davenport, Iowa police to face charges that he had kidnapped and murdered a 10 year old girl in Des Moines. After consul-tation between Williams' attorney and the Des Moines police, it was agreed that the Davenport officials would not question the prisoner while he was being transferred to Des Moines. The prisoner was then arraigned in Daven-port and the *Miranda* warnings given. During the trip to Des Moines the prisoner expressed an unwillingness to be interrogated in the absence of his attorney but stated he would tell the whole story after seeing his attorney in Des Moines. However, responding to one of the arresting officers' pleas that they stop and locate the body of the girl because her parents were entitled to a "Christian burial" for the girl who had been abducted on Christmas Eve, the prisoner made several incriminating disclosures and led the officers to the body. The prisoner was convicted on the basis of the evidence resulting from his disclosures.

In a 5–4 decision, the United States Supreme Court sustained the contention that the evidence in question had been wrongly admitted at the trial. The majority opinion by Justice Stewart held that the prisoner had been denied his constitutional right to the assistance of counsel under the Sixth and Fourteenth Amendments, and in light of the prisoner's assertion of his right to counsel, there was no reasonable basis for finding that the prisoner had waived that right. Among the dissenters, Chief Justice Burger contended that the prisoner had made a valid waiver of his rights, and his disclosures were therefore voluntary and uncoerced.

Miranda, like *Mapp,* is far from a perfect solution to the problem of curbing police and prosecutorial lawlessness without endangering the safety of the community by freeing dangerous criminals. The Burger court, conservative by nature, and sensitive to the justifiable concern of the public over the increase in violent crime, has chipped away at both of these decisions, but it is fair to say that more has been preserved than has been struck down. To the relief of many liberals, and the disappointment of conservatives, the Burger court, to date, has not overturned either *Mapp* or *Miranda* because for all their faults, no one has yet suggested a better way of preventing official incursion on personal rights that would be dangerous, not only to suspects in criminal cases, but to every person in the United States.

FAIR TRIAL AND THE RIGHT TO COUNSEL

The right to counsel, as enunciated in *Miranda* and *Escobedo,* is an adjunct of the right to silence specified in the Fifth Amendment. This is a recent and innovative use of the right to counsel. Traditionally, this right concerned efforts to ensure counsel for the accused *at the time of the trial.* The Sixth Amendment to the United States Constitution provides that an accused shall "have the assistance of counsel for his defense." It is quite clear that this clause means, at the very least, that in a federal trial a defendant who wishes to provide himself with counsel may not be denied the privilege. What is not clear, however, is the degree of obligation on the part of the federal government to provide counsel for an accused too poor to pay for his own lawyer.

As early as 1790, in the Federal Crimes Act, Congress ordered the courts to assign counsel for the defendant in all capital cases. The obligation was not considered to extend to noncapital cases, however, and until 1938, if a defendant charged in federal court with a noncapital crime could not or would not retain a lawyer for his trial, the federal government made no attempt to rectify the situation. In that year, in *Johnson v. Zerbst,* [63] the United States Supreme Court declared that the Sixth Amendment deprives the federal courts of the power to convict a defendant unrepresented by counsel, unless the defendant knowingly and intelligently waives the right. Since the *Johnson* case, counsel has been provided for all accused persons in federal courts.

The right to counsel in the state courts was initially established as a *federal* right in the first Scottsboro case, *Powell v. Alabama.* [64] The case involved nine black boys charged with the rape of two white girls while all were traveling on a freight train through northern Alabama. The boys were charged in an atmosphere so hostile that it was widely understood that only the certainty that the defendants would be convicted and hanged prevented the local residents from lynching the defendants on the spot. The case first came to trial without counsel. A small group of interested blacks attempted to procure counsel for the defendants, who were terrified and virtually illiterate. When the attempt proved unsuccessful, the trial judge appointed all the members of the local bar to act as counsel for the defendants.

In fact, the boys were unassisted by counsel when they went to trial on the capital charge of rape. News of the trial began to appear in the New York press, and the case became somewhat of a political cause celèbre when the defendants were quickly found guilty and sentenced to death despite the very weak case presented by the prosecution. The NAACP, the Communist party, and other interested groups raised funds on behalf of the Scottsboro boys which were used to retain Samuel S. Leibowitz (later appointed to the New York State Supreme Court) to defend the boys. Leibowitz appealed the verdict of the first trial on the ground that Powell had been denied due process of law when he was convicted of a capital crime without the assistance of counsel. The United States Supreme Court agreed that "the failure of the trial court to give [the defendants] . . . reasonable time and opportunity to secure counsel was a clear denial of due process."[65] Furthermore, the Court added, if the defendants were unable through their own efforts to procure counsel, it was incumbent upon the state to provide counsel for them. The Court refused to consider whether this obligation applied to all criminal trials or only to those involving capital offenses, but simply decided, on the basis of the facts of the *Powell* case, that the conviction could not stand.

> Whether this would be so in other criminal prosecutions, or under other circum-
> stances, we need not determine. All that it is necessary to decide, as we do decide,
> is that in a capital case, where the defendant is unable to employ counsel, and
> is incapable adequately of making his own defense because of ignorance, feeble
> mindedness, illiteracy, or the like, it is the duty of the court, whether requested
> or not, to assign counsel for him as a necessary requisite of due process of law.[66]

The *Powell* decision was too closely tied to the facts of that case to permit a substantial broadening of the right to counsel in state courts. Left unanswered were the issues of whether the right applied in noncapital cases as well as in capital cases, and whether it applied to defendants less helpless than the Scottsboro boys. Ten years later, in *Betts v. Brady,* [67] a Maryland case, an indigent defendant was convicted of robbery without benefit of counsel despite his request for legal representation at the trial. The Maryland law provided counsel for poor defendants in capital cases only. The United States

Supreme Court held that Betts had not been denied due process of law by the failure of the state to provide him with counsel. The Sixth Amendment, the Court declared, was not automatically incorporated into the concept of due process of the Fourteenth Amendment, and therefore, counsel could be denied at the discretion of the state where it was felt that the trial on the whole had been fundamentally fair.

Although the majority of the Court, in considering the *Betts* case, seemed to think that Betts was reasonably capable of defending himself in court, the facts when more closely examined do not support this conclusion. Although Betts was a man of normal intelligence, and grasped the principles of cross-examination, he was obviously incapable of analyzing the state's case against him, and pointing out its weaknesses.

> For example, the robbery victim testified: The robber "had on a dark overcoat and a handkerchief around his chin and a pair of dark amber glasses. . . . I told the police that I wasn't sure I could identify him without the glasses and the handkerchief, after seeing him when it was almost dark that evening." The *only* man in the line-up the day the victim came to the jail to identify the robber was Betts. And he could only be identified when he put on the dark coat, the smoked glasses and the handkerchief. . . .
>
> No coat or dark glasses or handkerchief was ever offered in evidence. . . . Although the matter is not entirely free from doubt—because neither trial judge nor prosecutor seemed to care much and Betts evidently failed to realize how this would weaken the State's case—a careful study of the record warrants the conclusion that the following occurred: The victim described to the police the various items the robber was supposed to have worn; the police obtained the requisite coat, glasses, and handkerchief and placed them on Betts; the victim then made his indentification, based largely on the coat, glasses, and handkerchief the police had put on Betts.[68]

The realities of the criminal justice process are such that very few open-minded observers could accept the Court's reasoning in *Betts*. It was obvious then, and became even more so with the passing years, that no one could receive a fair trial without the presence of his own attorney. Certainly, no one suggested that middle-class or upper-class defendants would be likely to go voluntarily to trial without benefit of counsel. After years of unhappiness with the *Betts* decision, and several decisions modifying the dictum therein, the Court finally seized upon an appeal *in forma pauperis* by one Clarence Gideon, for his conviction on a breaking and entering charge in Florida, as a vehicle for reconsideration of the *Betts* rationale. Gideon had requested counsel at his trial and had been denied an attorney because Florida, like Maryland, provided counsel for indigents in capital cases only. When his appeal reached the United States Supreme Court, the Court appointed Abe Fortas to argue the case for Gideon. In deciding the case, the Court finally overruled *Betts*, holding that the right to counsel is a fundamental right, and therefore an integral part of the concept of due process. By implication the Court also held that the Sixth Amendment right to counsel is subsumed and made applicable to the states through the due process clause of the Fourteenth Amendment.[69]

Gideon, (one of the few major criminal procedure decisions of the Warren court to meet with general approval) left, however, certain issues unresolved. Gideon himself was charged with a felony. Did defendants charged with misdemeanors have similar rights to counsel at trial? In *Argersinger v. Hamlin,*[70] the Burger court held that "no person may be imprisoned for any offense . . . unless he was represented by counsel at his trial."[71] Any defendant sentenced to jail or prison thus, must have counsel at trial. Expressly left open by the *Argersinger* majority, was the question of the right to counsel in prosecutions *not* involving imprisonment. The tenor of the decision, however, suggests that the Court is leaning towards a further extension of the right to counsel at trial.

Another related issue is the right of a defendant to conduct his own defense. May the state force a lawyer on a defendant who insists he does not want one? In *Faretta v. California,*[72] the United States Supreme Court held that an accused person has a constitutional right to defend himself if he wishes to. Justice Blackmun, along with Chief Justice Burger and Justice Rehnquist, dissented, commenting:

> If there is any truth to the old proverb that "One who is his own lawyer has a fool for a client," the Court by its own opinion today now bestows a *constitutional* right on one to make a fool of himself.[73]

The *Gideon* decision was confined to a defendant's rights at his trial. Did the principle of providing equal access to justice for the rich and for the poor also apply to a defendant's rights to *appeal* his conviction? As early as 1956, the United States Supreme Court, in *Griffin v. Illinois,*[74] held that all indigent defendants, under the Due Process and Equal Protection clauses, must be furnished free transcripts at least where allegations were made and not denied that manifest errors occurred at the time of the trial. Justice Black observed

> . . . There can be no equal justice where the kind of trial a man get depends on the amount of money he has. Destitute defendants must be afforded as adequate appellate review as defendants who have money enough to buy transcripts.[75]

Seven years later, at the same time *Gideon* was handed down in 1963, the Court, in *Douglas v. California*[76] extended *Griffin* to include not only the right of a free trial transcipt and a waiving of the fees required for an appeal, but the right to an attorney for a first appeal made *as of right.* However, in *Ross v. Moffitt*[77] the Burger court refused to intervene in those states where no provision was made to provide counsel for *discretionary* appeals. Justice Rehnquist explained the reasoning of the court.

... [A] defendant needs an attorney on appeal not as a shield to protect him against being "hailed into court" by the State and stripped of his presumption of innocence, but rather as a sword to upset the prior determination of guilt. This difference is significant for, while no one would agree that the State may simply dispense with the trial stage of proceedings without a criminal defendant's consent, it is clear that the State need not provide any appeal at all. The fact that an appeal *has* been provided does not automatically mean that a State then acts unfairly by refusing to provide counsel to indigent defendants at every stage of the way. Unfairness results only if indigents are singled out by the State and denied meaningful access to the appellate system because of their poverty. ...[78]

As of the present moment, thus, every defendant in every criminal case in every court, state and federal, in the United States, if charged with an offense punishable by imprisonment, is entitled to the assistance of counsel at the trial stage of his case, and also at such times prior to the trial as are necessary for the effective preparation for the trial. He is also entitled to counsel for at least one appeal where state or federal law makes provision for such appeal. His rights to have counsel appointed for him for a discretionary appeal have no constitutional basis, however, and even if one rejects Rehnquist's argument that this is not an unfair discrimination against an indigent defendant, there are difficulties in equalizing access to the appellate process for defendants of modest means. Everyone, as Rehnquist pointed out, has a right to a trial, no matter how weak his case. Not every case presents an obvious ground for appeal, however, and the search for an attorney who can find the proper legal arguments for an appeal may well be expensive, and in many cases fruitless. For most defendants, the quest for justice must inevitably end at the trial court level.*

The presence of an attorney is not the only requisite for a fair trial for the defendant, of course. As important, if not more so, is the right of the defendant to be judged by a jury unprejudiced against him. The problem of prejudice in regard to juries stems basically from two sources: either the jury may be biased by the race, religion, sex, or socioeconomic status of the jurors; or its prejudice may stem from jurors' having fixed or relatively fixed opinions with regard to the guilt of the accused prior to the trial. Regarding bias which stems from race or class considerations, the most thorny problem of the

---

*The United States Supreme Court has not yet addressed itself to the right of an indigent defendant to the services of private investigators and/or expert witnesses such as handwriting experts, pathologists, psychologists, and the like. In some case, such witnesses are essential to the defense case, as, for example in the Sheppard murder case, where the defendant after winning a new trial because of the inflammatory publicity surrounding his original trial, was able to establish his innocence largely on the basis of testimony given by pathologists retained by the defense. A much more serious problem relating to the access of the poor to the courts, is the complete failure of most communities to provide any kind of free legal assistance to litigants in *civil* cases such as divorce proceedings, landlord-tenant disputes, consumer fraud cases and the like. Poor people in many areas are virtually excluded from the relief available from the courts by their inability to retain counsel.

American criminal justice system has been the persistent, widespread discrimination against blacks in the selection of juries.

Following the Civil War, state laws that specifically restricted jury rolls to
white males were struck down by the United States Supreme Court as violating the Fourteenth Amendment.[79] The southern states then retreated to a
policy of unofficial discrimination against blacks, whereby blacks were excluded from juries in practice though not in law. Thus, in the second Scottsboro case, *Norris v. Alabama,*[80] Attorney Leibowitz was able to show through
questioning hundreds of witnesses that no black had served on a jury in the
Alabama county involved within the memory of the oldest living residents,
white or black, and no such service by blacks appeared in any of the court
records. He was also able to demonstrate that there were in the county a
sizeable number of fully qualified blacks who had never been called for
service. On appeal, the United States Supreme Court upheld Leibowitz's
contention that discrimination against blacks could be established by inference from established practice, even though no expressed statutory prohibition existed.

Since the *Norris* case, it is clear that some blacks must appear on the jury
rolls in every jurisdiction in which blacks reside. How many, of course, is
another question, and there is considerable evidence that in some areas to-
kenism has replaced the earlier policy of unofficial total exclusion; that is, one,
or a handful of blacks will be added to the jury rolls in areas where the black
population warrants far greater representation. The courts have thus far been
unable effectively to cope with this kind of discrimination. They have been
able to assure each defendant the right to be tried before a jury on which it
was *possible* for blacks to sit. No defendant, however, has a right at this point
to a jury on which one or more blacks *does* sit. From the point of view of black
defendants (or conceivably even white defendants), it is probably unfair to
be tried before a jury whose racial composition is not representative of the
racial composition of the population at large. It is not clear, however, how the
courts can remedy this situation, and most likely such conditions cannot be
rectified in the absence of willingness on the part of administrative officials
to do so.

Not only blacks are discriminated against by the jury selection system. Poor
people are probably vastly underrepresented on all juries throughout the
United States. The degree to which this is true depends on the particular jury
system used, and systems vary not only from state to state, but from federal
district to federal district. For many years, for example, federal jurors were
chosen under the "key man" system, whereby a prominent member of the
community recommended other outstanding citizens as veniremen. Another
widely used method for both state and federal jury selection is the use of tax
rolls, voting lists, telephone subscriber lists, and the like, all of which tend
to represent propertied, employed, home-owing citizens at the expense of
poorer people.

In 1949, during the prosecution of Eugene Dennis and his fellow leaders of the American Communist party, the defense attorneys tried to challenge the validity of the jury by establishing that poor people, women, blacks, Jews, blue-collar workers, and members of the American Labor party had been excluded from the jury rolls. The judge rejected their contention that the jury · selection was invalid; nevertheless, the defense contention that the jury was unrepresentative was probably true. In March 1968, a federal jury reform act was passed, which requires a random selection of jurors from a "fair cross-section of the community," and forbids discrimination on the basis of race, color, sex, national origin, or economic status. How this is to be accomplished, however, is not altogether clear, and as in the case of racial discrimination, the courts find it difficult to cope with the problem of socioeconomic discrimination in jury selection.

Women present a somewhat special problem in terms of jury selection. Until recently, in many states women could not be compelled to serve on juries, and in some others were not even called for jury service unless they voluntarily entered their names on the jury rolls. Such regulations undoubtedly stemmed from concern for women's domestic responsibilities, especially in regard to the care of young children. Nevertheless, such practices created juries which by their very nature were unrepresentative. In 1975, however, the United States Supreme Court ruled, in *Taylor v. Louisiana*[81] that women could not be excluded as a group from jury service, nor called for service in a manner different from potential male jurors. This decision should result in juries that are more balanced in terms of their male-female ratio. There are, however, other less obvious factors which tend to make juries unrepresentative of the communities from which they are drawn. Judges tend to excuse from service those for whom such service is an economic hardship or a matter of great inconvenience, so that juries frequently have disproportionate numbers of government employees, or employees of large corporations willing to continue salary payments during the period of jury service. Self-employed people, teachers, and manual laborers, among others, are found on juries far less frequently than public utility employees, clerical workers, and corporation officials. Another factor, frequently overlooked, is the manner in which both prosecutors and defense attorneys exercise their peremptory challenges. For a variety of reasons, blacks, women, and young people (along with unusually well-educated or prestigious individuals) are more often challenged than others and juries as finally selected are generally skewed in terms of the number of white middle-aged males.

Juries may also be prejudiced by the jurors having formed opinions as to the guilt or innocence of the accused before the trial. Prejudice on the part of individual jurors is normally handled reasonably effectively through the device of challenging, either for cause or peremptorily. Much more serious, however, is the problem which arises when the entire panel of veniremen may have attitudes antagonistic toward the accused, because of either strong local pretrial sentiment stemming from the status of the defendant or excessive ill-considered pretrial publicity relating to the crime and the defendant. Some trials, such as the Scottsboro trial or the *Frank* trial in Georgia[82] in 1915, are conducted in an atmosphere so filled with hostility to the defendants as to be virtually legal lynchings. In the *Frank* trial, for example, the defendant was a New York-born Jewish manager of the local textile mill, accused of raping a girl employee. The judge gave tacit recognition to the rampant xenophobia and anti-Semitism of the local population by requesting the defendant and his attorney to remain away from the courtroom when the verdict was brought in, lest there be a lynching if a verdict other than guilty as charged were returned. Frank was convicted, and appealed unsuccessfully to the United States Supreme Court on the ground that the atmosphere surrounding the trial had prevented him from receiving a fair trial. Some nights later, while in prison awaiting execution, Frank was taken from the state prison farm by a mob and lynched. His perception of the atmosphere in which his trial was conducted was apparently accurate.

It is unlikely that the United States Supreme Court today would be as insensitive to the claims of a defendant in circumstances similar to Frank's as it was in 1915. Eight years later, in *Moore v. Dempsey,*[83] a case involving black sharecroppers accused of murdering white men who had terrorized the black community, the Court substantially agreed with Holmes's comment in the earlier *Frank* case that "lynch law [is] as little valid when practiced by a regularly drawn jury as when administered by one elected by a mob intent on death."[84]

More troublesome today are cases involving juries inflamed, not by the mere status of the defendant, but by extensive pretrial publicity unfavorable to him as a person and as a defendant. The ultimate in situations of this kind was the publicity given to the arrest of Lee Harvey Oswald for the assassination of President John F. Kennedy in 1963, in Dallas, Texas. It is highly questionable whether, had Oswald lived and gone to trial, an unprejudiced jury could have been impanelled anywhere in the United States, much less in Texas. The quantity and quality of mass media coverage of the crime and the subsequent search for and arrest of the suspect had such enormous, almost universally felt impact that it is doubtful there existed twelve adult Americans of normal intelligence who had open minds as to the guilt or innocence of Oswald. The issue was not joined, of course, because of the assassination of Oswald himself, an act stemming in part, at least, from the self-same publicity.

Oswald's case, fortunately, is unique, but the problem of pretrial prejudicial publicity is not. More typical are cases such as *Irvin v. Dowd,*[85] where reports that the defendant offered to plead guilty if promised a ninety-nine year sentence were widely circulated. Local newspapers also described the accused as the "confessed slayer of six," a parole violator, and a fraudulent check artist. Some 90 percent of the veniremen, when questioned, admitted to some opinion as to his guilt. In *Rideau v. Louisiana*,[86] shortly before the defendant's arraignment and trial, a local TV station broadcast, at three different times, a twenty-minute film of the accused in the presence of the sheriff and two state troopers, admitting in detail, in response to leading questions by the sheriff, the commission of various offenses. Most widely publicized of all was the case of Dr. Samuel Sheppard, a wealthy young osteopath accused of murdering his wife.[87]

Sheppard's family lived in a suburb of Cleveland and operated an osteopathic hospital in the vicinity. The Cleveland press quite early took the position that Sheppard was guilty, and that any investigatory action on the part of law enforcement officials pointing in any direction other than Sheppard's guilt was an attempt to shield wealthy and influential people from the processes of the law, and thus was evidence of corruption. The pretrial publicity given the investigation was intense and virulent.

> Charges and countercharges were aired in the news media besides those for which Sheppard was called to trial. In addition, only three months before trial, Sheppard was examined for more than five hours without counsel during a three-day inquest which ended in a public brawl. The inquest was televised live from a high school gymnasium seating hundreds of people. Furthermore, the trial began two weeks before a hotly contested election at which both Chief Prosecutor Mahon and Judge Blythin were candidates for judgeships.[88]

Not only was pretrial publicity extensive and detrimental to the accused, but the trial was run in the atmosphere of a Roman circus. Reporters were permitted to sit inside the bar, and the goings and comings of the representatives of the mass media created so much confusion that not only could the testimony of witnesses not be heard, but Sheppard was forced to leave the courtroom to consult with his attorney.

> The fact is that bedlam reigned at the courthouse during the trial and newsmen took over practically the entire courtroom, hounding most of the participants of the trial especially Sheppard. . . . The erection of a press table for reporters inside the bar is unprecedented. The bar of the court is reserved for counsel, providing them a safe place in which to keep papers and exhibits, and to confer privately with client and co-counsel. . . . Moreover, the judge gave the throng of newsmen gathered in the corridors of the courthouse absolute free rein. Participants in the trial, including the jury, were forced to run a gauntlet of reporters and photographers each time they entered or left the courtroom.[89]

The names of the jurors, with their addresses and their pictures, appeared in the newspapers both before and during the trial, and the jury itself, although sequestered in the course of the trial, was permitted to make telephone calls freely to friends and relatives outside.

Sheppard was convicted of his wife's murder and, after ten years of motions and appeals (made possible, in part, by his personal wealth), finally succeeded in obtaining from the United States Supreme Court a reversal of his conviction on the grounds that he had not received a fair trial because of the uncontrolled prejudicial publicity surrounding his trial. He was retried by the state of Ohio and acquitted.

In reaction to the Sheppard, Ruby, and Oswald cases, and to the potential for a miscarriage of justice inherent in the mass media coverage of each of them, a good deal of public discussion was engendered as to how such coverage could be restricted to best protect the rights of defendants. In 1967, the Reardon Committee of the American Bar Association made a series of recommendations which would severely restrict statements to the press by law enforcement officials, including police, prosecutors, and court attachés, as well as defense counsel. Such matters as the defendant's prior criminal record, statements including confessions which he might have made, the identity of witnesses, their potential testimony, and speculations as to the guilt or innocence of the accused would all be prohibited. In general, only such details as might be necessary for the apprehension of a fugitive or for the protection of the community would be released. The obvious feeling of the committee was that the less publicity surrounding any trial the better. The proposed restrictions would be enforced either by internal departmental disciplinary procedures against law enforcement officials, by bar association proceedings against private attorneys, or by the use of the contempt power of the judge against reporters and others.

Representatives of the mass media, understandably, disagreed with many of the suggestions of the Reardon Committee. For one thing, the use of the contempt powers of the courts against reporters, while in line with British practice, runs counter to American tradition. On the whole the United States Supreme Court has been reluctant to sustain convictions of reporters for contempt, that is, publication that does not actually obstruct the business of the court. "A judge of the United States," as Justice Holmes once remarked, "is expected to be a man of ordinary firmness of character,"[90] and presumably, therefore, able to shield his courtroom from unwarranted interference or influence by the press.

More important, however, the representatives feel that publicity is not only not necessarily evil, but is an essential good in a democratic society. While willing to concede that excesses and abuses frequently occur in the coverage of trials, they feel that to virtually do away with press coverage of police investigators and trials is to throw out the baby with the bathwater.

Public discussion of major problems in the court of public opinion has proved historically to be a far more potent method of correction of inbred evil or advocating needed change than legal processes limited to the courtroom alone. We should go slowly about adopting rules that would have prevented Attorney General Richmond Flowers of Alabama from commenting on the hand-picked

Liuzzo murder jury, Estes Kefauver from exposing the violent crimes and cor-
rupting influence of the Mafia, or Senator Walsh from denouncing the Teapot
Dome Scandal. Nor do I think that Clarence Darrow's great debate on freedom
of education in the period preceding the *Scopes trial* should have been stricken
from our history.[91]

The critics of the ABA Report correctly point out that the press is a
watchdog against official corruption, and while harm may befall an individual
defendant through improper press coverage, far greater harm may befall all
defendants should public surveillance of police and prosecutorial practices be
relaxed.

The point may be illustrated by a consideration of pretrial confessions.... If a
confession is truly voluntary, it will be admitted at trial, and the damage that the
press may bring about by prior publication will be inflicted against principle but
not practicality. If, however, the confession is coerced and is *not* admitted at trial,
then pretrial news of the confession may hurt the defendant's chances of getting
an impartial jury. But it also constitutes a highly necessary and perhaps the only
notice to the public of police misfeasance. There has been harm to the defendant,
perhaps avoidable. But which was the greater harm to him, the coercion of a
confession, or the publication that a confession was made?[92]

On balance, it would appear that excessive restriction of press coverage
may well be a greater social evil than totally unrestricted press coverage.
There seems no need, however, to select between two such dire alternatives.
Recognition of the problem by attorneys, reporters, and law enforcement
officials and willingness to set reasonable voluntary standards for restraints
should do much to eliminate the worst excesses of the type in evidence at the
Sheppard trial. Trial judges, moreover, have sufficient power, if they care to
use it, to sequester and insulate the proceedings in their courtrooms from the
adverse effects of prejudicial press coverage. Certainly, the circuses that were
permitted to take place under the appellation of trials in the cases cited above
have had a salutary effect in alerting all concerned to the dangers of improperly influencing the judicial process through unrestricted publicity.

The situation does not appear to be so unmanageable as to warrant officially imposed silence, which may lead to even graver evils. It is instructive
to recall that at the height of the Watergate scandal, John Mitchell and
Maurice Stans were acquitted in New York City of charges of obstruction of
justice in connection with an investigation of illegal campaign contributions,
even though the prosecution's case was fairly strong, and public opinion was
quite hostile to the defendants. Similarly, although a predominantly black
Washington, D.C. jury (blacks were considered to be very hostile to the
Nixon administration) convicted Mitchell, Haldeman, and Ehrlichman of
conspiracy to obstruct justice by covering up the Watergate break in, their
codefendant, Kenneth W. Parkinson was acquitted. Even jurors who have

been exposed to extensive pretrial publicity, can, apparently, if handled properly by the presiding judge, render a fair verdict.

The issue, nevertheless, is troublesome and some judges attempt to restrict press coverage of cases brought before them. In a recent case in Nebraska[93] involving an accused mass-murderer who had received extensive adverse pretrial publicity, the trial judge imposed a total ban on all news coverage of pretrial procedures including the preliminary hearing and the selection of jurors. The press and broadcasting media were forbidden to report not only any statements made by the accused which might implicate him, but court proceedings which were open to the public.

The Nebraska Press Association appealed the gag order to the United States Supreme Court as an unconstitutional prior restraint on the press, and the high court, in an opinion written by the Chief Justice, unanimously reversed the Nebraska court. While some of the justices were willing to examine the facts of the case to determine whether the circumstances warranted such press restriction, a majority seemed to express doubt that such prior restraint could ever be justified. While the press was understandably and justifiably relieved by the decision in the *Nebraska Press Association* case, nevertheless, the handwriting is on the wall. If news coverage becomes so inflammatory as to make the proper handling of defendants impossible, there will be further attempts at restraining the media, some of which may succeed. There is no reason to suppose, however, that the news media are incapable of responsible coverage of criminal proceedings, or that a *modus vivendi* between the courts and the newspapers is impossible to reach.

One last consideration in relation to a fair trial is that the right to a jury trial inheres in the seriousness of the punishment for the charged offense rather than the appellation given that offense within a particular penal code. The constitutional provisions regarding jury trial are clearly intended to protect accused persons from serious punishment until after adjudication by *juries.* Traditionally, this has been taken to mean that those prosecuted for felonies have a right to a trial by jury. Recently, however, the United States Supreme Court has broadened this concept to include the right of jury trials in misdemeanor cases where the permissible punishment may be as long as two years in prison. In *Duncan v. Louisiana,*[94] the conviction of a defendant accused of simple battery, a misdemeanor punishable under Louisiana law by two years imprisonment and a three hundred dollar fine, was reversed because the accused's request for a jury trial had been denied by the trial judge. In reversing the conviction the court, after some discussion of the relationship of the Fourteenth to the Sixth Amendment, recognized that some crimes are too petty to warrant jury trials, and defined this category as including at least those where the specified punishment was a maximum of six months imprisonment. The six months standard was later reaffirmed in *Baldwin v. New York.*[95] The *Duncan* and *Baldwin* decisions are regarded with some horror by state and local officials, not so much for the principles they have enunciated as for the practical problems they have created. With court calendars already filled to bursting, the prospect of large numbers of additional cases requiring jury trial is unattractive, to say the least. Should the situation become sufficiently desperate, there is some likelihood that certain misdemeanor punishments may be revised downward to remove them from the required jury trial category. However, two recent cases may have somewhat diminished the constitutional burden that the state courts must and should carry. *Williams v. Florida,*[96] held that a twelve-man jury was a historical accident, and accordingly, a six-man jury in criminal cases does not violate the Sixth Amendment, as applied to the states via the Fourteenth. *Apodaca v. Oregon,*[97] upheld the constitutionality of less-than-unanimous jury verdicts in state criminal cases.

DOUBLE JEOPARDY

The notion behind the constitutional prohibition against double jeopardy is that the state may not get two bites at the apple. A defendant may be tried only once for a particular crime, and the state must then either convict him or forever hold its peace, so to speak. The principal complication that has arisen in the United States, however, stems from the fact that we live in a federal system where there is not one sovereign, but two; not merely federal law, but state law as well.

The Fifth Amendment says, "Nor shall any person be subject for the same offense to be twice put in jeopardy of life or limb." This means quite clearly that if John Robber holds up a federally insured bank in New York State, New York State may try him only once for the crime of bank robbery. The difficulty is, however, that such a robbery is also a federal crime. The federal government may also try Mr. Robber only once. Neither sovereignty has had "two bites of the apple;" nevertheless, Mr. Robber has been tried twice for the same offense. Thus far the United States Supreme Court has upheld the practice of double prosecutions by different sovereignties as not violative of the Fifth and Fourteenth Amendments although in *Benton v. Maryland*[98] the Court ruled that the double jeopardy clause of the Fifth Amendment is applicable to the states through the Fourteenth Amendment. Double prosecutions are a very real problem and violate the spirit, if not the letter, of the Constitution. The federal government, for its part, has attempted administratively to remedy the situation by a voluntary decision on the part of all attorneys general since 1959 not to try federal cases where there has already been a state prosecution for substantially the same act. The states, however, have not reciprocated, and continue double prosecutions not only where a federal prosecution has taken place, but even where local or municipal prosecution has taken place for an act that is simultaneously violative of a local or municipal code.

Another type of multiple prosecution sometimes occurs when the criminal act committed can actually be thought of as more than one act. For example, if while robbing the bank, Mr. Robber takes money first from the teller and then from each of three customers standing in line, his bank robbery can be thought of as four separate criminal acts. If the state were to prosecute him for the robbery of the teller and fail to convict him, should it have an opportunity to try him subsequently for the robbery of each customer? A 1970 case that came to the United States Supreme Court illustrates this problem. *Ashe v. Swenson*[99] arose out of a robbery of a group of poker players by three or four men. Ashe had originally been charged with the robbery of player No. 1, a Mr. Knight. The trial judge instructed the jury that if they thought that Ashe had been one of the robbers they must convict him, even if he had not personally robbed Knight. The prosecutor's case was poorly presented and Ashe was acquitted. Subsequently, Ashe was indicted for the robbery of player No. 2, a Mr. Roberts. This time, the state's case was stronger and Ashe was convicted. He thereupon appealed his conviction to the United States Supreme Court on double jeopardy grounds, contending that his acquittal at his first trial established that he was not one of the robbers, and therefore the state could not try him again, simply by switching victims. The United States Supreme Court agreed, noting that the state, in its brief, had frankly admitted that it had treated Ashe's first trial and his acquittal merely as a dry run for the second trial:

> ... "No doubt the prosecutor felt the state had a provable case on the first charge and, when he lost, he did what every good attorney would do—he redefined his presentation in the light of the turn of events at the first trial." ... [100]

This is what the constitutional guarantee forbids. The general rule is that separate offenses require separate evidence for conviction; that is, if the evidence for all offenses is identical, only one conviction can be obtained.

Jeopardy normally attaches with the swearing in of the first juror at the beginning of the trial. When a person has been acquitted or convicted by a court of competent jurisdiction he may not be retried for the same offense. If, however, the jury fails to reach a verdict, or a mistrial is declared, the accused is not considered to have been placed in jeopardy, and trial proceedings may be reinstituted. (The prosecution may not, of course, for tactical reasons, interrupt the trial and ask for a mistrial if things are going badly for the state. Otherwise, any district attorney who detected an unfavorable response on the part of the jury could throw in the sponge and hope for better things with a subsequent jury.) If the court is later determined not to have had proper jurisdiction, or to have been improperly constituted in some way, the accused may also be retried.

CAPITAL PUNISHMENT

In the United States, the death penalty was a legally and socially acceptable punishment imposed for a variety of serious offenses (chiefly premeditated murder and rape) in many states, from 1789 to 1967, when a moratorium on executions was declared by the federal courts pending resolution of legal challenges to its constitutionality. The popularity and social acceptability of the death penalty, however, declined steadily in the thirty years preceding the moratorium. In the 1940s, an average of 128 people per year were executed; by 1967, only 2 executions took place. The decline in the use of the death penalty reflected growing controversy over its morality and effectiveness. This controversy was translated in legal terms into court challenges to the constitutionality of capital punishment statutes.

The primary ground for attack was that execution, in the twentieth century, was a cruel and unusual punishment forbidden by the Eighth Amendment. Some critics argued that the death penalty *per se* was cruel and unusual: that the state had no right to take a life even as a penalty for murder. Others argued that the manner in which the death penalty was imposed was improper—that judges and juries received insufficient guidance as to the circumstances under which the death penalty would be appropriate. Challenges were also mounted, on due process grounds, to the practice of preventing potential jurors who opposed the death penalty from sitting in capital cases. The death penalty was also attacked on Equal Protection grounds since statistics showed that it was far more frequently applied to blacks than to whites, particularly in rape cases. Of the 455 persons executed for rape since 1930, 90 percent were black. (The death penalty has also been used principally against poor defendants: very few middle- or upper-class persons have been executed in American history.)

As a result of numerous law suits brought by legal defender groups, such as the ACLU and the NAACP, on behalf of condemned prisoners, the appellate courts issued an increasing number of stays of execution until by 1968, no executions were carried out anywhere in the United States. During this same period, several of these cases were accepted for hearing by the United States Supreme Court, which, in 1971, rendered two significant decisions. In *McGautha v. California*[101] and *Crampton v. Ohio,*[102] petitioners claimed that permitting the jury to impose or withhold the death penalty as it saw fit without any governing standards, violated due process. In addition, in the Ohio case, Crampton contended that allowing the jury both to determine guilt and impose the death penalty in a single proceeding created an "intolerable tension" between his right not to testify against himself in the matter of determining his guilt, and his right to be heard on the issue of punishment. The Court, with Brennan, Douglas, and Marshall dissenting, struck down both challenges, holding that it was unnecessary and impossible for specific standards to be enacted for the guidance of the judges and juries in imposing the death penalty, and that the pressure on Crampton to plead his case on the sentencing issue did not conflict with his right not to incriminate himself.

The following year, however, the position of the Court in *McGautha* and Crampton was substantially modified when three cases headed by *Furman v. Georgia*[103] reached the Court. At stake were not only the lives of the three petitioners, but the lives of almost 600 prisoners facing execution throughout the United States. Two of the three cases were from Georgia, one involving murder and one rape, and one involving rape was from Texas. All of the defendants were black and had been convicted after a jury trial. In each case, the imposition of the death penalty had been at the discretion of the judge or jury. *Certiorari* was limited to the question, "Does the imposition and carrying out of the death penalty constitute cruel and unusual punishment in violation of the Eighth and Fourteenth Amendments?" In a *per curiam* 5–4 opinion, the Court struck down the laws of thirty-nine states as well as several federal statutory provisions, and held that the imposition and carrying out of the death penalty under the arbitrarily and randomly administered system then current, violated the Eighth and Fourteenth Amendments. Each member of the five man majority wrote a concurring opinion stating his own position on the issue. Douglas said that while capital punishment might be constitutional, when applied arbitrarily or capriciously, it was unacceptable. The historical record showed most of those executed to have been poor, black, or ignorant; other defendants in similar cases had been given prison terms. Justice Brennan, on the other hand, condemned the death penalty itself as being unusually severe and degrading and serving no purpose that imprisonment could not. Stewart objected to the death penalty because its imposition was as random as being struck by lightning, and White, agreeing with Stewart in substance, found that there was no meaningful way of distinguishing the few cases where execution was used from the many in which it was not. Marshall, like Brennan, held the death penalty itself to be unconstitutional as "morally unacceptable to the people of the United States." The dissenters, led by Justice Burger, disagreed with Marshall and argued that there was no evidence justifying the overriding of the legislative judgment of thirty-nine states. Powell agreed that deference should be shown to the judgments of legislatures, but suggested that in some rape or homicide cases the death penalty might be grossly excessive.

The *Furman* decision left unanswered two questions: (1) was the death penalty *per se* cruel and unusual punishment, and (2) if it was not, under what procedures might it be constitutionally imposed? Five cases, *Gregg v. Georgia*, [104] *Proffitt v. Florida*, [105] *Jurek v. Texas*, [106] *Woodson v. North Carolina*, [107] and *Roberts v. Louisiana*, [108] all decided in 1976, attempted to resolve these questions.

In a 7–2 decision, the Court held, first of all, that the punishment of death was *not* necessarily, under all circumstances, a cruel and unusual punishment prohibited by the Eighth and Fourteenth Amendments. The Court then went on to define the constitutional standards for the imposition of the death penalty. In *Gregg,* the Court upheld the conviction and death sentence of the defendant who had been convicted under a recently enacted Georgia statute providing for a bifurcated jury trial: a first trial for the purpose of determining guilt; and a second trial to determine whether the death penalty should be imposed. The Georgia statute also provided that judge and jury be given information as to aggravating and mitigating circumstances surrounding the crime. It specified the types of aggravating circumstances to be considered, among them murder committed during the commission of another capital felony; murder committed for money; and murder that was "outrageously vile." In order to impose the death penalty, the jury must have found at least one aggravating circumstance. In *Gregg* the jury found two. In addition to the bifurcated trial and the guidelines to the jury for the imposition of the death sentence, the Georgia Supreme Court also was required to review every death sentence for evidence of prejudice or disproportionality. Given the Georgia statutes' procedural protection against arbitrary and capricious imposition of the death penalty, the Court upheld Gregg's death sentence, and let stand on similar grounds, the death sentences of Proffitt and Jurek, sentenced under similar Florida and Texas statutes.

The two remaining cases, *Woodson v. North Carolina* and *Stanislaus Roberts v. Louisiana,* involved death sentences imposed under state statutes which *mandated* execution for any person convicted of a variety of homicidal offenses. No provision was made in either statutory scheme for consideration of either aggravating or mitigating circumstances, or the personal circumstances of the accused—age, mental capacity, or the presence or absence of drug addiction or alcoholism. On these grounds Justice Stewart, writing for the five man majority, held the Louisiana and North Carolina statutes to be unconstitutional. Stewart pointed out that historically, states had rejected mandatory death penalties as being excessively harsh and rigid, and juries had frequently refused to convict under such laws. A state could not eliminate excessive jury discretion in this area by simply mandating the death penalty for a broad range of offenses. Justices Burger, White, Rehnquist, and Blackmun dissented from Stewart's opinion. To them, the North Carolina and Louisiana statutes were constitutionally as acceptable as those of Georgia, Texas, and Florida which the Court had upheld. They saw no objection to a mandatory death sentence for a specifically defined range of offenses. Brennan and Marshall wrote a separate concurring opinion, restating their *Gregg* position: that the death penalty *per se* was unconstitutional—a cruel relic of a less civilized past which society should eliminate.

The *Woodson—Stanislaus Roberts* opinion did not consider the question of the constitutionality of a mandatory death sentence for a very narrowly defined range of crimes. The following year, in *Harry Roberts v. Louisiana,* [109] the Court considered a death sentence imposed under a state statute which mandated execution for anyone convicted of the intentional killing of a police officer engaged in the performance of his lawful duties. While the Court agreed that the offense was far more narrowly defined than in the *Stanislaus Roberts* case, the majority held to the earlier decision that the failure to consider aggravating and mitigating circumstances as well as the personal characteristics of the defendant violated the Eighth and Fourteenth Amendments.

> As we emphasized repeatedly in Stanislaus Roberts ... it is essential that the capital-sentencing decision allow for consideration of whatever mitigating circumstances may be relevant to either the particular offender or the particular offense. Because the Louisiana statute does not [do so], it is unconstitutional.[110]

Blackmun, White, and Rehnquist dissented, protesting that under the plurality opinions of the 1976 cases, the Louisiana provision with its narrowly restricted mandate would be constitutional. Further, as they read it, even the instant decision (*Harry Roberts*) did not rule out all mandatory death sentences, but only those where no opportunity was given for the consideration of mitigating and aggravating circumstances.

Shortly after *Harry Roberts,* the Court modified further the power of the states to impose the death penalty. In *Coker v. Georgia,*[111] an escaped convict who had been serving life terms for murder, rape, and kidnapping, and an additional sentence for aggravated assault, robbed and tied up a man and then raped and abducted his wife. The jury, after convicting him, found sufficient aggravating circumstances to warrant the imposition of the death penalty, which on appeal was upheld by the Georgia Supreme Court. The United States Supreme Court reversed the Georgia court on the question of the death sentence, holding that "a sentence of death is grossly disproportionate for the crime of rape, and is therefore forbidden by the Eighth Amendment as cruel and unusual punishment." The majority felt that where the victim was an adult woman who had not been subjected to excessive brutality or suffered lasting injury, the crime of rape, though serious, did not warrant the death penalty, even in the presence of aggravating circumstances. Burger and Rehnquist dissented complaining that the interpretation of the majority opinion might be overly broad.

> The clear implication of today's holding appears to be that the death penalty may be properly imposed only as to crimes resulting in the death of the victim. This casts serious doubt upon the constitutional validity of statutes imposing the death penalty for a variety of conduct which, though dangerous, may not necessarily result in any immediate death, e.g., treason, airplane hijacking, and kidnapping.[112]

Taken together, the death penalty opinions of the United States Supreme Court indicate a court enormously uncomfortable with the notion of assuming responsibility for the execution, not only of the appellants in the cases before them on appeal, but of the 600 convicted persons awaiting execution in death rows throughout the country. Although the Court in *Gregg* held explicitly that the death penalty in some circumstances was constitutional, it subsequently defined those circumstances so narrowly, that as a practical matter, capital punishment has become quite difficult to impose. Coker for example, had a long history of rape and murder: in 1971 he had raped and murdered a young woman; a few months later he kidnapped, raped, and severely beat a sixteen-year-old girl. In 1974, he escaped from prison and raped another sixteen-year-old girl. Certainly, if a criminal's past history constitutes an aggravating circumstance, Coker's qualifies. Yet the Court refused to permit Coker's execution. The reluctance of the Court actually to allow executions was reaffirmed by two 1978 appeals from Ohio where, once again, the Court found fault with the manner in which the Ohio courts had handled the mitigating circumstances surrounding the crimes.[113] Barring a substantial change in the membership of the court, it seems likely that capital punishment will continue theoretically to be constitutional. It also seems likely that its actual use will be difficult and infrequent.

CONCLUSION

In the last decade and a half, the United States Supreme Court has made more changes in criminal procedure than had been made by the Court in the previous 175 years of its existence. Critics of the Court have charged bitterly that these changes have "coddled criminals" and have reflected an undesireable attitude of permissiveness toward bad conduct. A fair minded review of what the Court has actually done will show that these contentions are not true. The Court has not created any new rights for the criminals; it therefore cannot have coddled criminals or been permissive of their evil ways. *What the Court has done is to equalize the rights of rich suspects and poor suspects.* The Court has not created any new rights, but it has extended to the poor, illiterate, and ignorant accused those rights which have long been known and enjoyed by the middle- or upper-class defendant. The *Miranda* decision created not one right or privilege that was not known and used by defendants who were either experienced or sufficiently affluent to hire good counsel promptly.*

Nevertheless, the critics are right in accusing the Warren court of having

---

*The criminal procedure decisions which have most outraged the public have had surprisingly little effect on the fate of the defendants involved. Miranda, Escobedo, and Mrs. Mapp were all subsequently sentenced to prison. Miranda was convicted of possession of stolen goods in 1967, and sentenced to twenty to thirty years in prison; Escobedo was convicted in federal court of narcotics law violations in 1968 and given a twenty-two year sentence; and Mrs. Mapp was convicted in New York City of possession of narcotics found in her home after a police search with a valid search warrant, and was sentenced to twenty years to life.

created a revolution in the field of criminal procedure. By extending the rights of the rich to the poor, enormous *practical* problems have been created. *Poor people commit more, and more serious crimes, than rich people,* and by giving the poor the treatment that has traditionally been reserved for the rich, the Court is overloading to the point of breakdown our criminal justice system. It is also forcing our society to declare whether it really believes in equality before the law. Many citizens and public officials who are appalled at crowded court calendars, lengthy appellate proceedings, overcrowded prisons, and the need for more and better police work—all of which are to some extent the results of the higher standards enunciated by the Court—have evaded the fundamental issue through rather mindless criticisms of the Court as being soft on criminals. If, however, the criminal justice system is in difficulty today, and it is, the causes are far more basic than weak minds and bleeding hearts on the United States Supreme Court. Either we must abandon the notion of equality before the law without regard to race, color, or socioeconomic status, or we must find another way to *stop creating so many criminals.* While it is true that each individual in a free society has a personal responsibility to obey the law (as a corollary to society's obligation to respect each individual's personal rights), it is only realistic to recognize that, in a statistically predictable number of cases, this responsibility will be evaded or ignored. Either we must improve the socialization process so that fewer young people and adults turn to crime, or we have to restructure our criminal codes so that fewer kinds of actions may be deemed criminal. We must return to the realization that the basic purpose of a criminal code is not to legislate morality, but to legislate against only those forms of immorality which are seriously and objectively known to be socially disruptive. Every society everywhere protects itself against murderers and rapists; not every society must protect itself against gamblers, prostitutes, and drug users.

In fact, in many areas relating to criminal procedure, the United States Supreme Court has taken away rights that suspects previously enjoyed. The standards for legal searches and seizures have been lowered and made more flexible; the rules for the admission of evidence in criminal cases (outside of statements by the accused) have been made less rigid; and wiretapping and eavesdropping have been legalized.

Nevertheless, the record of the Warren court with regard to criminal procedure is, on the whole, one of the high-water marks of American history. Despite the legitimacy of much of the criticism of the United States as a violent, machine-dominated, materialistic, inhuman society, the attempt to protect the rights of the most despised members of society—criminals—is surely an indication that we are more decent, more civilized, and more truly libertarian than many critics, on both the right and the left, are willing to admit. After all, the point about *Miranda* is not what the decision did for Ernesto Miranda, but what it did for the rest of us.

Selected Readings

Abraham, Henry J. *The Judicial Process.* 3rd ed. New York: Oxford, 1975.

Association of the Bar of the City of New York. *Mr. Justice Jackson: Four Lectures in His Honor.* New York: Columbia University Press, 1969.

Cox, Archibald. *The Role of the Supreme Court in American Government.* New York: Oxford, 1976.

Cox, Archibald. *The Warren Court.* Cambridge: Harvard University Press, 1968.

Dash, Samuel; Knowlton, Robert; and Schwartz, Richard. *The Eavesdroppers.* New Brunswick, N.J.: Rutgers University Press, 1959.

Dinnerstein, Leonard. *The Leo Franks Case.* New York: Columbia University Press, 1968.

Dorsen, Norman, ed. *The Rights of Americans.* New York: Vintage Books, 1971.

Ernst, Morris L., and Schwartz, Allan U. *Privacy: The Right to Be Let Alone.* New York: Macmillan, 1962.

Friendly, Alfred, and Goldfarb, Ronald L. *Crime and Publicity.* New York: Twentieth Century Fund, 1967.

Lewis, Anthony. *Gideon's Trumpet.* New York: Random House, 1967.

Meltsner, Michael. *Cruel and Unusual: The Supreme Court and Capital Punishment.* New York: Morrow, 1974.

Miller, Arthur R. *The Assault on Privacy: Computers, Data Banks, and Dossiers.* Ann Arbor, Mich.: University of Michigan Press, 1971.

Niederhoffer, Arthur, and Blumberg, Abraham S., ed. *The Ambivalent Force.* 2nd ed. New York: Holt, Rinehart and Winston, 1976.

Pollack, Harriet, and Smith, Alexander B. *Civil Liberties and Civil Rights.* St. Paul, Minn.: West, 1978.

Pritchett, C. Herman, and Westin, Alan F., ed. *The Third Branch of Government.* New York: Harcourt, 1963.

Radzinowicz, Leon, and Wolfgang, Marvin E., ed. 2nd ed. *Crime and Justice, Volume II: The Criminal in the Arms of the Law.* New York: Basic Books, 1977.

Skolnick, Jerome H. *Justice Without Trial.* New York: Wiley, 1966.

Westin, Alan F. *The Anatomy of a Constitutional Law Case.* New York: Macmillan, 1958.

Westin, Alan F. *Privacy and Freedom.* New York: Atheneum, 1967.

Williams, Edward Bennett. *One Man's Freedom.* New York: Atheneum, 1962.

Notes

1. For a good discussion of the rules of jurisdiction and procedure of the United States Supreme Court, see Henry J. Abraham, *The Judicial Process,* 3rd ed. (New York: Oxford, 1975), pp. 169–243. See also Chapter 1.

2. *Uveges v. Pennsylvania,* 335 U.S. 437 (1948), at 449–450.

3. 372 U.S. 335 (1963).

4. Anthony Lewis, *Gideon's Trumpet* (New York: Random House, 1964). Although written by a journalist rather than a lawyer or constitutional scholar, this is probably one of the best constitutional case studies ever written. Several interesting, though shorter, case studies can be found in Pritchett and Westin.

5. Edward Jay Epstein, *Agency of Fear* (New York: Putnam, 1977), pp. 18–19.

6. *Wolf v. Colorado,* 338 U.S. 25 (1949).

7. 342 U.S. 165 (1952).
8. 347 U.S. 128 (1954).
9. *Mapp v. Ohio,* 367 U.S. 643 (1961).
10. 392 U.S. 1 (1968).
11. 392 U.S. 40 (1968).
12. 392 U.S. 40 (1968).
13. *Terry v. Ohio,* at 13–14.
14. For further discussion of this point, see Jerome H. Skolnick, *Justice Without Trial* (New York: Wiley, 1966), Chap. 10.
15. 394 U.S. 721 (1969).
16. *Warden v. Hayden,* 387 U.S. 294 (1967).
17. 412 U.S. 291 (1973).
18. 412 U.S. 218 (1973).
19. 414 U.S. 218 (1973).
20. For a full discussion of this issue, see Ruth G. Weintraub and Harriet Pollack, "The New Supreme Court and the Police," in Arthur Niederhoffer and Abraham Blumberg (ed.) *The Ambivalent Force,* 2nd ed., New York: Praeger, (1976), pp. 257–268.
21. 423 U.S. 411 (1976).
22. 428 U.S. 543 (1976).
23. 428 U.S. 465 (1976).
24. 439 U.S. 128 (1978).
25. 277 U.S. 438 (1928).
26. Ibid., 2 at 470.
27. *Nardone v. United States,* 302 U.S. 379 (1937).
28. *Nardone v. United States,* 308 U.S. 338 (1939).
29. 344 U.S. 199 (1952).
30. 355 U.S. 96 (1957).
31. Edward Bennett Williams, *One Man's Freedom* (New York: Atheneum, 1962), pp. 113–114.
32. *Goldman v. United States,* 316 U.S. 129 (1942).
33. 365 U.S. 505 (1961).
34. 343 U.S. 747 (1952).
35. 373 U.S. 427 (1963).
36. *Hoffa v. United States,* 385 U.S. 293 (1966), at 300–302. There was vigorous dissent from Justices Warren and Douglas who felt it was basically unfair for the government to use a paid informer as a stool pigeon, especially when, as was true of Partin, he was in prison facing indictment for serious crimes. Douglas remarked that a man may have to assume the risk that a friend will turn against him, but the planting of an undercover agent constituted an unlawful breach of privacy by the government.
37. 388 U.S. 41 (1967).
38. 389 U.S. 347 (1967).
39. 407 U.S. 297 (1972).
40. Ibid., at 320–321.
41. *New York Times,* May 19, 1977.
42. Herman Schwartz, *Taps, Bugs, and Fooling the People* (New York: Field Foundation, 1977), (a pamphlet).
43. Ibid., p. 16.
44. For an excellent discussion of the origins of the right against self-incrimination, see Leonard W. Levy, *Origins of the Fifth Amendment* (New York: Oxford, 1968).
45. Levy, p. viii.
46. 297 U.S. 278 (1936).
47. *Ashcraft v. Tennessee,* 322 U.S. 143 (1944).
48. 360 U.S. 315 (1959).

49. *Spano v. New York*, at 320–321.

50. As quoted in Williams, p. 127.

51. *Escobedo v. Illinois*, 378 U.S. 478 (1964).

52. Ibid., at 490–491.

53. For an excellent brief discussion of the effect of *Miranda* on police practice, see "The Impact of *Miranda* in Practice," in Livingston Hall, Yale Kamisar, Wayne R. LaFave, and Jerold H. Israel, *Modern Criminal Procedure*, 4th ed. (St. Paul, Minn.: West 1974), pp. 592–596.

54. Sidney E. Zion, *New York Times*, November 20, 1965, p. 1. Also note "Interrogations in New Haven: The Impact of Miranda," 76 *Yale Law Journal* 1521 (July 1967).

55. For a discussion of the relationship of procedural protections, the urban courts, and the inadequate handling of criminal suspects, see Alexander B. Smith and Harriet Pollack "The Courts Stand Indicted in New York City," 68 *Journal of Criminal Law and Criminology* 252 (June 1977).

56. 401 U.S. 222 (1971).

57. 420 U.S. 714 (1975).

58. 423 U.S. 96 (1975).

59. 429 U.S. 492 (1977).

60. 420 U.S. 714 (1975) at 725.

61. 423 U.S. 96 (1975) at 118.

62. 430 U.S. 387 (1977).

63. 304 U.S. 458 (1938).

64. 287 U.S. 45 (1932).

65. Ibid., at 71.

66. Ibid.

67. *Betts v. Brady*, 316 U.S. 455 (1942).

68. William B. Lockhart, Yale Kamisar, and Jesse H. Choper, *Constitutional Rights and Liberties*, 2nd ed. (St. Paul, Minn.: West, 1967), p. 225.

69. *Gideon v. Wainwright*, 372 U.S. 335 (1963).

70. 407 U.S. 25 (1972).

71. Ibid., at 37.

72. 422 U.S. 806 (1975).

73. Ibid., at 852.

74. 351 U.S. 12 (1956).

75. Ibid., at 19.

76. 372 U.S. 353 (1963).

77. 417 U.S. 600 (1974).

78. Ibid., at 610–611.

79. *Strauder v. West Virginia*, 100 U.S. 303 (1879).

80. 294 U.S. 587 (1935).

81. 419 U.S. 522 (1975).

82. *Frank v. Mangum*, 237 U.S. 309 (1915).

83. 261 U.S. 86 (1923).

84. *Frank v. Mangum*, at 350.

85. 366 U.S. 717 (1961).

86. 373 U.S. 723 (1963).

87. *Sheppard v. Maxwell*, 384 U.S. 333 (1966).

88. Ibid., at 354.

89. Ibid., at 355.

90. *Toledo Newspaper Co. v. United States*, 247 U.S. 402 (1918), at 424.

91. Judge George C. Edwards, as quoted in Hall, Kamisar, LaFave, and Israel, 3rd ed. p. 1180, fn.

92. Alfred Friendly and Ronald L. Goldfarb, *Crime and Publicity* (New York: Twentieth Century Fund, Inc., 1967), p. 240.

93. *Nebraska Press Ass'n v. Stuart,* 427 U.S. 539 (1976).
94. 391 U.S. 145 (1968).
95. 399 U.S. 66 (1970).
96. 399 U.S. 78 (1970).
97. 406 U.S. 404 (1972).
98. 395 U.S. 784 (1969).
99. 397 U.S. 436 (1970).
100. Ibid., at 447.
101. 402. U.S. 183 (1971).
102. Ibid.
103. 408 U.S. 238 (1972).
104. 428 U.S. 153 (1976).
105. 428 U.S. 242 (1976).
106. 428 U.S. 262 (1976).
107. 428 U.S. 280 (1976).
108. 428 U.S. 325 (1976).
109. 431 U.S. 633 (1977).
110. Ibid., at 637.
111. 433 U.S. 584 (1977).
112. Ibid., at 621.
113. *Lockett v. Ohio,* 438 U.S. 586 (1978); *Bell v. Ohio,* 438 U.S. 637 (1978).

chapter **9**

after conviction: probation, parole, and imprisonment

"He (the convicted felon) has as a consequence of his crime, not only forfeited his liberty but all of his personal rights except those which the law in its humanity accords to him. He is for the time being the slave of the State."

    Rufflin v. Commonwealth (1871)

"I suspect that all the crimes committed by all the jailed criminals do not equal in total social damage that of the crimes committed against them."

    Karl Menninger, *The Crime of Punishment*

The criminal justice process does not end when the defendant is convicted or pleads guilty. He must be punished. Unfortunately, we have not yet developed a theory of what constitutes punishment, or how and on whom it should be imposed. We do not even have consensus on whether punishment (as opposed to therapy or rehabilitation) is necessary at all. Some people think that all criminals (particularly those who have committed outrageous crimes) are sick. They believe in a "disease" theory of crime which implies that criminals should be "treated" rather than punished. Most people, however, believe that at least some offenders, under some circumstances should be punished. But how? Under what circumstances? For what reason? To accomplish what objectives? Should we, for example, punish for vengeance? Do we punish for retribution, because every crime must be balanced by a suitable punishment? Do we punish in the hope that others will be deterred from future crime? Do we punish to protect society by removing a dangerous criminal from our midst? Do we punish in the hope that the criminal will be

205

rehabilitated and turned from his evil ways? Or, do we punish because, when punishment is imposed on the transgressor, the societal bonds are made stronger?[1]

We do not have a clear-cut or consistent philosophy of punishment. Our penal codes generally provide judges with a number of alternative methods for disposing of convicted criminals. Felons may be sentenced to death for serious crimes or imprisoned for periods ranging from a year to life. At the other end of the spectrum, minor transgressors may receive suspended sentences or fines, or may be made to pay reparations or make restitution to victims. Judges also have the option of placing convicted persons on probation, where they will be supervised for a period of time fixed by the court. Criminals who are serving prison sentences may also become eligible for parole after serving their minimum sentences. These judicial options however, are frequently not exercised with any consistent pattern. Consider for example, the following five cases which, though the defendants' names are fictionalized, are taken from the records of a criminal court of a major American city:

Case 1.   Adams, a dull nineteen-year-old youth of a working-class family, was arrested minutes after he accepted a ride from a friend who was driving a stolen car. Adams had had one previous appearance in juvenile court, and had adjusted well after that incident. Indeed his parents, in an effort to improve the boy's situation, had moved from their old high-delinquency neighborhood to a better residential district. Adams was made to plead guilty to a felony and was committed to a reformatory with a five-year maximum sentence.

Case 2.   Baker, an eighteen-year-old boy, while practicing a quick draw with a pistol, accidently killed his sweetheart. He had no previous court record but was committed to a reformatory with a maximum sentence of five years.

Case 3.   Chavez, a twenty-one-year-old man recently arrived from Puerto Rico, impregnated a fifteen-year old girl who had willingly cohabitated with him, evidently with the thought of future marriage. Chavez had no prior record, but his school record was poor, and his work history spotty. He was sentenced to three years in prison for statutory rape.

Case 4.   Downs, in a paroxysm of rage, killed his drunken wife who had nagged and irritated him beyond endurance. Downs had an excellent employment record and was the father of several young children. Following his plea of guilty to manslaughter, he was placed on probation.

Case 5.   Edwards, an eighteen-year-old boy with a poor school and work record, participated in the armed robbery of a supermarket. Despite his unpromising previous behavior, he was placed on probation.

The sentences imposed in the first three cases, whatever else may be said about them, can hardly be thought rehabilitative. In Case 1, the defendant and his family had already made substantial efforts toward his rehabilitation; in Case 2, the defendant had no criminal record at all, and seemed at worst to have been guilty of poor judgment; in Case 3, the defendant apparently had no sense of moral wrong in connection with his offense since he was acculturated in a different social setting. Considering the realities of treatment of offenders in reformatories, it is far more likely that antisocial tendencies would be encouraged in the defendants rather than the opposite by the sentences imposed. The judge in Case 4, on the other hand, avoided committing the defendant to a prison, even though he had admittedly killed a person in a fit of rage. In Case 5 the judge was also apparently willing to risk repeated antisocial conduct by the defendant in hopes of achieving some other goal. One can only speculate on the motives of the judges involved in these cases, but certainly the judges of Cases 1, 2, and 3 seem to have been primarily oriented toward vengeance and retribution, whereas the judges of Cases 4 and 5 seem to have been influenced by a desire to rehabilitate the criminals.

THEORIES OF CRIME CAUSALITY

Both disparity in sentencing and the lack of a consistent philosophy of punishment, stem, in large part, from our inability to develop an acceptable theory of causation of criminal behavior. Historically, various assumptions about why people commit antisocial acts have been made. Early in man's history it was thought that a criminal was possessed of the devil. Accordingly, various rites and ceremonies were elaborated to exorcise the evil spirit. To this day this concept has some vitality, as witness the TV comedian, Flip Wilson, who provokes laughter whenever he has done or said something of a hostile nature by saying, "The devil made me do it."

In the eighteenth century the classical school of criminology assumed that people chose a course of action because it yielded them pleasure. If they committed a crime then the punishment should consist of just enough pain to cancel out the pleasure derived from the criminal act. Classical theory was not based on empiricial research, but was simply an attempt to explain and control criminality. Its focus was on the crime and not the criminal. Cesare Beccaria, the founder of this school, assumed that the criminal had free will in making the hedonistic calculations involved in committing a crime. In writing his *Essays on Crime and Punishment* in 1764, Beccaria reacted against the unnecessary cruelty and unequal sentences imposed at that time. He believed that punishment should be applied equally to all those commiting the same crime, making no exceptions for age, sanity, position, or circumstances. The penal law, he felt, should specify the punishment so that anyone about to commit an illegal act should know the amount of pain to be endured as a consequence. Jeremy Bentham, the English legal philosopher, who was a major proponent of the classical school, in 1825 published *An Introduction to the Principles of Morals and Legislation*. This book along with Bentham's activities proved to be an important influence on English penal practices in the nineteenth century.

The essential rigidity of the classical school in handling all criminals uniformly soon made it imperative that some flexibility be introduced into penal practices. This led to the development of the neoclassical school which not only made exceptions in the cases of children, mental incompetents, and the insane because they were unable to calculate pleasure and pain, but also took into consideration the mitigating circumstances behind the commission of a crime and was less punitive than the classical school.

Some criminologists however questioned the psychology underlying the classical and neoclassical schools and out of these doubts the positivist school, which rejected the concepts of free will and individual responsibility developed. The first of the positivists in sociology was Auguste Comte (1798–1857) who said "man's behavior is caused by social or psychological forces outside his consciousness and therefore beyond his control." An Italian physician, Cesare Lombroso (1835–1909), thought that he had explained crime scientifically when he asserted that persons with a certain shape head or other physical stigmata tended to commit crime. (Nevertheless, he did not overlook the social factors which might influence the development of a criminal.)

Other positivists looked to social, psychological, or economic factors, or a combination of these elements in explaining criminality. Basically, the positivist criminologists explained criminal behavior by attributing it to forces beyond the criminal's control. Consequently, they believed that by changing these pressures, the criminal would become law-abiding. The classicists, on the other hand, believed that a person committed a crime of his own free will and therefore should be punished. The positivists nevertheless, believed that a dangerous criminal might be put to death or imprisoned, not as punishment, but to protect society.

The distinction between the classical and positivist schools was succinctly drawn by Clarence Ray Jeffrey:

> The Classical School defined crime in legal terms; the Positive School rejected the legal definition of crime. The Classical School focused attention on crime as a legal entity; the Positive School emphasized determinism. The Classical School theorised that punishment had a deterrent effect; the Positive school said that punishment should be replaced by a scientific treatment of criminals calculated to protect society.[2]

In a sense, except for the classical and neoclassical points of view, all other points of view (including the sociological, psychological, economic, and demographic explanations of criminal behavior) are positivist, since they are concerned with scientific explanations for criminality, and focus on causative factors outside the criminal and beyond his free will. In the nineteenth century for example, social scientists Adolphe Quetelet of Belgium and Andre M. Guerry of France founded the cartographic school, which theorized that crime was caused by conflicts of values arising when legal norms failed to take into consideration the behavioral norms specific to the lower socioeconomic classes, various age groups, and interest groups living in certain geographic areas. Early adherents of this school, which flourished between 1830 and 1880, saw crime rooted in poverty, misery, and depravity but still held the individual responsible for his behavior. Later proponents merged with the socialist school.

The socialist school of criminology which was based on the writings of Karl Marx and Friedrich Engels began about 1850 and emphasized *economic* determinism. This school was basically interested in economics and only incidentally in crime causation. Postulating that poverty is the result of capitalist ownership of the means of production and the consequent exploitation of the working class, the socialist theorists asserted that poverty caused the poor to resort to crime. Utilizing statistical studies, this group demonstrated that crime rates vary with variations in economic conditions.

In the twentieth century, some positivists attempted to explain crime by setting up typologies of criminal behavior. Criminologist Donald R. Cressey studied embezzlement and tried to describe it in such detail that its etiology would become clear. His results were only partially satisfactory, because as one critic said, his "analysis instructs us about embezzlement, but does not provide a causal explanation [of the crime itself]."[3]

Another modern *sociological* school of positivism asserts that our institutions are criminogenic, and crime, therefore, is an adaptive response to a bad situation. Crime is associated with social, economic, and commercial development and grows as a nation increases its use of technology, brings masses of people together in urban centers, and increases the level of their education and standard of living.

(A)s you expand the bounds of human freedom and economic and social potential, you equally expand the bounds of potentiality for non-conformity and delinquency and crime. As legitimate opportunities increase so also do illegitimate opportunities. As our economic insights now stand, industrialization seems to carry with it urbanization, which in turn carries with it the anonymity, isolation, frustration, discontent, and the enormous criminogenic potential of the city.[4]

All those exposed to the above conditions, however, do not commit crimes. Although many studies have shown a relationship between slums, poor health, unemployment, poor education, broken family life, rejected and neglected children, and crime and delinquency, the vast majority of those subjected to these influences emerge as law-abiding citizens. This fact in itself refutes any allegation that the above factors are "causes" of crime.

Still other contemporary positivists think *psychological* factors are more important than sociological factors in causing crime, though both play a part. The psychological school is a continuation of Lombrosian theory without Lombroso's emphasis on physical appearance. When the Lombrosian school fell into disrepute, its logic and methodology were retained by the mental testers school, except that feeblemindedness was postulated as a cause of crime rather than physical traits. The pioneer American psychologist, H. H. Goddard, in 1914, asserted that the mentally retarded were unable to evaluate the consequences of their behavior, hence they became involved in criminal acts. Goddard's tests showed that criminals were feeble-minded and the feeble-minded were criminals. However, when mental testing became more standardized and objective, with cultural factors being taken into consideration along with comparable control groups, this point of view was discredited and the school of mental testers fell into disrepute.

They were succeeded by the psychiatric school which, at first, postulated psychoses, epilepsy, and "moral insanity" as contributing to crime. However, in time, emotional disturbances, acquired through social interaction rather than biological inheritance were considered to be crime producing factors.

The psychological theories assume that inherent in human beings are impulses of an antisocial nature. Deep in the unconscious are hostile, aggressive forces which each person must learn to control. Those who have not learned to control these drives "act" them out in the form of criminal behavior. Criminals grapple with psychological conflicts and their criminal acts relieve them of the tension and anxiety of the conflicts. Crime is thus a psychological problem solving act.

It is probably fair to say that positivist theories of crime causation and punishment have been predominant in the twentieth century as evidenced by the emphasis on therapeutic and rehabilitative programs of all kinds and the extensive development of probation and parole. Cases 4 and 5, *supra,* illustrate the positivist approach to handling a convicted felon. Downs, who killed his drunken wife while in a fit of rage, was placed on probation in the hope that the strength of character he showed in other aspects of his life would prevent his committing future crimes. Edwards, the eighteen-year-old armed robber, was placed on probation so that he might be helped through therapy to lead a conforming life.

On the other hand, the classical and neoclassical schools have never quite disappeared from the penal codes, and from our attitudes towards crime. Underlying our laws, and in the minds of most people, is the feeling that a crime must be atoned for through the punishment of the criminal. Even where the punishment of the criminal serves no useful rehabilitative or deterrent purpose, there is frequently a strong feeling that the wrong-doer must be punished. The German architects who designed Auschwitz, for example, were brought to trial and convicted more than twenty-five years after the close of World War II. From a positivist point of view punishment at that point was meaningless. The defendants were old men who would certainly never design another extermination camp. Nor would their punishment deter future architects from designing future barbarities. Yet, most people felt that these war criminals should be punished because the great wrong they did had to be proclaimed as such by the severity of the punishment inflicted on them. While the positivist and classical schools are useful conceptual schemes, in the real world, neither is completely satisfactory, and most people's attitudes are a somewhat inconsistent amalgam of the two.

SENTENCING

If there is no agreement on what causes crime, there can be no agreement on how criminals should be handled. If criminals are sick they should be treated, but if they are bad they should be punished. Judges, juries, probation, parole, and corrections officials do not handle all cases in a uniform manner but vacillate, sometimes unpredictably, between these two polar positions. One cause of sentence disparity, thus, is the lack of a consistent theory of crime causation and punishment.

There are, however, at least three other causes for sentence disparity which warrant examination. The expectations of a particular community are a second major variable in sentencing procedures. An area as large as the United States, or indeed as large as many of the larger states, is heterogeneous both geographically and culturally. What is an appropriate sentence for holding up a drugstore in Chicago may be totally inappropriate for the same offense in Cornwall Bridge, Connecticut. Forcible rape sentences vary considerably from community to community, depending on the section of the country and on the race of the victim as compared to that of the criminal. In small towns where informal social controls over the individual tend to be quite strong and effective, sentences for the offender who flouts those controls tend to be more severe. Conversely, the anonymity, or even anomia, of the big city tends to soften the sharpness of social disapproval of the criminal, which reflects itself in shorter, less severe sentences. Racial, ethnic, and other class prejudices that are idiosyncratic to particular communities will also affect the severity of punishment.

A third major variable in sentencing is the personality of the judge himself. Very little has been written about how the judge as a person influences the judge as a judge. Criminologists Winick, Blumberg, and Gerver, in a study of judicial psychology, list some of the personal variables that affect the decision-making process: age, sex, ethnic background, nationality, religion, race, marital status, socioeconomic status, law school, and background of legal practice. In another study, Smith and Blumberg related judicial personality factors to the context in which judicial decisions are made, that is, the socio-legal courtroom milieu.[5]

Personality variables are particularly significant in the area of sentencing, since there are very few formal guidelines or standards to narrow the range of alternatives available to the judge. Unless he comes to his position in the criminal court with a background of experience in sentencing, there are few places where he can seek guidance aside from the wide limits defined in the statutes and the specific precedents established in reported judicial decisions. An American judge, unlike some of his continental counterparts, receives training only as a lawyer, not as a judge. Certainly the law school curricula do not focus on the special needs of judges sitting in criminal court. There is, in short, no specific preparation for this highly important position in our society, and an intuitive understanding of the requirements of sentencing is as much as can be expected or hoped for from any newly appointed sitting judge.

A fourth factor contributing to sentence disparity stems from the pressures engendered by the day-to-day operations of the criminal courts. In many urban jurisdictions, the courts, and sometimes the prison and detention facilities, are so overloaded that defendants must be disposed of at almost any cost. Frequently this means that some serious offenders are given inappropriately light sentences; others, who have committed crimes no more reprehensible, but for whom a courtroom, jury or prison cell can be found, will be punished much more severely. It is well known that in many urban jurisdictions as many as 90 percent of felony cases are handled through plea bargaining. What is not so well known is that increasingly plea bargaining has tended to become sentence bargaining, that is, the defendant bargains, not so much for the formal label that will eventually be attached to his offense in the final judgment of the court, as for the sentence that will be imposed. He doesn't care if his offense is called robbery or attempted grand larceny. He cares only if he will go to prison rather than be placed on probation, or if he knows he is to go to prison, for how long. So desperate is the condition of many of our urban courts that pragmatic necessity has become the overriding cause of sentence disparity in recent years. In addition to the tremendous pressure on the courts, in many states, there is an acute shortage of prison beds which has a very similar effect in creating sentence disparities.

HANDLING SENTENCE DISPARITY

Since the latter part of the nineteenth century, it has been customary in the United States for legislatures, reflecting the growing predominance of the positivist philosophy of crime causation and punishment, to prescribe not one, but a range of punishments for a given offense. Armed robbery, for example, might carry a punishment of 5–10, or even 1–20 years in prison. In addition to the wide range of prison sentences possible for a given offense, the possibility of either probation in lieu of imprisonment, of parole in lieu of part of a prison sentence, has added further flexibility to the handling of an individual offender. It is this legislatively created flexibility which makes possible the phenomenon of sentence disparity.

Underlying the positivist philosophy is the notion that sentence disparity is a positive good, that is, that since individuals and their circumstances differ, sentences should also. In recent years, however, many segments of society have become increasingly critical of disparate sentences. Some groups, who have returned to the thinking of the early classical school, feel that punishment should fit the crime, not the criminal. A murder deserves "X" years in prison, a robbery "Y" years. What difference does it make why the crime was committed or by whom? The impact on the victim and on society is the same.

Besides this criticism, which stems from the notion of punishment as retribution or vengeance, other criticisms of sentence disparity have surfaced. Some critics complain that the notion of rehabilitation which underlies flexible sentencing is fine theoretically, but in practice does not work. Sociologist Robert Martinson, in a 1974 study, evaluated 231 rehabilitative programs, and using the criterion of the impact of these programs on recidivism, he concluded that, with a few isolated exceptions, they were ineffective and could not "overcome or even appreciably reduce the powerful tendency for offenders to continue in criminal behavior." Martinson's research suggested that rehabilitation was not a realistic goal for correctional systems and therefore punishment should be based on other grounds, principally protection of the community or revenge.*

Another objection to disparate sentencing has been raised by inmates who see fellow prisoners who have committed the same crime, but who have been sentenced to shorter prison terms. Even where, from the point of view of the judges or parole officials, the disparity in sentencing is justified by the differences in the circumstances of the offenders involved, from the point of view

---

*Many social scientists and legislators who joined the "nothing works" Martinson bandwagon which advocated scrapping all treatment programs, were either unaware that Martinson had reported a few programs which had positive outcomes or, like Martinson, they disregarded these positive results which held out promise for the rehabilitation of criminal offenders. However, in a subsequent study reported by Selwyn Raab in the *New York Times* of November 7, 1976, p. 61, Martinson and his colleague Judith Wilks reversed their earlier judgment that nothing worked and announced new conclusions stemming from a later research project involving former inmates of correctional institutions. They found that released prisoners under parole supeervision had a return rate of 25.3 percent compared with 31.5 percent for those discharged without parole supervision. Martinson and Wilks emphasized the same results in an article "Save Parole Supervision" (*Federal Probation,* September 1977, pp. 23–27) in which they concluded, "The evidence seems to indicate that the abolition of parole supervision would result in substantial increases in arrest, conviction, and return to prison." In respect to the three dimensions of rearrest, new convictions, and new prison sentences, the parolees demonstrated better results as compared to inmates released after serving their full sentences: rearrest-parolees 24.5 percent v. maximum/sentence discharged inmates 42.9 percent; new convictions-parolees 19.7 percent v. maximum sentence discharged prisoners 29.9 percent; and, new prison sentences parolees 10.5 percent v. maximum sentence prisoners 14.8 percent.

of the inmate serving a term for armed robbery who sees another armed robber released years before he can hope for a release, the situation is enormously frustrating. Inmate frustration, in turn, creates problems for prison administrators, so that they too, object to widely varying sentences.

Finally, many critics have pointed out that it is wrong, on both theoretical and practical grounds, for public officials in a democratic society to be permitted to wield power with a discretion that is virtually unchecked. Traditionally, the decisions of parole boards are final and unappealable; they are not required to state on what grounds parole will be granted or on what grounds it will be refused. The inmate whose parole has been denied has no way of knowing why his request was denied, nor what he can do to remedy the situation. Many inmates, particularly blacks and political radicals, feel that the unchecked discretionary power of the parole board has been widely used either for racist purposes, or to enforce a servile political conformity on inmates.

Similarly, judges have a very great range of sentencing options, for the application of which they are largely unaccountable. If a judge, out of ignorance, or personal prejudice, imposes a sentence markedly deviant from the norm, there is little the unfortunate recipient can do. Federal District Judge Marvin Frankel discusses this problem at length in his book *Criminal Sentences.* [7] In the federal system, sentences are generally unreviewable on appeal.* (Even if they were subject to appellate review, as they are in many states, such review is not a practical way of handling large scale sentence disparity.) Frankel deplores the total lack of training for sentencing, the absence of guidelines for judges, and the lack of consultation or interaction between and among judges on the same bench in regard to case disposition.

Finally, one of the most widespread and impassioned objections to sentencing disparity, is not so much a criticism of disparity as such, as a protest that dangerous criminals are underpunished—are not incarcerated for sufficient periods of time to protect the community from their depredations. This last criticism probably stems more from the adverse effects of overcrowding and excessive plea bargaining than from deliberately conceived legislative or administrative policy. Many of the horror stories in the press, of violent crimes committed by recently released offenders, relate, not to criminals released or placed on probation after rehabilitation therapy, but to dangerous felons permitted, because of crowding in the courts, to plead to minor charges, and then sentenced minimally in accordance with the terms of the plea bargain. "Rehabilitated" criminals do recidivate unfortunately, but much recidivism is by offenders who simply have been incarcerated for inappropriately short lengths of time.

In response to widespread criticism of our sentencing system, several large

*Federal sentences are reviewable only if the trial judge has relied on improper factors or failed to evaluate properly the facts relevant to sentencing. See *U.S. v. Daniels* 446 F.2d 967 (1971).

scale studies have been undertaken which have resulted in a number of recommendations for reform. The Committee for the Study of Incarceration, a group of scholars and high level government administrators, issued a report, *Doing Justice*,[8] written by its executive director Andrew von Hirsch, a professor at Rutgers University. The von Hirsch group found sentence disparities intolerable and recommended a return to flat sentencing, that is, specific, relatively short punishments (for example, 18 months for breaking and entering) for all offenders, with minimal flexibility for first offenders, recidivists or a very few others in special circumstances. Flat sentencing has the virtue of simplicity and satisfying the understandable desire of the community for criminals being given their "just deserts." Nevertheless, the scheme as proposed was excessively rigid, and did not address itself to the major question of precisely what punishments should be imposed for what crimes.

Another approach to the sentencing problem was made in a study commissioned by the Twentieth Century Fund, *Fair and Certain Punishment* by Professor Alan Dershowitz of Harvard Law School.[9] The Dershowitz group developed the notion of a "presumptive sentence." Normally, when legislatures assign a punishment for a particular crime, such as armed robbery, the legislators attempt to imagine the entire range of circumstances under which such a robbery might occur, and assign a correspondingly wide range of punishment. The Dershowitz group suggested that the procedure be reversed: that the legislature conceive of the average or typical armed robbery and assign a particular fixed punishment for such an offense. This fixed punishment would be the "presumptive sentence," which could be varied by the sentencing judge only in consideration of specifically cited aggravating or mitigating circumstances. This scheme has the virtue of flexibility and yet retains the capacity for minimizing sentence disparity. It is, however, fairly complicated, especially in establishing the legislative categories for punishments and aggravating and mitigating circumstances.

A very different approach to the sentencing problems was developed by Leslie T. Wilkins, a professor at S.U.N.Y., Albany, and a group of colleagues. Using probation department records in Denver, Newark, Des Moines, and the state of Vermont, they divided the previous five years' caseload into categories based on the offense committed.[10] They then analyzed each offender's record to determine the correlation, if any, between a predetermined list of over 200 variables relating to the case, and the actual sentence given. These variables included a wide range of factors relating both to the offense and the offender. The Wilkins group found that only a very few variables were relevant to the sentencing decision, principally the age and previous criminal record of the offender, and aggravating or mitigating circumstances relating to the offense. By assigning weights or scores to these relevant variables, they were then able to develop a sentence model which stated in tabular form the sentence actually given for each type of offense in over 85 percent of the cases processed in the five year period studied. The tabular form consisted of a series of grids in which the vertical axis measured offense scores, and the horizontal axis measured offender scores. Each box of the matrix contained a sentence or range of sentences (See Table 9–1).

Taken together, the grids developed for a particular court (frequently referred to as sentencing guidelines) represented the sentencing experiences for that court for the five preceding years, with an 85 percent likelihood that the sentence in any particular case would fall within that grid. The study essentially converted sentencing data for a particular court into graphic form that made it readily available to those who wished to know what had actually transpired in terms of sentencing in that court. Thus, using the grid developed by the study, a judge in any individual case could find an appropriate sentence simply by properly scoring both the offender and the offense.

The sentencing guidelines approach (developed by Wilkins and his group) is a very attractive approach in many ways. To begin with, it is relatively easy to put into operation in that it can be implemented by administrative fiat and does not require enabling legislation. It can also be confined to a single small jurisdiction so that pilot studies are relatively easily undertaken. It is also noncontroversial politically, that is, it does not espouse any particular philosophy of punishment (for example, whether punishment should be geared to the offense or the offender), but simply attempts to continue the experience of the past in the most rational way possible. Because it is nonideological, it tends not to arouse opposition from groups committed to, for example, pro-

TABLE 9–1.[11] Demonstration Guidelines for Felony 4 Offenses Denver District Court (Feasibility Study)

		Offender Score			
	-1 -7	0 2	3 8	9 12	13+
10–12	Indet. Min. 4–5 year max.	Indet. Min. 8–10 year max.	Indet. Min. 8–10 year max.	Indet. Min. 8–10 year max.	Indet. Min. 8–10 year max.
8–9	Out	3–5 month work project	Indet. Min. 3–4 year max.	Indet. Min. 8–10 year max.	Indet. Min. 8–10 year max.
6–7	Out	Out	Indet. Min. 3–4 year max.	Indet. Min. 6–8 year max.	Indet. Min. 8–10 year max.
3–5	Out	Out	Out	Indet. Min. 4–5 year max.	Indet. Min. 4–5 year max.
1–2	Out	Out	Out	Out	Indet. Min. 3–4 year max.

Offense Score (vertical axis label)

Colorado uses a Penal Code that contains five levels of felonies (with Felony 1 being the most serious and Felony 5 the least serious) and three levels of misdemeanors. Typical crimes that fall within the Felony 4 category are manslaughter, robbery, and second degree burglary. The statutory designated maximum incarcerative sentence for a Felony 4 offense is 10 years. No minimum period of confinement is to be set by the court. The term "out" refers to a nonincarcerative type of sentence such as probation, deferred judgment, or deferred prosecution. (See Appendix G for further information regarding the Denver Demonstration Model.)

tection of defendants' rights, or law and order advocates. Because it builds on past experience, it has less impact on parole, probation, and prosecutors, and corrections than do other sentencing systems which enact changes which diverge sharply from previous paractice.

Essentially, these guidelines create mathematical models of the reality of sentencing which are simple, comprehensible, valid in terms of the real world, and easy to use for purposes of comparison and instruction. They are excellent for the socialization and instruction of new judges, especially judges in isolated areas. They may alert idiosyncratic judges that they are out of the mainstream of sentencing practice. The mathematical model facilitates appellate review of sentences in that it enables comparisons of sentencing practice from different courts and different areas. It also makes possible comparisons of sentencing practice in the same court during different periods of time. It facilitates conscious changes in sentencing policy. It also provides judges with a yardstick for measuring the presentence recommendations made by the probation department.

Most of the advantages of the sentencing guidelines approach derive from the fact that this approach is primarily descriptive—an attempt to depict and, to some extent, rationalize what has actually been done in a given court or courts. Unfortunately, the disadvantages of the sentencing guideline approach stem from the same source: if past practice was flawed or inadequate, the problems thereby created will be present in the implementation of the new system. To begin with, the sentencing grid is set up in such a way that 85 percent of all past sentences will fall within the confines of the model. In order for this to happen, however, the range of punishments in each square of the grid, in many cases, must be considerable. For example, in Table 9–1, offenders with a score of 9–12 who commit an offense which scores 8–9 could be given a sentence within a range of an indeterminate minimum to an 8–10 year maximum. This may well represent an improvement if the system had previously permitted sentences of from one year to life in prison, but from the point of view of the offender who wants to be sure that he is not penalized by an excessively strict judge, or from the point of view of those critics who want to be sure that every offender gets his just deserts in terms of equal imprisonment for an equal offense, this surely is an inordinately wide range of punishment. Furthermore, prison administrators would still have to deal with the problem of similar offenders serving dissimilar sentences.

To some extent, the guidelines approach creates its own definition of sentencing disparity. If a grid is created which encompasses 85 percent of past sentences and projects that 85 percent of future sentences will fall within its purview, then by definition, all such sentences are nondisparate. If, however, the range of punishments within each box of the grid is so wide as to permit a ten year difference between offenders similarly situated, then, in the real world, such sentences might be considered disparate even though in terms of the sentencing guidelines scheme they are not. Conceivably, of course, the range of punishment within each box might be far narrower. In that case, however, the likelihood is that the number of sentences falling within the limits of the sentencing grid would be far smaller, for example, perhaps only 60 percent instead of 85 percent.

The fact that this approach can be used in a single jurisdiction, or even a single court, can also sometimes be disadvantageous in that sentencing reform in a single court or jurisdiction will have no effect on sentencing disparities between courts. If, for example, the scheme is used successfully in Denver but is not used, or is used with a different set of grids in Boulder, the Colorado State Penitentiary may still receive offenders who have received widely different sentences for similar offenses. If, on the other hand, the Denver grid were to be imposed on Boulder, questions would arise as to the validity of selecting Denver as the model for the sentencing scheme, and also as to the appropriateness of using the same scheme in two communities which have different needs and traditions. Sentencing satisfying to the community in an urban area, for example, may be very unsatisfactory in a rural area.

Another serious criticism of the sentencing guideline approach is that the grids are based on sentences imposed for charges to which there has either been a plea of guilty or conviction by a judge or jury. These sentences may or may not be related closely to the criminal conduct involved because between the commission of the crime and the adjudication of guilt, many steps in the criminal justice process transpire, the most important of which is plea bargaining. The reduction in the charge may or may not be appropriate, depending on many factors including the degree of overcrowding in the court. In many jurisdictions, the plea bargain struck may be realistic and appropriate in terms of the strength of the prosecution's case, the circumstances of the offense and the background of the offender. In other jurisdictions, the bargain may be unduly influenced by the need of the prosecutor and court to dispose of cases on the calendar. Where such undesirable pressures exist, and charges are inappropriately reduced, the concommitant resulting sentences will be disparate with relation to sentences imposed in other less pressured courts. Urban courts are generally extremely overcrowded and attempting to use their past experience as the basis for developing sentencing grids would simply perpetuate plea bargaining excesses. On the other hand, imposing a sentencing grid developed in a less crowded court system on such an urban court, might result in chaos and breakdown of the system because of overloading.

Despite the lack of field testing, and despite obvious criticisms such as those above, the simplicity and administrative feasibility of the Wilkins scheme have attracted many adherents. Initial reaction to the idea has been quite favorable in many communities. Several areas of the country, including Denver County, Colorado, Vermont, Cook County Circuit Court (Chicago), Maricopa County (Phoenix), and Philadelphia Court of Common Pleas have developed some form of sentencing guidelines. Similar action is contemplated in New Jersey, Michigan, Minnesota, Massachusetts, Wisconsin, Florida, Louisiana, and Ohio. This type of grid is also being used in some jurisdictions for parole decisions.

Other reforms to deal with the sentence disparity problem have been implemented recently in various jurisdictions, though no single scheme has caught fire in the manner of the Wilkins sentencing guidelines. Several states, including California, Indiana, and Maine, have changed their penal codes to incorporate some type of flat or definite sentencing. In many of these states, the parole board has been abolished in all but name, although its function may have been assumed by another body. Other states have experimented with mandatory minimum punishments for certain offenses. New York, for example, enacted laws mandating a life sentence for some type of drug offenses. These Rockefeller drug laws have proved to be disastrous in terms of effectiveness and impact on the criminal justice system. Severe punishment has fallen disproprotionately on minor drug dealers rather than on the major drug ring organizers who were the laws' intended target. Through eliminating the possibility of plea bargaining in many drug cases, the laws have created severe congestion in the courts and have tended to overcrowd the prisons as well. The United States Supreme Court declined to hear a challenge to their constitutionality in January 1979. Later that year, the state legislature modified the harshest provisions of these laws.[12]

PROBATION AND PAROLE

Probation work is social service carried on in a court setting. The probation officer has two main functions. He prepares a presentence investigation designed to give the judge sufficient social and legal background concerning an adjudicated guilty defendant to enable the judge to impose a sentence which reflects both the severity of the crime and the potential behavior of the defendant in light of his past. If the judge places the defendant on probation, the probation officer is then charged with the responsibility of supervising the defendant (probationer) while he remains at liberty in the community. Supervision entails assisting the defendant in adjusting to his home and his community; helping him get employment; counseling in resolving psychological or other problems; making referrals to other agencies when needed; and supervising the activities of the probationer so that he will refrain from violating the conditions of probation or committing new crimes. The conditions of probation generally involve keeping regular hours, maintaining steady employment, supporting dependents, refraining from frequenting bars, remaining sober, and reporting to the probation office when required to do so. Some jurisdictions have more and some have fewer conditions. A judge may also impose specific conditions such as refraining from particular employment; paying fines, reparations, or making restitution; or other specific directives.

Although the historical backgrounds of probation and parole are dissimilar, in function, on a day-to-day basis, the jobs of probation and parole officers cannot be distinguished.[13] Parole, according to one definition, is

> conditional release, usually by a board of parole or a board of managers, of an inmate from a penal or reformative institution after he has served a part of the sentence imposed upon him.[14]

Probation is a judicial function, presided over by a judge, while parole is an administrative function performed by an independent board of parole, board of managers, or some other body. The parole officer prepares preparole reports designed to assist parole boards in making decisions concerning the release of inmates prior to the maximum expiration of their sentences. The material in the probation and parole reports is similar, although in probation more emphasis is given to a discussion of the crime, while in the parole reports relatively greater attention is paid to an inmate's home and employment programs. The parolee on release is met with conditions similar to that faced by the probationer, and the casework and counseling services are the same for probation and parole.

Probation in the United States and England dates from 1841, and parole had its beginnings some years later. Despite their well-established character however, probation and parole practices have been reshaped by the same ferment that is affecting so much of the criminal justice system. In the past decade, defendants questioned procedures never challenged before. Did a defendant, for example, have a right to counsel at probation or parole revocation hearings? Did a defendant have a right to see the presentence investigation report which was used by the judge in sentencing? Did an inmate have a right to see the preparole report prepared for the use of the parole board? Was there a right to cross-examine the witnesses who gave testimony in a probation violation hearing? Might an offender present witnesses on his own behalf, or rebut the testimony offered in probation or parole hearings? On what grounds might probation or parole be revoked? Most basic of all, did an individual have a right to probation or parole at all?

Whether one is entitled to probation or parole depends on whether probation and parole are considered to be privileges extended to those worthy of them at the mercy and discretion of the state; or, on the other hand, whether probation and parole are considered merely available alternative forms of punishment subject to the same due process requirements as any other forms of punishment.* Is the granting of probation or parole an act of grace compa-

---

*While recent United States Supreme Court decisions have tended to move away from the old "slave of the state" philosophy in relation to prisoners and to extend to both prisoners and parolees an increasing number of procedural rights, a recent decision, *Greenholtz v. Inmates* (decided May 29, 1979), seems somewhat retrogressive. In that case the Court in a 5–4 decision

rable to the commutation of a sentence, or does it have only the same procedural significance as the levying of a fine or the commitment to a penal institution? The traditional view of the courts was that a defendent had no rights after conviction other than the right to the maximum sentence prescribed by law for the offense for which he was convicted. This view has changed.

In *Mempa v. Rhay* [15] two petitioners challenged the right of the state of Washington to revoke their probation at hearings at which the defendants were not assisted by legal counsel. Mempa, aged seventeen, after having pleaded guilty to joy-riding, had been placed on probation with a deferred sentence. Some months later, the prosecutor moved to revoke probation on the ground that Mempa had been involved in a burglary. At the hearing, to which Mempa was accompanied by his stepfather, the state made no offer of counsel for the probationer.

> At the hearing Mempa was asked if it was true that he had been involved in the alleged burglary and he answered in the affirmative. A probation officer testified without cross-examination that according to his information petitioner had been involved in the burglary and had previously denied participation in it. Without asking petitioner if he had anything to say or any evidence to supply, the court immediately entered an order revoking petitioner's probation and then sentenced him to 10 years in the penitentiary. [16]

The other petitioner, Walkling, had been convicted of burglary and placed on probation for three years. Two years later he was arrested, charged with forgery and grand larceny, and brought before the court for a hearing on a petition by the prosecuting attorney to revoke his probation. Walkling requested and received a short continuance so that he might obtain a lawyer. When the hearing was called, however, the attorney did not appear and the proceedings continued with Walkling unrepresented by counsel.

> A probation officer presented hearsay testimony to the effect that petitioner had committed the acts alleged in the 14 separate counts of forgery and 14 separate counts of grand larceny that had been charged against petitioner previously at

---

held that the states are free to administer their parole systems in any manner they choose, with no requirement that inmates be allowed to participate in parole board hearings or be informed of the reasons for denial or parole. The Federal Appeals Court had held in a Nebraska case that inmates' "conditional liberty interest" in being released on parole entitled them to protection of the Constitution's due process clause. Chief Justice Burger, writing for the majority, overruled the appeals court, holding that "the state holds out the *possibility* of parole provides no more than a mere hope that the benefits will be obtained."

In a similar vein, a week later the high court in a 7–0 decision, held that parole commissions are not bound by the wishes of the sentencing judge as to when parole should be granted, and prisoners denied parole had no right to challenge that denial on the ground that the sentencing judge expected that parole would be granted at a particular time (*United States v. Addonizio,* June 4, 1979).

the time of his arrest. The court thereupon revoked probation and imposed the maximum sentence of 15 years on Walkling. . . . Because of the failure of the State to keep a record of the proceedings, nothing is known as to whether Walkling was advised of his right to appeal. He did not, however, take an appeal.[17]

On appeal the U.S. Supreme Court reversed the petitioners' convictions and remanded the cases to the Washington courts for further hearings. The basis for the reversal was largely that an accused person is entitled to counsel at every stage of a criminal proceeding. The decision, thus, might have been regarded as nothing more than an extension of the *Gideon* decision, but in fact proved to be an important first step in broadening the postadjudicatory rights of probationers, prisoners, and parolees.

The Warren court, for ten years, had been assiduous in protecting the rights of accused persons. The only important segment of the criminal justice system that it had not reached were the postadjudicatory processes: probation, parole, and penal confinement. This area is characterized, moreover, by both broad legislative delegations of power to relevant officials and an almost total absence of formal constitutional safeguards. With the exception of the prohibition against cruel and unusual punishment, no section of the U.S. Constitution relates to postadjudicatory rights.[18] The courts in general were loath to review the decisions made in probation, parole, and corrections cases, primarily because probation and parole had been looked upon as privileges extended to the convicted defendant, and imprisonment was frequently considered to have effectively nullified all of the prisoner's personal rights for the duration of his or her sentence. The result was that decisions in this area were made by a variety of officials, virtually uncontrolled either by previously established legislative or constitutional standards, or by *post hoc* judicial review.

As criminologist Fred Cohen commented in 1968:

A combination of extremely broad legislation, narrow judicial review, and the consignment of most of the legally relevant issues to matters of privilege rather than of right has created a situation of virtually uncontrolled, unreviewable discretion in the administration of the correctional process. . . .

There is no area of law, except perhaps the civil commitments of the mentally ill, where the lives of so many people are so drastically affected by officials who exercise a virtually absolute, unreviewed discretion. As the Court becomes increasingly aware of this situation, through a steady increase in the number of appeals that raise peno-correctional issues, the discretion factor alone could stimulate the Court's reformative energy.[19]

It was difficult however, for the Court to extend the procedural protections of accused persons to probationers and parolees, without evaluating the impact of the system on the individuals concerned. Were probation and parole programs punitive or rehabilitative? Was the probation or parole hearing an

adversary proceeding, or was there an identity of interest between the probationer or parolee and the officials charged with overseeing their lives? These
questions were precisely analogous to the questions the Court attempted to
resolve in the extension of procedural rights to juveniles. In the *Gault, Kent,*
and *Winship* cases, the Court extended some of the procedural rights of adult
defenders to children at a juvenile court hearing, but the Court has not yet
made up its mind whether the juvenile hearing is essentially rehabilitative or
punitive in its impact on the child. The basic contradiction in juvenile cases
is still obvious: children are in fact punished in the name of rehabilitation,
but to view the process as purely punitive and extend to it all the procedural
safeguards associated with true adult adversary proceedings would be to
eliminate the rehabilitative ideal completely—to throw out the baby with the
bathwater. The same contradictions apply to parole and probation programs.
While rehabilitative in intent, many of the conditions, including provisions
for automatic revocation of probation or parole without procedural safeguards, are punitive in fact. However, to extend to probation revocation
hearings the same range of procedural safeguards applicable to the original
trial of the accused is to remove some of the flexibility which is desirable in
a rehabilitative program. At the same time, to make such revocation possible
almost at the whim of administrative officials is to punish, not rehabilitate,
without due process.

The underlying conceptual difficulties are admirably illustrated by a response in the *Georgetown Law Journal* to an opinion of Judge Burger (now
Chief Justice Burger) of the U.S. Court of Appeals for the District of Columbia. The issue, in *Hyser v. Reed,*[20] was whether a parolee was entitled to
assigned counsel at a parole revocation hearing. Justice Burger, for the majority, argued that,

> The Bureau of Prisons and the Parole Board operate from the basic premise that
> prisoners placed in their custody are to be rehabilitated and restored to useful
> lives as soon as . . . that transition can be safely made. . . . Thus there is a genuine
> identity of interest . . . in the prisoner's desire to be released and the Board's
> policy to grant release as soon as possible. Here there is not the attitude of
> adverse, conflicting objectives as between the parolee and Board inherent be-
> tween prosecution and defense in a criminal case. Here we do not have pursuer
> and quarry but a relationship partaking of *parens patriae.* In a real sense the Parole
> Board in revoking parole occupies the role of parent withdrawing a privilege
> from an errant child not as a punishment but for misuse of the privilege.[21]

to which the *Georgetown Law Journal* responded,

> It is submitted that the view that parole revocation proceedings do not involve
> adversary interests is invalid. When the Board maintains that a parolee has done
> a specific act for which his parole may be revoked and he denies it, there are
> undeniable adverse objectives; this falls far short of a genuine identity of inter-

ests. . . . Furthermore, the revocation process presents basic similarities to the consequences of a criminal trial. The possibility of a parolee losing his conditional liberty is the most obvious similarity. . . . In the analogous area of juvenile courts, the Supreme Court, rejecting an argument that *ex parte* juvenile proceedings are totally non-adversary in their determinations of delinquency, recently recognized that adverse interests do in fact lurk beneath the *parens patriae* surface.[22]

Recently, parolees have been given greater rights. In January 1971, the New York State Court of Appeals, in the case of *Menechino v. Warden*[23] extended the right to counsel in parole revocation hearings. Subsequent decisions of courts in other jurisdictions asserted that parole revocation was inherently an adversary situation and therefore required that the procedural safeguards in *Mempa v. Rhay* be likewise mandated for parolees. Later, in *Morrissey v. Brewer*,[24] the U.S. Supreme Court held that there was no identity of interest between parolees and the parole board, and therefore, parolees facing parole revocation were entitled to minimum due process safeguards including a two stage parole revocation procedure: (1) a preliminary hearing conducted by an impartial hearing officer (not the parole officer involved) near the place of alleged parole violation to determine whether there is probable cause to believe that the parolee has violated the conditions of his parole; and, if there is, (2) a revocation hearing (months later and held in prison) to evaluate the contested facts and evidence. The parolee has the right to receive written notice of hearings and their purpose; a statement of the charges against him; the right to speak and present witnesses and evidence on his own behalf; and the right to confront adverse witnesses unless the hearing officer rules that revealing witnesses' identity would be harmful.* Despite these procedural protections, however, the Court was careful to distinguish parole revocation proceedings from normal criminal trials.

> There is no thought to equate this second stage of parole revocation to a criminal prosecution in any sense. It is a narrow inquiry; the process should be flexible enough to consider evidence including letters, affidavits, and other material that would not be admissible in an adversary criminal trial.[25]

Morrissey did not clarify the right to counsel at parole revocation hearings. This issue was raised in *Gagnon v. Scarpelli*[26] in relation to a probation revocation proceeding. The Court held that both probationers and parolees are entitled to *Morrissey* type hearings, but that indigent probationers or parolees have no automatic right to be represented by appointed counsel at these hearings. (The Court reserved decision on whether a probationer had a right to be represented by retained counsel in cases where the state was not obliged

---

*These rights do not apply to parolees who have been convicted of another crime while on parole or who do not deny the allegations of parole violation. In such cases the parolee is automatically returned to the institution from which he was released.

to provide appointed counsel for indigents.) The Court once again emphasized the difference between a criminal trial, which is an adversary proceeding, and a revocation hearing in which the state is represented by a hearing officer whose orientation is quite different from that of a prosecutor. Nevertheless, the Court held that while the presence of counsel would probably be undesirable and constitutionally unnecessary in most revocation hearings, where a probationer or parolee claims either that he has not committed the alleged violation or that there were mitigating circumstances surrounding the violation, counsel presumably should be provided by the state. The right to counsel must be determined on a case by case basis.

More recently, in 1976, the U.S. Supreme Court in *Moody v. Daggett,*[27] curtailed some of the parolee's rights which had been spelled out in *Morrissey*. While on parole from a federal prison, a parolee named Moody shot and killed two persons on the Fort Apache Indian Reservation. Moody pleaded guilty to manslaughter and murder and was given two 10-year sentences to run concurrently. These two crimes constituted obvious violations of the terms of parole. Accordingly, the U.S. Board of Parole issued, but did not execute, the parole violator warrant which was merely lodged with the prison officials as a detainer. When Moody requested that the Board execute its warrant immediately so that any imprisonment imposed for violation of his earlier parole (for his rape conviction) could run concurrently with his manslaughter and murder sentences, the Board refused, and affirmed its decision to allow the warrant to remain unexecuted. Previously, similar decisions by the Board had been appealed to the various U.S. Courts of Appeal which had handed down decisions some of which sustained the Board and others reversed the Board. In *Moody*, the U.S. Supreme Court held that parolees imprisoned for federal crimes committed while on parole, and clearly constituting parole violations were not constitutionally entitled to an immediate parole revocation Morrissey-type hearing where a parole violation warrant had been issued and lodged with the institution of his confinement as a "detainer" and not executed. The Court explained,

> The revocation hearing mandated by *Morrissey* is bottomed on the parallel interests of society and the parolee in establishing whether a parole violation has occurred and, if so, whether under all the circumstances the quality of that violation calls for parole revocation. The issue before us here, however, is not whether a Morrissey-type hearing will ever be constitutionally required in the present case, but whether a hearing must be held at the present time, before the parolee is taken into custody as a parole violator. We hold that there is no requirement for an immediate hearing.[28]

The state courts are not necessarily bound to follow this decision. In New York, for example, in *Beattie v. New York State Board of Parole,*[29] a similar question was presented to the New York Court of Appeals (the highest appellate court in that state) which ruled that a parolee held on an unrelated criminal charge is entitled to a *prompt* final revocation hearing, that is, within a reasonable time.

Another due process problem in relation to probation is the right of a defendant to see the presentence investigation report on him prepared by the probation department for the judge's consideration before sentence is passed. The interest of the defendant in this report is obvious: he wants to know what information the probation department gathered so that he can assess its accuracy and fairness. Many probation officials, on the other hand, are reluctant to reveal the contents of the report lest such revelation expose those who gave adverse information about the defendant to reprisal from him or his friends. If a wife or a mother, for example, knows that the defendant will find out what she said about him, she may be afraid to give adverse information to the probation officer. On the other hand, if she knows he will never see the report, she is free, if she is feeling vengeful, to concoct untrue stories about him.

The confidentiality of a presentence investigation was affirmed in 1949 by the United States Supreme Court which held in *Williams v. New York*[30] that there was no denial of due process when a trial judge based his severe sentence on the contents of a presentence investigation without disclosing its contents to the defendant or giving him an opportunity to rebut it. In that case the jury had returned a verdict of guilty of Murder First Degree with a recommendation for mercy, a recommendation that the judge had the option of disregarding. Because the information gathered by the probation officer demonstrated that Williams was a dangerous individual who had committed other crimes for which he had not been arrested, the judge disregarded the jury's recommendation and sentenced Williams to be executed. In writing the 7–2 majority opinion, Justice Black recognized that there were sound historical and practical reasons for different evidentiary rules governing trial and sentencing procedures.

> Under the practice of individualizing punishments, investigational techniques have been given an important role. Probation workers making reports of their investigations have not been trained to prosecute but to aid offenders. Their reports have been given a high value by conscientious judges who want to sentence persons on the best available information rather than on guesswork and inadequate information. To deprive sentencing judges of this kind of information would undermine modern penological procedural policies that have been cautiously adopted throughout the nation after careful consideration and experimentation. We must recognize that most of the information now relied upon by judges to guide them in the intelligent imposition of sentences would be unavailable if information were restricted to that given in open court by witnesses subject to cross-examination. And the modern probation report draws on information concerning every aspect of a defendant's life. The type and extent of this information make totally impractical if not impossible open court testimony with cross-examination. Such a procedure could endlessly delay criminal administration in a retrial of collateral issues.[31]

In dissenting, Justice Murphy observed, "due process of law included at least the idea that a person accused of crime shall be accorded a fair hearing throughout all the stages of the proceeding against him."[32]

Williams was modified seventeen years later, in 1966, by the decision in *Kent v. United States.*[33] *Kent* was a case which had originated in the juvenile court of Washington, D.C. and which had subsequently been waived to the adult court. At the time of waiver the juvenile court judge refused Kent and his attorney access to the social history contained in his probation record on which the decision to waive had been based. The probation record was then forwarded to the adult court. The United States Supreme Court, on appeal, held that the juvenile court's refusal to grant access to a significant part of the probation record to Kent's attorney was a denial of due process. The following year, one Francis Eddie Specht who had been convicted and sentenced for indecent liberties under the Colorado Sex Offender Act to an indeterminate sentence of from one day to life, succeeded, on appeal, in reaching the United States Supreme Court. There, in a unanimous decision, the Court ruled that the trial court could not impose that type of indeterminate sentence without the full panoply of protections which due process guarantees in state criminal proceedings.[34] Under the then prevailing Colorado statute, the maximum sentence for a conviction for indecent liberties was ten years unless the judge believed that a person convicted of a specified sex offense "if at large, constituted a threat of bodily harm to members of the public, or is an habitual offender and mentally ill." The judge so believed, and imposed a one year to life sentence. In distinguishing *Specht* from *Williams,* Justice Douglas commented,

> The case is not unlike those under recidivist statutes where an habitual criminal issue is "a distinct issue" . . . on which a defendant "must receive reasonable notice and an opportunity to be heard." . . . Due process, in other words, requires that he be present with counsel, have an opportunity to be heard, be confronted with witnesses against him, have the right to cross-examine, and to offer evidence of his own. . . . None of these procedural safeguards we have mentioned is present under Colorado's Sex Offenders Act. We therefore hold that it is deficient in due process as measured by the requirements of the Fourteenth Amendment.[35]

It appears, however, that the impact of *Williams* will continue to be felt. In December 1977, in *United States v. Fatico,* a United States District Court judge in the Eastern District of New York, prohibited the introduction of hearsay evidence in a sentencing proceeding. The Government appealed from the order and won in the United States Court of Appeals for the Second Circuit in June 1978. The Circuit Court cited *Williams* and held that the use in sentencing of information supplied by an unidentified informant, where there is good cause for nondisclosure of his identity and the information he furnishes is subject to corroboration by other means, is not unconstitutional.[36]

Practice with reference to permitting defendants to read their presentence reports varies throughout the United States. The federal government and New Jersey (among other jurisdictions) permit the defendant and his lawyer to see the presentence report.[37] In New York, the defendant and his attorney may see the report, which will then also be made available to the prosecutor. The court may withhold certain types of sensitive or irrelevant material, but must notify the defendant of such withholding. Withholding is also subject to appellate review.[38]

The state of the law in relation to probation and parole procedural rights is not yet in its final form. The 1970s have seen tremendous growth of judicially designed and imposed procedural protections for probationers and parolees, but the impact of these changes in the real world of administrative practice is not yet fully apparent. As in the handling of juveniles, there is a need to balance fairness to offenders and the attempt to rehabilitate them with the need of the community for protection.

PENAL CONFINEMENT

Like probationers and parolees, prisoners increasingly are using the courts to define and to enlarge their personal rights. The traditional view of the courts was that individuals, once legally consigned to prison, had no rights and that they were, for the duration of their sentences, in effect "the slaves of the state." Reformers, civil libertarians, and others concerned with the rights of inmates, however, argued that only those rights necessary to effectuate the sentence of the court should be lost to prisoners and that they should retain all others. Inmates, in other words, must be restrained to the extent necessary to keep them in a penal institution, but beyond that they should retain control over their personal lives. Dozens of questions concerning the extent to which prison administrators might restrict the activities of their charges have been raised, since prison is, after all, probably the most total of total institutions.

Enormous discretion is left to correctional administrators to define the conditions of imprisonment. They determine the way in which the offender will live for the term of imprisonment; how he is fed and clothed; whether he sleeps in a cell or a dormitory; whether he spends his days locked up or in relative freedom; what opportunity he has for work, education, or recreation. They regulate his access to the outside world by defining mailing and visiting privileges. They define rules of conduct and the penalties for violation of such rules. And increasingly, they make classification decisions—assigning different prisoners to different kinds of correctional programs. This may involve decisions to place prisoners in different institutions or to grant certain prisoners relative freedom in the community, as for example, on educational or work-release programs.[39]

Whether a prisoner has a right to receive unlimited quantities of uncensored mail; whether he has a right to give legal advice to other inmates; whether he has a right to practice actively any religion he chooses; whether he has a right to advance and support political opinions while in prison—the answers to all these questions depend, not so much on the letter or even the spirit of the Constitution and the laws, as on society's view of the purpose of imprisonment. Is an offender sentenced to prison to punish him, to keep him out of circulation, or to rehabilitate him? When he is sent to prison, is the imprisonment itself the punishment, or is the prison simply the locus of further punishment?* As previously indicated, we do not have a simple, clear-cut philosophy of corrections. When pushed, most people will assert that rehabilitation is probably the most important goal to be achieved, but the reality of our corrections system is such that vengeance and possibly a desire to quarantine dangerous offenders are obviously far more important goals. Not only does society permit prisoners to be housed and fed in inhuman and degrading conditions, but underneath the seeming apathy which accounts for the slowness of prison reform is a seldom expressed, though widely prevalent feeling that whatever inmates suffer, it is probably no more than what they deserve. One cannot read any of the massive literature relating to prison conditions without becoming aware that the public probably does not wish things to be any different. Dr. Karl Menninger called his recent book on corrections *The Crime of Punishment* and states that the crimes committed by society against prisoners in the name of corrections are greater than the crimes these prisoners had committed against society.[40]

If the purpose of prison is punishment, prisoners should have very few rights, since after all, the purpose of confining them is to make them suffer, and there is little point in mitigating that suffering by defining personal rights. Prison personnel, to be sure, should not be degraded by having to administer punishments too barbarous or grisly, but according to this philosophy prisoners who have been sent away to suffer should be permitted to do so. On the other hand, if the purpose of the prison sentence is to keep offenders out of circulation and away from the public for a given period of time, there is no reason why inmates should not enjoy all personal rights except those which would permit them to leave their place of confinement at will. If the purpose of imprisonment is rehabilitation, however, then it is *essential* that inmates not be deprived of their personal rights more than is absolutely necessary, since the primary goal of rehabilitation is to restore a sense of dignity and integrity to those who are already degraded in the eyes of society. As Menninger points out, if one hopes that on release prisoners will re-enter society as decent men living with other decent individuals, they must be treated in the way that we expect them to treat others on their

*The distinction between being committed to prison as punishment or for punishment is the difference between Sing Sing, where prisoners were simply held in custody, and certain southern prison systems where inmates were forced to work on a chain gang.

release. Humiliating or degrading programs and punishments are thus entirely counterproductive since they confirm in the inmates their own sense of lack of self-worth and make them even more vicious than they already are.

Hundreds of court suits aimed at vindicating the rights of prisoners reached the state and federal courts during the 1970s. A handful of these cases reached the United States Supreme Court. Although in many of these cases, inmates won significant legal victories, it is difficult to assess what the practical impact on prisons has been, since correctional institutions are, to a large extent, closed institutions well shielded from the public view, and prison administrators, like all administrators, tend to drag their feet in implementing decisions that are distasteful or inconvenient. Nevertheless, significant changes have occurred.

As early as 1944, in *Coffin v. Reichard,*[41] the Federal Court of Appeals for the Sixth Circuit, declared that a convicted offender retained all rights except those which must be denied or limited to make possible the running of the institution in which he was confined. No "generous sweep," moreover, ought be given to pleas of administrative convenience made by prison officials. While *Coffin* was binding only in the Sixth Circuit, several more recent United States Supreme Court decisions have adopted its philosophy. In *Pell v. Procunier,*[42] for example, the Court held that

> A prison inmate retains those First Amendment rights that are not inconsistent with his status as a prisoner or with the legitimate penological objectives of the corrections system.[43]

Despite this brave statement, however, the Court went on to uphold a California regulation forbidding reporters to interview inmates, as a reasonable rule which infringed neither the inmate's freedom of expression nor the reporters' right to carry out their assignments. Justices Brennan, Marshall, and Douglas dissented vigorously. In a related case, *Procunier v. Martinez,*[44] however, the Court invalidated certain kinds of prisoner mail censorship in the California prisons, albeit on the narrow ground of the infringement of nonprisoners' First Amendment rights. (Every letter sent to, or received by, a prisoner involves a nonprisoner who is either the sender or the recipient. The Court struck down prison mail censorship by upholding the nonprisoner's First Amendment rights.) Brennan, Marshall, and Douglas would have reached the same result directly by upholding the First Amendment rights of the prisoners themselves.

Other First Amendment suits have alleged infringement by prison officials of the free exercise of religion, particularly of Black Muslims whose revolutionary ideology and religious rituals are often seen as inimical to prison discipline by those in charge of institutions. Muslims and Orthodox Jews also have sued for a diet consistent with their religious needs. Some of these suits have been successful. Another interesting First Amendment claim was made unsuccessfully in *Jones v. North Carolina Prisoners' Labor Union*[45] in which the United States Supreme Court upheld a state prison regulation prohibiting inmates from soliciting other inmates to join a prisoners' labor union, and barring all meetings of the union and certain kinds of union mailings. Justices Marshall and Brennan dissented.

Prisoners' suits have also been mounted under the Due Process clause of the Fifth Amendment and under the Sixth, Eighth, and Fourteenth Amendments. In *Johnson v. Avery*[46] the United States Supreme Court upheld the right of inmates to receive the help of "jailhouse lawyers," (fellow inmates with some expertise in law, usually self-taught). Prison administrators generally forbade this type of legal assistance as being harmful to prison morale in focusing the attention of inmates on faults in the prison or criminal justice systems and encouraging false hopes of release. Jailhouse lawyers, however, were frequently the most accessible, and sometimes, the only form of counsel available to prisoners. In 1977, the high Court further enlarged the right to legal assistance in *Bounds v. Smith*[47] holding that

> The fundamental constitutional right of access to the courts requires prison authorities to assist inmates in the preparation of filing of meaningful legal papers by providing prisoners with adequate law libraries or adequate assistance from persons trained in the law.[48]

Chief Justice Burger and Justices Rehnquist and Stewart failed to see any necessary correlation between access to the courts and access to lawyers and law libraries.

Inmates have also challenged prison procedures in disciplinary hearings. Does an inmate have a right to the procedural protections of the judicial process if he is charged with either an offense against prison rules or a violation of the criminal statutes? In *Wolff v. McDonnell*[49] the United States Supreme Court held that due process requires that an inmate at a disciplinary hearing be given written notice of the charges against him, and be permitted to call witnesses and present documentary evidence unless such witnesses or evidence were unduly hazardous to the safety of the institution or the goals of the correctional program. An inmate has no right, however, to confront his accusers or to have an attorney. The Court restated the limitation on the right of confrontation and the right to counsel in *Baxter v. Palmigiano*[50] where the inmate was charged with a crime, not simply an infraction of prison discipline.*

*A different and provocative point of view on the impact of the prisoners' rights movement has been expressed by Charles Silberman (*Criminal Violence, Criminal Justice,* New York: Random House, 1978). Silberman, the director of the Study of Law and Justice, a Ford Foundation research project, maintains that the most serious threat to a prisoner's well being is the danger of attack by one of his fellow inmates. He cites statistics showing the incidence of homosexual rapes, stabbings, beatings, and other types of assaults, all of which have markedly increased due to an increasing proportion, in recent years, of violent criminals in the prison population. The situation

Another successful legal challenge against prevailing prison administrative practices was mounted by an inmate who claimed that New York State statutes regulating the transfer of prisoners to an institution for the criminally insane provided for fewer procedural safeguards than were afforded those who were not prisoners facing involuntary confinement in a mental hospital, thus denying prisoners equal protection of the laws.[51] The Federal Circuit Court agreed that the prisoner was entitled to an examination by independent, outside physicians, and a hearing at which he could produce witnesses and evidence. He was entitled moreover to judicial review of the proceedings before his transfer and to a periodic administrative review of the need for his continued confinement in the mental institution.

In a related case, *Baxtrom v. Herold,* Baxtrom challenged the New York State practice of continuing the confinement of insane criminals after the expiration of their prison sentences without affording them a jury trial on the question of their sanity.[52] Such trials were afforded to dangerous persons who were civilly committed. The United States Supreme Court held unanimously that Baxtrom, when his sentence had expired, was entitled to the same procedural protection before further confinement as a civilian who faced initial commitment to a mental institution. As a result of the Baxtrom case nearly 1,000 prisoners who had been declared too dangerous to be placed in a civil hospital were reclassified and released either to their homes or to civil hospitals. Only seven had to be returned to the prison hospital.

As one author has noted, the Baxtrom cases were almost as pure as Ivory Snow; they were 99 28/100 percent free from mental illness.[53]

Perhaps the most important and wide-ranging challenges of all, however, have been to the living conditions which prisoners frequently are forced to endure: the overcrowding, lack of sanitary facilities, lack of medical care, vulnerability to attacks by other inmates, and the generally unhealthy, degrading, and physically hazardous environment of many prisons. In *Gates v.*

---

has been further complicated by explosive racial tensions. Black prisoners, who frequently constitute the majority of inmates, seek to assert their dominance through sexual and other types of abuse against white prisoners. They are often very well organized and claim to look on the prison experience as simply a continuation of their lives on the street. So violence prone are these inmates that discipline has become a very serious problem. The unarmed guards, outnumbered and fearful for their own safety, tend to overlook all but the most serious infractions of discipline. On the other hand, the use of incentives and rewards to induce inmates to follow the rules has been severely limited because the privileges that were once at the disposal of the warden to dispense to the well-behaved, are now available to all as a matter of right. So constrained have prison administrators become in their ability to secure conforming behavior through special privileges, that, according to Silberman, the prisoners' rights movement has resulted in greater rather than less emphasis on physical punishment, since segregation, limitation of the normal diet and the like are the only weapons left to administrators. Silberman's point is not that prisoners should not have legally enforceable rights; rather he seeks to point out the complexity of problems involved in the confinement of very dangerous and violent prisoners.

Collier[54] Justice Tuttle of the Fifth Circuit, after describing some of the dreadful conditions in the Mississippi State Penintentiary at Parchman, Mississippi, ordered both immediate and long-range relief for the inmates. The immediate relief directed prison officials to end the censorship of prison mail; to abolish corporal punishment; to decently clothe and feed and provide for the sanitary needs of inmates in solitary confinement; to provide adequate medical care for inmates; to protect inmates against attack by other inmates; to abolish the use of trustees in custodial positions; and to renovate physical facilities so as to remove health hazards. Prison officials were also directed to undertake long-range plans to improve prison housing, water and sewer systems, and fire-fighting and hospital facilities. In a similar type of case, Judge Morris Lasker of the Federal District Court SDNY ordered New York City to close the Tombs, a jail used as a pretrial detention facility and remand center, because of the poor condition of the physical plant and the hardships forced on prisoners incarcerated there, most of whom were awaiting trial.[55]

These challenges to prison and jail conditions were brought under the Eighth Amendment ban on cruel and unusual punishment. The United States Supreme Court has not yet ruled on this issue, but it is hard to believe that the high Court, or any other federal or state appellate court, can continue to look away from the frequently dehumanizing and degrading conditions in the correctional institutions. The general movement of the courts seems to be towards a declaration that all prisoners have a right to decent living conditions, clean bedding, good food, and the opportunity for rehabilitative treatment. Certainly, the courts have been far more active in protecting prisoners' rights than either the legislatures or administrative officials.

Obviously the courts alone cannot do the whole job, and we may be worse off than ever if they attempt to do so without cooperation from other branches of government. The legislature and administrative officials however, cannot be expected to act without some prodding from the public itself, which must become aware of the needs for intelligent handling of prisoners. The hope is, as Dr. Menninger has put it, that

> The public will grow increasingly ashamed of its cry for retaliation, its persistent demand to punish. This is its crime, *our* crime against criminals—and incidentally our crime against ourselves. For before we can diminish our sufferings from the ill-controlled aggressive assaults of fellow citizens, we must renounce the philosophy of punishment, the obsolete, vengeful penal attitude. In its place we would seek a comprehensive, constructive social attitude—therapeutic in some instances, restraining, but preventive in its total social impact.[56]

Selected Readings

Abadinsky, Howard. Probation and Parole. Englewood Cliffs, N.J.: Prentice-Hall, 1977.

Blumberg, Abraham S. *Criminal Justice.* New York: New Viewpoints/Franklin Watts, 1967.

Carter, Robert M., and Wilkins, Leslie T. ed. *Probation, Parole, and Community Correc-. tions.* 2nd ed. New York: Wiley, 1976.

Citizens' Inquiry on Parole and Criminal Justice. *Prison Without Walls.* New York: Praeger, 1974.

Dressler, David. *Practice and Theory of Probation and Parole.* 2nd ed. New York: Columbia University Press, 1969.

Fox, Vernon. *Introduction to Corrections.* 2nd ed. Englewood Cliffs, N.J.: Prentice-Hall, 1977.

Frankel, Marvin E. *Criminal Sentences.* New York: Hill & Wang, 1972.

Gaylin, Willard. *Partial Justice.* New York: Knopf, 1974.

Goldfarb, Ronald L., and Singer, Linda R. *After Conviction.* New York: Simon & Schuster, 1973.

Haft, Marilyn G., and Hermann, Michele. *Prisoners' Rights.* New York: Practicing Law Institute, 1972.

Hart, H. L. A. *Punishment and Responsibility.* New York: Oxford, 1967.

Kerper, Hazel B., and Kerper, Janeen. *Legal Rights of the Convicted.* St. Paul, Minn.: West, 1974.

Killinger, George G., and Cromwell, Paul F. Jr., ed. *Corrections in the Community.* 2nd ed. St. Paul, Minn.: West, 1978.

Killinger, George G.; Kerper, Hazel B.; and, Cromwell, Paul F. Jr. *Probation and Parole in the Criminal Justice System.* St. Paul, Minn.: West, 1976.

Kittrie, Nicholas N. *The Right to Be Different.* Baltimore: Penguin, 1973.

Menninger, Karl. *The Crime of Punishment.* New York: Viking, 1968.

Mitford, Jessica. *Kind and Usual Punishment.* New York: Knopf, 1973.

Morris, Norval. *The Future of Imprisonment.* Chicago: University of Chicago Press, 1974.

Morris, Norval, and Hawkins, Gordon. *The Honest Politician's Guide to Crime Control.* Chicago: University of Chicago Press, 1970.

National Advisory Commission on Criminal Justice Standards and Goals. *Corrections.* Washington, D.C.: U.S. Government Printing Office, 1973.

President's Commission on Law Enforcement and Administration of Justice. Task Force Report: *Corrections.* Washington, D.C.: U.S. Government Printing Office, 1967.

Radzinowicz, Leon, and Wolfgang, Marvin E., ed. *Crime and Justice Volume III: The Criminal in Confinement.* 2nd ed. New York: Basic Books, 1977.

Report of the Twentieth Century Fund Task Force on Criminal Sentencing. *Fair and Certain Punishment.* New York: McGraw-Hill, 1976.

Rossett, Arthur, and Cressey, Donald R. *Justice by Consent.* Philadelphia: Lippincott, 1976.

Sellin, Thorsten. *Capital Punishment.* New York: Harper & Row, 1967.

Silberman, Charles E. *Criminal Violence, Criminal Justice.* New York: Random House, 1978.

Smith, Alexander B., and Berlin, Louis. *Introduction to Probation and Parole.* 2nd ed. St. Paul, Minn.: West, 1979.

Smith, Alexander B., and Berlin, Louis. *Treating the Criminal Offender.* Dobbs Ferry, N.Y.: Oceana Publications, 1974.

Stanley, David T. *Prisoners Among Us.* Washington, D.C.: Brookings Institute, 1976.

Toch, Hans, ed. *Legal and Criminal Psychology.* New York: Holt, Rinehart and Winston, 1961.

von Hirsch, Andrew. *Doing Justice.* New York: Hill & Wang, 1976.

Yochelson, Samuel, and Samenow, Stanton E. *The Criminal Personality, Volume I—A Profile for Change; Volume II—The Change Process.* New York: Aronson, 1977.

Zimring, Franklin E., and Hawkins, Gordon J. *Deterrence.* Chicago: University of Chicago Press, 1973.

Notes

1. For a brief discussion of philosophies of punishment, see Martin P. Golding, *Philosophy of Law* (Englewood Cliffs, N. J.: Prentice-Hall, 1975), chs. 4–5.

2. Clarence Ray Jeffrey, "The Historical Development of Criminology," in Hermann Mannheim (ed.) *Pioneers in Criminology,* 2nd edition (Montclair, New Jersey: Patterson Smith, 1972), p. 460.

3. Norval Morris and Gordon Hawkins, *The Honest Politician's Guide to Crime Control* (Chicago: University of Chicago Press, 1970), p. 47.

4. Ibid., p. 49.

5. Charles Winick, Israel Gerver, and Abraham Blumberg, "The Psychology of Judges," in Hans Toch, ed., *Legal and Criminal Psychology* (New York: Holt, Rinehart and Winston, 1961), pp. 141–145; Alexander B. Smith and Abraham Blumberg, "The Problems of Objectivity in Judicial Decision-Making," *Social Forces* 46, no. 1 (September 1967): 96–105.

6. Robert Martinson, "What Works?-Questions and Answers about Prison Reform," *The Public Interest* (Spring 1974), p. 49.

7. New York: Hill and Wang, 1973.

8. New York: Farrar, Strauss, 1976.

9. New York: McGraw-Hill, 1976.

10. Leslie T. Wilkins, Jack M. Kress, Don M. Gottfredson, Joseph C. Calpin and Arthur M. Gelman, *Sentencing Guidelines: Structuring Judicial Discretion* (Washington, D.C.: National Institute of Law Enforcement and Criminal Justice, Law Enforcement Assistance Administration, February 1978).

11. Ibid., p. xv.

12. *New York Times,* January 8, 1979, p. B 16.

13. For a complete and full description of probation and parole, including their historical background, see Alexander B. Smith and Louis Berlin, *Introduction to Probation and Parole,* 2nd ed. (St. Paul, Minn.: West, 1979).

14. *Manual for Probation Officers in New York State,* 6th ed. (New York State Great Meadow Correctional Institution, 1960), p. 1308.

15. *Mempa v. Rhay,* 389 U.S. 128 (1967).

16. Ibid., at 131.

17. Ibid., at 132–133.

18. See Heinz R. Hink, "The Application of Constitutional Standards of Protection to Probation," 29 *University of Chicago Law Review* 483 (1962).

19. Fred Cohen, "Sentencing, Probation, and the Re-Habilitating Ideal: *The View from Mempa v. Rhay,"* 47 *Texas Law Review* 1 (1968).

20. *Hyser v. Reed,* 318 F. 2nd 225 (D.C. Cir., 1963).

21. Ibid., at 237.

22. Note, "Parole Revocation in the Federal System," 56 *Georgetown Law Journal* 705 (1968): at 721–723

23. 27 N.Y. 2d 376 (1971).

24. 408 U.S. 471 (1972).

25. Ibid., at 489.

26. 411 U.S. 778 (1973).

27. 429 U.S. 78 (1976).

28. Ibid., at 86.

29. 39 N.Y. 2d 445 (1976).

30. 337 U.S. 241 (1949).

31. Ibid., at 249–250.

32. Ibid., at 253.

33. 383 U.S. 541 (1966).

34. *Specht v. Patterson,* 386 U.S. 605 (1967).

35. Ibid., at 610–611.

36. 579 F.2d 707, 2d Cir. (1978).

37. Regulations concerning presentence reports in the United States courts are found in U.S. Code, Title 18, Appendix-Crimes and Criminal Procedures, Rule 32(c), p. 4506 and Publication No. 105, *the Presentence Investigation Report,* Division of Probation Administrative Office of the United States Courts, Washington, D.C. 20544. For New Jersey see, *New Jersey v. H. Kunz,* 66 N.J. 128 (1969).

38. New York State *Criminal Procedure Law,* Articles 390.20, 390.30, 390.40, 390.50, 400.10.

39. President's Commission on Law Enforcement and Administration of Justice, *Task Force Report: Corrections* (Washington, D.C.: U.S. Government Printing Office, 1967), p. 84.

40. Karl Menninger, *The Crime of Punishment* (New York: Viking, 1968).

41. 143 F2d 443 (1944).

42. 417 U.S. 817 (1974).

43. Ibid., at 822.

44. 416 U.S. 396 (1974).

45. 433 U.S. 119 (1977).

46. 393 U.S. 483 (1969).

47. 430 U.S. 817 (1977).

48. Ibid., at 828

49. 418 U.S. 539 (1974).

50. 425 U.S. 308 (1976).

51. *Schuster v. Herold,* 410 F 2d 1071 (2d Cir. 1969). Cert. denied 396 U.S. 847 (1969).

52. 383 U.S. 107 (1966).

53. *Schuster v. Herold,* at 1086.

54. 501 F 2d 1291 (5th Cir. 1974).

55. *Rhem v. Malcolm,* 507 F 2d 333 (2d Cir. 1974).

56. Menninger, p. 280.

appendix

a note on crime statistics

It is well known that the statistics dealing with crime and delinquency are manifestly unreliable. A large number of all crimes are undetected and therefore, not reported, other crimes are detected but not reported; and still other crimes are reported but not recorded. For the most part, crime statistics measure not crime, but crime *known to the police*—a very different figure indeed—and the statistics generated relate not to crimes committed but to crimes recorded by the police, arrests, convictions, and commitments to correctional institutions. At best, these statistics should be used with a great deal of caution in drawing conclusions respecting the actual number of crimes committed, and should be considered only as a rough index of the number and kinds of crimes actually committed. Crime statistics are affected, moreover, not only by the number of crimes committed, but by efforts made to enforce the law. If the public becomes concerned over drug traffic, the number of arrests and convictions for drug offenses will rise, not necessarily because more violations of the drug laws have occurred, but because greater efforts to stamp out violations have been made.

Of the official measures of crimes, the one which best reflects the number of crimes committed is crimes known to the police (crimes reported and recorded by the police). While this measure is markedly lower than the actual number of crimes committed, it is the best estimate available and is utilized by law enforcement and other criminal justice agencies to estimate operating costs, to assign personnel and for other important policy decisions. In addition, the same figures are relied upon by legislative bodies in considering budgets and changing laws relating to crime. Scholars also must rely on crimes known to the police for their research and writing.

Since 1930, the FBI has assumed responsibility for attempting to develop and refine methods of recording criminal data for the United States. The data and statistics are contained in the FBI's *Uniform Crime Reports* which are published annually. The bureau records crime in two categories: Part I is concerned with violent crimes—murder, forcible rape, robbery, and aggravated assault; and property crimes—burglary, larceny-theft, and auto theft (a total of seven crimes). The FBI utilizes these data to calculate a crime index to be used in comparing rates of crime. Part II crimes are less serious and consist of a range of crimes including arson, fraud, embezzlement, drunkeness, prostitution, and so on. Part II data contain only arrest information while Part I crimes are reported in greater detail. The data upon which the UCR are based are gathered by the FBI from state, city, and other local criminal justice systems. The FBI recognizes the limitations of these data and does not guarantee the UCR's accuracy.

The late Edwin H. Sutherland and Donald R. Cressey cite six reasons why the number of crimes known to the police is not an adequate index of crime.

1. The number of crimes known to the police is actually much smaller than the number actually committed . . .
2. The number of crimes known to the police is a reasonably accurate index of crime only if the police are honest, efficient, and consistent in making their reports. . . .
3. The value of crimes known to the police as an index of crime is sharply limited by the fact that the ratio of crimes committed reported and recorded varies according to the offense. . . .
4. The organization of control agencies affects the volume of crime known to the police . . . The sheer number of police officers obviously affects how much crime is processed. . . .
5. Variations in the criminal law may affect the volume of crimes known to the police, reducing the value of the measure for comparative purposes . . .
6. The number of crimes known to the police must, for purposes of comparison, be stated in proportion to the population or to some other base, and the determination of this base is often difficult. . . .[1]

The Uniform Crime Reports are supplemented by crime statistics gathered by various organizations for a variety of purposes: the annual report of the Federal Bureau of Prisons, *Federal Prisons,* gives data on persons convicted of violating federal laws; the United States Department of Health, Education, and Welfare publishes *Juvenile Court Statistics;* The Federal Deposit Insurance Corporation, the Treasury Department, and the Department of Justice publish statistical data on violations of certain federal laws; individual states publish their own criminal justice data, including data on prisoners in state correctional institutions; the American Bankers Association keeps records of offenses against banks, fidelity bonding companies maintain records of their losses due to different kinds of crime; and other organizations keep crime records for their specific purposes. These data are focused on special crimes and criminals, and add to, but do not supplant the data supplied by UCR.

Over the years government agencies and other organizations attempted to uncover the true extent of crime. Surveys were conducted in Cleveland in 1922; Missouri in 1926; Illinois in 1929; Oregon in 1932; and on the federal level (The Wickersham Report) in 1939–40, all of which demonstrated that crime was underreported by the UCR. In addition, surveys based on self-reports showed that criminality is more widespread than had been suspected.

In 1967, in order to develop a method of measuring the extent of criminal behavior more accurately than the UCR, the President's Commission on Law Enforcement and Administration of Justice requested that three victimization surveys be conducted. The most significant and widely known of these was conducted by the National Opinion Research Center (NORC). In this survey, interviews were conducted in 10,000 households in the United States containing 33,000 eligible interviewees. In each household, one knowledgeable person was asked whether any member of the household had been the victim of an FBI Part I offense (index crime) in the past year. If such a victim was identified, he was interviewed and the relevant police record was then examined to determine whether the crime had been reported. The results of the NORC survey cannot be considered completely accurate since victims' memories may have been faulty and their accounts of crimes distorted. Moreover, some crimes, such as murder, particularly of unattached males, are difficult to discover through interviews. Nevertheless, a comparison of UCR data and the NORC reports revealed that only 50 percent of all major crimes had been reported. (See Table A-1).

The survey was designed to inquire into crimes against individuals and their property (Part I—UCR index crimes). It was not concerned with victimless crimes: drug laws violations, gambling, or prostitution. The NORC crime rate was higher than UCR in all except automobile theft and willful homicide.

Automobile theft may be reported more frequently than it occurs because automobile owners sometimes file a complaint with the police when an auto

TABLE A-1. Comparison of Survey and UCR Rates (Per 100,000 population)

Index Crimes	NORC survey 1965-66	UCR rate for individuals 1965[1]	UCR rate for individuals and organizations 1965[1]
Willful homicide	3.0	5.1	5.1
Forcible rape	42.5	11.6	11.6
Robbery	94.0	61.4	61.4
Aggravated assault	218.3	106.6	106.6
Burglary	949.1	299.6	605.3
Larceny ($50 and over)	606.5	267.4	393.3
Motor vehicle theft	206.2	226.0	251.0
Total violence	357.8	184.7	184.7
Total property	1,761.8	793.0	1,249.6

[1] "Uniform Crime Reports," 1965, p. 51. The UCR national totals do not distinguish crimes committed against individuals or households from those committed against businesses or other organizations. The UCR rate for individuals is the published national rate adjusted to eliminate burglaries, larcenies, and vehicle thefts not committed against individuals or households. No adjustment was made for robbery.

is not found because the owner forgets where it has been parked, or another member of the family has driven the car away without notifying the owner. In these cases, the owner, believing the car to have been stolen, may file a report with the police immediately for insurance purposes. Homicide is relatively so small a figure that an error of a few numbers will distort the meaning of the sample. Nevertheless, despite official underreporting of most crimes, the rank order of frequency of these serious offenses reported by the victim (NORC) is, except for homicide and auto theft, the same as the UCR. Because it was felt that NORC surveys had value, victimization surveys were continued in 1972, designed in accordance with the objectives specified by the statistics division of the Law Enforcement Assistance Administration (LEAA). They have been conducted by the Bureau of the Census. These surveys are called the National Crime Surveys (NCS).

Victimization studies are an important measure of the extent of crime to use along with crimes reported to the police (UCR). Nevertheless, the important *caveats* of victimization studies are those of any public poll: how representative the sample was; cheating and bias of the people interviewed; and whether the questions asked had the same meaning for all subjects. Two researchers who analyzed victimization and attitude data feel that "... the NCS is not an ultimate data source. It has many limitations that can only be overcome and gaps that can only be filled by treating it as a complement to, rather than as a replacement for, other data sources."[2]

The chief problem with crime statistics is not merely that crime is *under-reported,* but that we have a *distorted* picture of the kinds of law breaking that occur. The nonviolent crimes of the middle and upper class, sometimes described as white-collar crime, are markedly underreported as compared with the UCR Part I index crimes which are mainly committed by the poor, many of whom are black or Hispanic. On the other hand, the negotiations and accommodations that take place throughout the arrest, prosecution, and sentencing phases of the criminal justice system tend to minimize the seriousness of the UCR Index crimes which have been committed.

Finally, external pressures on those who compile crime statistics can also produce distortions. When police departments find it expedient to show an increase in productivity, for example, more arrests are made and reported. *Crime* may not have increased, but arrests have.

Thus, it is very difficult for us to know who is committing what kinds of crimes and to what extent crime has been committed. Without such knowledge the quest for an effective theory of crime causation is thwarted and the efficient allocation of resources in the criminal justice system is impossible.

Notes

1. *Criminology,* 10th ed. (Philadelphia: Lippincott, 1978.) pp. 31–35.
2. James Garofalo and Michael J. Hindelanz. *An Introduction to the National Crime Survey.* (Washington, D.C.: U.S. Government Printing Office, 1977), p. 33.

Index